THE ART OF GETTING GOOD GRADES CAN BE LEARNED

Nowadays when so much depends on the grades you get in school—job, salary, social status—you owe it to yourself to get the best possible grades you can.

Getting good grades is not just a matter of long, hard hours of study. It is an art, an art which can be learned with surprising ease with the help of this unique book. Here is how you can begin to get better grades by:

- Getting more out of what you read by learning to scan.
- Learning to prepare for each of the four different kinds of tests.
- Mastering the five different shortcuts to developing "an ear" for languages.
- Learning how to correct the ten most common faults in writing.

Here is how you can learn literally dozens of other invaluable shortcuts to better grades—not next week, or next month, but starting right now.

HOW TO STUDY BETTER AND GET HIGHER MARKS

BY EUGENE H. EHRLICH

in charge of
READING AND STUDY HABITS IMPROVEMENT PROGRAM,
SCHOOL OF GENERAL STUDIES / COLUMBIA UNIVERSITY

*This low-priced Bantam Book
has been completely reset in a type face
designed for easy reading, and was
printed from new plates. It contains the complete
text of the original hard-cover edition.*

NOT ONE WORD HAS BEEN OMITTED.

HOW TO STUDY BETTER AND GET HIGHER MARKS
*A Bantam Book / published by arrangement with
Thomas Y Crowell Company*

PRINTING HISTORY
Crowell edition published October 1961
2nd printing......................November 1961
3rd printing...................... June 1962
*Bantam edition published May 1963
2nd printing*

For permission to reprint copyrighted material, grateful acknowledgment is
extended to the following:
Thomas Y. Crowell Company for pages 11-13 from *Laboratory Manual in
Elements of General Chemistry* by Joseph A. Babor, W. L. Estabrooke, and
Alexander Lehrman.
Harper & Brothers for material from *Evolution in Action* y Julian Huxley,
Daisy Miller by Henry James, and *The Direction of Human Development* by
M. F. Ashley Montagu.
Harvard University Press for material from *American Politics in a Revolu-
tionary World* by Chester Bowles, © Copyright 1956 by The President and
Fellows of Harvard College.
Harcourt, Brace & World, Inc., for material from *In the Name of Sanity* by
Lewis Mumford, copyright 1954 by Lewis Mumford, and *An Introduction
to Logic and Scientific Method* by Morris R. Cohen and Ernest Nagel, copy-
right 1934 by Harcourt, Brace & World, Inc.
Houghton Mifflin Company for material from *The Coming of the New Deal*
by Arthur M. Schlesinger, Jr., *Fundamentals of General Psychology* by
John Frederick Dashiell, *Analytic Geometry* by John Wesley Young et al.,
The American Nation by John D. Hicks, and *The Human Use of Human
Beings* by Norbert Wiener.
Longmans, Green and Company for material from *English Social History* by
G. M. Trevelyan.
The Macmillan Company for material from *Principles of Chemistry* by Joel
H. Hildebrand and Richard E. Powell, and *An Introductory Course in
College Physics* by Newton Henry Black and Elbert Payson Little.
McGraw-Hill Book Company, Inc., for material from *Apes, Angels, and Vic-
torians* by William Irvine, copyright © 1955 by William Irvine, *Botany:
Principles and Problems* by Edmund W. Sinnott and Katherine S. Wilson,
and *Geology Principles and Processes* by William H Emmons.
Oxford University Press for material from *Freedom, Loyalty, Dissent* by
Henry Steele Commager, copyright 1954 by Oxford University Press, Inc.
Penguin Books Ltd. for material from *Memory: Facts and Fallacies* by
I. M. L. Hunter.
Pocket Books, Inc., for material from *The Pocket History of the United States*
by Allan Nevins and Henry Steele Commager, copyright 1942, 1951, ©
1956 by Allan Nevins and Henry Steele Commager.
Prentice-Hall, Inc., for material from *Calculus* by Lyman M. Kells.
Simon and Schuster, Inc., for material from *The Causes of World War Three*
by C. Wright Mills.
University of Nebraska Press for material from *Constraint and Variety in
American Education* by David Riesman, copyright 1956 by the University
of Nebraska Press.
D. Van Nostrand Company, Inc., for material from *Physics* by Erich Haus-
mann and Edgar P. Slack, copyright 1941 by D. Van Nostrand Company,
Inc., Princeton, New Jersey.
The Viking Press for material from *The American Democracy* by Harold
Laski, copyright 1948 by The Viking Press, and *The Challenge of Man's
Future* by Harrison Brown, copyright 1954 by Harrison Brown.

*Bantam Books are published by Bantam Books, Inc. Its trade-mark,
consisting of the words "Bantam Books" and the portrayal of a bantam, is registered in the United States Patent Office and in other
countries. Marca Registrada. Printed in the United States of America. Bantam Books, Inc., 271 Madison Ave., New York 16, N. Y.*

ACKNOWLEDGMENTS

I wish to acknowledge assistance given me in various ways in the writing of this book.

Professor Louis Hacker of Columbia University first suggested the book more than seven years ago when he was Dean of the School of General Studies. He and the late Professor Irving Lorge, Teachers College, Columbia, helped in the early discussions and planning, as did my two colleagues, Professors John Middendorf and Ernest Griffin.

President Peter Sammartino, Fairleigh Dickinson University, gave me the opportunity to establish the first reading clinic at that institution. Professor Ruth Strang, formerly of Teachers College, Columbia, supervised my first work in reading. Dr. John Haanstra, International Business Machines Company, helped by his discussions of study problems of science students.

Mrs. Dorothy Pace and Dr. Daniel Murphy, who teach in our reading and study habits program, have given encouragement and counsel all through our many years of association. Gorton Carruth, Editor of Reference Books, Thomas Y. Crowell Company, made an awkward manuscript a book.

To all, my thanks. To Irving Lorge, remembrance.

TO NORMA

PREFACE

This book shows you *exactly how* to improve your memory, write good papers, study effectively in *all* your courses, and get higher marks on examinations. If you apply the information you read here, you will be able to realize your full potentialities as a student. This book is not just for the student who makes poor grades. It is for every student who wants to do better: for the good student who wants to be outstanding, as well as for the mediocre student who wishes to improve.

- Do you do well in class but badly in examinations?
- Do you find it hard to concentrate?
- Do you stumble when it comes to writing reports?
- Do you forget the next day what you learned the day before?
- Do you worry constantly about whether you are doing good work?
- Do you work too slowly?
- Do you waste time when you go to the library?
- Do you take confusing, unsystematic notes?
- Do you do well in some subjects, badly in others?

If your answer is "yes" to any of the above questions, this book will give you many valuable pointers which will save you time and energy.

CONTENTS

CHAPTER 1

HOW TO HAVE ENOUGH TIME
FOR YOUR STUDIES

YOU must have time for reflection and exploration if you are going to profit fully from college life. You must find time to read more widely than required for course work alone. There are clubs to join, newspapers, magazines, theater groups, sports, and other extracurricular activities. They are important too. Constant scrambling to keep up, worry about whether you are learning effectively, the desperation of being swamped by assignments—all are harmful to your work and disagreeable as well. You can avoid these pitfalls and enjoy college if you read this book carefully and put its suggestions to work.

The importance of good grades

The grades you make in college will have a profound effect on your life after you leave school. Business and engineering students, language and English majors—in fact, all students —find this out when they look for jobs or apply for admission to graduate schools. Each spring, companies send recruiters to college campuses to interview seniors. While recruiters are interested in many things about you—your intelligence, personality, appearance, qualities of leadership—they are primarily interested in how well you have done in your courses.

Companies that have their pick of college graduates set their sights on the *top 10 per cent of the class. Usually they will not even interview anyone outside this select group.*

If you are thinking ahead to a career in law, medicine, or teaching, you must know that admission to a professional or graduate school is based primarily on college grades. As difficult as it is to be admitted to college, competition for acceptance into graduate schools is even greater.

How good are your work habits?

A good student must have good work habits. He does not have to be outstandingly intelligent, but he must know how to use his time. If an expert student could tell you exactly what he does, here is probably what the "secret of success" would look like.

In the classroom he:
- 1. Listens carefully
- 2. Thinks along with the teacher
- 3. Relates what he hears to what he already knows
- 4. Asks questions when he is puzzled
- 5. Makes notes that will be helpful in reviewing

In the library he:
- 6. Knows what he is after
- 7. Knows how to find what he is after
- 8. Has all his study gear with him
- 9. Gets right to work and wastes no time
- 10. Makes notes on what he finds

In his study he:
- 11. Has a good place in which to work
- 12. Has all his study materials at hand
- 13. Knows exactly what he is supposed to do
- 14. Gets right to work and wastes no time
- 15. Finishes his work on time

College demands good work habits. The course load is heavy, the competition keen. You cannot depend on your teachers to review materials you are supposed to cover on your own. Unless you study efficiently, you will be swamped with work and worry before your first college Christmas vacation.

To help yourself to pinpoint your strengths and weaknesses as a student, answer the following questions. The first fifteen deal with your basic skills as a student, the last ten with the pattern of your study. Read each question thoughtfully and check either *Yes* or *No* before each question.

1. YES NO Can you read as fast as most of the students in your classes?

2. YES NO   Can you get what you must from your reading without having to read over and over again?

3. YES NO   Do you take clear notes on what you read?

4. YES NO   Are you able to give a résumé today of something you read yesterday?

5. YES NO   Can you write effective examination papers?

6. YES NO   Can you write a clear sentence?

7. YES NO   Do you understand almost all the words you read and hear?

8. YES NO   Is your vocabulary still growing?

9. YES NO   Do you understand and use the writing patterns of books you read?

10. YES NO   Do you read footnotes?

11. YES NO   In reading a book, do you use the index, table of contents, foreword, and chapter titles?

12. YES NO   Do you know when you have studied a topic well enough to go on to another?

13. YES NO   Do you know how to outline?

14. YES NO   Do you know how to read a book you are going to review?

15. YES NO   Can you write a book review?

16. YES NO   Do approaching examinations cause you to worry unduly?

17. YES NO   Do you wait until the last moment before doing your work?

18. YES NO   Do you review regularly during a semester?

19. YES NO   Do you have special techniques for final review before a test?

20. YES NO   Do you set a definite goal for each study session?

21. YES NO   Do you have difficulty in concentrating on your work?

22. YES NO   Do you find it hard to get started on your work?

23. YES NO   Do you waste study time?

24. YES NO   Do you have trouble in completing your work?

25. YES NO   Do you carry a loose-leaf notebook with you at all times during the school day?

Did you answer *no* to any of the questions from 1 to 15? If so, you have a fundamental study problem. Close attention to the various subjects discussed in this book can help you to eliminate these problems by improving your study habits.

Did you give the "wrong" answers to any of the last ten questions? You can begin to change them to "right" answers immediately by carefully reading the rest of this chapter. The suggestions you will find there will help you to end the worries of half-completed work by organizing your study. Thus you will gain more time both for extra study in your major field of interest and for needed relaxation.

How to plan your study time

A good student will not only keep up in his studies, but will also have interesting extracurricular activities. And, all the while, he is thinking and wondering about his choice of career and how best to prepare for it. There is no doubt that a busy life requires planning. No scientist plunges into a research job without careful planning. No executive takes a step without careful thinking and planning. The student without a plan for his daily activities lives from one study crisis to the next. He has a miserable time. He learns less than he is capable of learning.

You have surely heard that the first year of college is the most difficult, that the drop-out rate is highest of all the four years. The greatest reason for this is that entering freshmen do not have a plan of study.

If you want to learn how to plan your study time, bear in mind the four steps in planning:

- 1. Find out what each course demands.
- 2. Prepare a tentative study plan.
- 3. Modify your plan as needed.
- 4. Lay out the final plan and *use* it.

Each step will now be discussed in detail.

1. FIND OUT WHAT EACH COURSE DEMANDS

Your first job in college each year is to find out the amount and kind of work that will be required of you for the rest of the year. The first six weeks of college can be a misleading period of peace and harmony for many students. Accustomed to high school routine, they are surprised to find that most of their college teachers make no day-to-day assignments. So they do practically no studying. They wake up one day faced with a big examination for which they have not begun to prepare, or with a paper they are not ready to write. *Don't be misled by the lack of daily assignments.* Your teachers expect work from the very beginning.

As a semester gets under way, then, estimate as best you can the work that you will have to do for each course you take.

Warning: The number of credits a course carries is only a rough guide to the amount of work it will demand. This is because, as in high school or prep school, students have varying abilities in different courses. If in high school you had to spend twice as much time on mathematics assignments as on social studies, roughly the same proportion will be required in college. Your history courses—and most of the social sciences—require only reading. If you are an excellent reader, you will find this to your liking and will not have to put in as many hours as the student who is only a fair reader. Of course, if you are a poor reader such courses will make heavy demands on your time.

Language study involves a great deal of drill work. Your knowledge of English grammar will also affect your scheduling of time here. If you have little experience with nouns, pronouns, and the like, plunging into the grammar of a language other than your own will call for long hours to master concepts you should already know.

Mathematics and science emphasize reasoning. Once again, you must take into account your aptitude for this kind of work in estimating your time. From your first assignments in these courses, you will begin to adjust your estimates to the situation.

Consider the work load you will have in typical freshman courses. The best study procedures for all subjects are discussed later in this chapter, so we will not concern ourselves now with how to study. We will consider here how to develop a realistic estimate of the time needed for each course.

In foreign languages, you will have to learn new vocabulary each week as well as a number of grammatical principles. In addition, there will be composition, translation, and study of pronunciation. Your first guesses as to time needed for all this may be far from the mark. In a few weeks, however, you will learn enough about doing your work so that you will know precisely how much time to put aside for it.

In mathematics, you will find that new principles are introduced each week. They must be mastered. To help you in the job, you will work a number of problems each week. There will be periodic tests to help you review and to spot any weakness in your understanding of the material that could make trouble for you later on.

Your English composition course will probably demand a theme each week. Its length will, of course, determine in part how much time you will have to allot for it—but so will your ability as a writer. There is also the question of finding material for theme assignments. There may be exercises to do in a workbook, and perhaps some reading in an anthology.

To help in estimating the time you will need for social science readings, time yourself on a chapter or two of a social science textbook to see how long it will take you to read. Don't forget that an integral part of the reading process will be taking notes on what you read. So you must include time for this in your estimate. Outline the first chapter of the book carefully to see how much time that requires. Do not be surprised if you are able to cover only fifteen pages or so in one hour. In fact, you can almost bet that your speed at the beginning will be closer to ten pages an hour.

So it goes with each of your courses. Time will have to be allowed for class attendance, homework, and the library. Estimate all the time required. Of course, these estimates will be revised, but *make a start right at the beginning of each semester.* Then keep records of how much time you actually spend on your work so that you can perfect your study plan early in the semester.

Begin planning your work as soon as you find out what your program is going to be. As a freshman, you will have little choice of courses; depending on your major field, you may have more choice as the years of college go by. Your freshman schedule may look like this:

	Mon.	Tues.	Wed.	Thurs.	Fri.	Sat.
9	English	Geology	English	Geology	English	Geology
10	Spanish	Economics	Spanish	Economics	Spanish	Geology
11		Economics				Geology
12						
1	Math.	Math.	Math.	Math.	Phys. Ed.	
2					Phys. Ed.	
3						

From your schedule of classes, prepare a study-plan work sheet that will contain a list of the courses you are taking, estimated study time for each course, and a record of actual time spent. For the program just described, the work sheet will look like that shown below.

As the weeks of the semester pass, you will know fairly well how much time to give each subject. Keep in mind that the early weeks in a new course can look hopeless because of the amount of new information you are expected to learn. It might almost be said that if the situation does *not* look grim, you are probably underestimating the amount of work you should be doing. In time, this feeling passes. For one thing, the basic concepts in a strange field are always more difficult to master than the concepts that are introduced later on. They represent a way of thinking you have never encountered before. In addition, you are learning the vocabulary of the

Course	Estimated Study Time	Actual Time Spent	
Economics			1st week
			2nd week
			3rd week
English			1st. week
			2nd week
			3rd week
Geology			1st. week
			2nd week
			3rd week
Mathematics			1st. week
			2nd week
			3rd week
Spanish			1st week
			2nd week
			3rd week
Physical Education			1st week
			2nd week
			3rd week

new subjects—so important a problem that it will be discussed fully in Chapter 2 of this book.

Do not overlook the day when you will face your first examination in each course. And there will be term papers, book reviews, and special reports. Your weekly schedule gives you time to take care of all of these.

2. Prepare a Tentative Study Plan

As the next step toward an effective study plan, you should prepare a tentative schedule. First fill in your class hours, as shown on page 6.

Using your estimate of the study time you will need for each course, add to your schedule the study hours. How do you decide where to place the sessions you must have? There are three principles to use as guides:

- 1. You remember best what you have just studied.
- 2. The amount of time you can spend profitably in study varies from course to course.
- 3. You do your best work during certain periods of the day.

Let us examine each principle in detail so that you can make the best use of this knowledge.

You Remember Best What You Have Just Studied

The more time you permit to elapse between study and a test of what you have learned, the less you will remember of it. In planning your schedule, make time for studying each subject as close as possible to the time its class meets.

Study Time Will Vary from Course to Course

The amount of time you can spend profitably in study varies from course to course. One student is so excited by mathematics that he can spend a whole afternoon doing problems, while another student tires so rapidly that he must quit in one hour. What a student likes, he has time and energy for.

Yet you will find that when there is a pressing need, you are able to study any subject for much longer periods than you can handle ordinarily. On the night before a test, for example, students often find that they can work longer and harder than they can ordinarily. As we discuss the way to use study time in Chapter 12, you will find out how to make use of this human characteristic.

Above all, don't waste time on many brief study periods.

Starting, getting warmed up, and stopping use more precious time than you may realize. Consider the work you will be doing in the library, for example. It is easy to forget the time consumed by such details as getting there and back, finding, checking out, and returning books. One extended visit to the library is often worth more than several hasty trips.

The same principle applies to jobs requiring a variety of equipment that needs to be set out and put away—making a drawing with ink and crayons for a biology class, for instance. It is wasteful to stop in the middle of a drawing only to get back to it in another sitting. Or why should you do your mathematics problems in two sittings when you can finish them off faster in one? Splitting a single assignment into two sessions makes you lose sight of the principle being taught in the assignment. Decide how much time you can spend efficiently on each subject and assign room in your study plan.

STUDY WHEN YOU ARE AT YOUR BEST

You do your best work during certain periods of the day. Study when you are at your best. Some students are night owls; they do their best work between seven P.M. and midnight. Others work better in the early morning. Some students work best right after meals but can do little in the half hour before eating.

You will find that the pace at which your body works, your sleeping habits, and your metabolism determine when you are most alert. A heavy meal, for example, often makes the student drowsy, while a light one invigorates. Exercise to the point of near-exhaustion calls for sleep afterwards, not mental work of the greatest difficulty. Once you know when you are able to study best, try to build your schedule around these hours.

Now you are ready to use the three principles in selecting study hours for your tentative study plan. Of course, you will find, as you plan, that you often have to make do, and settle for less than the best arrangement. After all, there are just so many hours a day for study.

A popular rule of thumb for estimating study time is two hours of study for each hour of class. This will help in apportioning your time. With a sixteen-hour class load, you will have to estimate thirty-two hours for hitting the books. Total—forty-eight. If you fit this amount into five days, you miss the advantage of Sunday night work for Monday classes. There is nothing more dangerous than staying away from a subject for two days and then sitting down to a quiz or recitation on it. Weekend study is a must.

As you go along in college, you learn to select your program each year in such a way that you will not be underworked in one semester and worked half to death in the next. Nothing can be worse for you as a student than a soft-touch semester that encourages loafing. Thus you should mix courses that are easy for you with courses that are difficult. You will also learn to choose class sections which meet at times that permit you to get the most out of hours left for study. Some students choose to leave whole days free in order to have large blocks of time available for study. Other students avoid free days because they have learned that they do not make good use of time when they do not have to get started early in the day. *It is unwise to stagger classes through the day with one-hour intervals for study between.* While this kind of schedule gives you convenient time for review between classes, it does not permit you to get your teeth into a difficult subject before it is time for your next class.

Every student asks, "When am I going to have time for fun if I work six or seven days a week?" A good question. You must have recreation if you are going to remain healthy and alert. The answer is that the load you start out with in a semester becomes easier after you have become used to your classes. But the best answer of all is that *proper organization and use of study time will leave you time for relaxation.* If you use your weekends wisely, you will find that your day-to-day load is easier to manage.

A final word on this matter before going into the next step in effective planning of time. If you are going to undertake varsity sports or if you are going to work at a part-time job, your life will have to be a miracle of organization. Precious few moments can be wasted in either case. For athletes and students who must work their way through school, life is real, life is earnest.

3. MODIFY YOUR PLAN AS NEEDED

It usually takes a few weeks to find out all you need to know about how much studying is required and how you can best apportion time. That is why the study-plan work sheet on page 7 has room for a three-week record of time spent on each course. Do not hesitate to adjust your tentative schedule until it works for you.

As the semester progresses, you will discover when there will be quizzes, when you will have extracurricular activities, and when you will be called on in class. As these become fixed points in your week, you will want to adjust your schedule accordingly.

Your original estimates of how long it takes to do certain tasks may turn out to be exaggerated, while other courses may demand much more time than you originally estimated. This is another reason for considering your study plan *tentative*. By the second week of a semester, your plan will be undergoing modifications if you are using it carefully. But by the third or fourth week, it should settle into a pattern that will be followed by and large for the remainder of the semester. You will see, however, that there will always be slight changes in your study plan. The early weeks of a semester may find you groping in the dark in certain courses. Gradually, however, you find that you can manage them, and you may take time away from these courses and use it for others.

4. Lay Out the Plan and Use It

Now you are ready to sign a contract with yourself for the studying you will do during the remainder of the semester. In addition to class and study time, you must schedule exercise and other recreation. Whatever you schedule, do the best you can for yourself, knowing that you can effectively do no more. This is your contract. Your routine is set. Pages 14–15 show how the schedule of one student worked out for him.

Write the final schedule clearly on a card and attach it to the wall directly in front of your desk. Make a copy for your notebook. After you have used the schedule for a few weeks, you will probably know it by heart. At any rate, you will be using your time well. You will never have to wonder, "What should I be doing now?"

The best tip-off to a person who is not making good use of his time is that he always seems to be ready for a break. Yet this person does not enjoy his brief relaxation because in back of his mind is the knowledge that final examinations, term papers, quizzes, and term grades are lying in wait for him.

THE STUDENT CALENDAR

In addition to the study plan, there is another valuable weapon in the student arsenal. This is a daily reminder and long-range planner called the student calendar. It is the repository for reminders of papers due, examination dates, book reviews, examination review dates, trips, dances, football games, and the like. It is your special events calendar to be used in conjunction with your study plan.

The student calendar should take the form of notes to be attached to the wall alongside your study plan. Such notes are preferable to a small book that might well be lost or tucked away in a desk drawer where it will never catch your eye. When a teacher assigns a paper, examination, or book review, make a note covering the assignment and put it up on your wall. Part of each entry is the date when the assignment will be due. Include also intermediate target dates for completing each step of the assignment.

For example, you may be assigned a book review that must be handed in by December 15. Your calendar will read:

HISTORY BOOK REVIEW

1. November 1—*select and obtain book*
2. November 15—*complete reading*
3. December 1—*complete first draft*
4. December 13—*complete revisions and type*
5. December 15—*hand in review*

Or you might use a large calendar pad that has enough space around each date for making notes.

The book list from which you will select might go up on the wall next to the calendar note. This is far better than keeping it apart from the assignment itself. When the time comes to begin work on the review, you have both things you need right in front of you.

Another entry will concern final examinations. (Chapter 12 discusses final examination strategy in detail.) The calendar will list review schedules, commencing well before examination time. It also will schedule dates for consulting old examinations that are available and for getting together with classmates to discuss the examination before you begin to review.

These devices will eliminate the pressure that can build up during a semester. Such pressure can ruin your college years by causing you to be constantly worried and fatigued. Now let us look at the program one student set for himself. This experience will help you make your own study plan.

	Sun.	Mon.	Tue.	Wed.	Thur.	Fri.	Sat.
9:00		English class theme		English class		English class	Hist. library
10:00		Math class	Chem. lab.	Math. class	Chem. study	Math. class Quiz	Hist. library
11:00		French class	Chem. lab.	French class	Chem. study	French class	Hist. library
12:00			Chem. lab.		Chem. study		
1:00		Chem. study		English workbook			French study
2:00	English vocab Type	Chem. class lecture	Hist. class	Hist. class	Chem. class Quiz	Hist. class	French study
3:00	French study				French study	Hist. library	
4:00	French study		English reading	Eng. write theme	French study	Hist. library	
5:00	French study			Eng. write theme		Hist. library	
6:00							
7:00		Hist. library					
8:00	Math study	Hist. library	Math. study	French study	Math. study		
9:00	Math study	Hist. library	Math. study	French study	Math. study		
10:00	Math study		Math. study		Math. study		
11:00							

How one student planned his study time

John S. was a college freshman. The first thing John did in planning his study was to write out his list of courses and estimate the amount of time he would need for studying every week. This was his original study plan:

COURSE	CLASS HOURS	ESTIMATED STUDY HOURS
Introduction to Chemistry	5	3
English Composition	3	5
Advanced French Reading and Conversation	3	9
Medieval European History	3	9
Introduction to Mathematics	3	8
totals	17	34

In chemistry, Monday classes were lectures, and John had felt that he did not have to prepare for them. This turned out to be an error. By *preparing for each lecture himself,* he was able to get much more out of the lecture than without preparation. He decided to read the textbook section covering the lecture topic *before* each lecture. By doing a good job on the material, he was able to use the lecture as a review session rather than a new learning experience. Concentrating the rest of his study time just before the Thursday quiz section turned out to be just what the doctor ordered. He had to add only one hour to his original study plan.

English themes were due on Monday, and time had to be made for writing well in advance of the due date. He knew that last-minute rushing did not work for him. Thus, when themes were assigned, he made notes on possible topics at once. He did his writing during the week. Sunday study time was reserved for editing and typing. He found that five hours were quite adequate.

French could be done at any time during the week provided his study was spaced adequately. He set up each study period as a combination of review of old material and study of new. Nine hours for French.

History meant the library. Not only would there be a great deal of reading, but it would be a kind of reading that John had never done before. Notes would have to be taken carefully and organized well so he would be able to study for important examinations. He would also need time for learning material that was covered in lectures. He wanted to make sure of doing a good job in history because he was considering it as a major. Nine hours of study.

There would be no quizzes in history, so there was no reason for trying to prepare just before class time. He set two goals for himself. First, he wanted to stay ahead of the lecturer, but not too far ahead. Secondly, he would review all the material of the semester at least once each week so that the mid-semester and final examinations did not overwhelm him.

Mathematics would mean daily recitations, frequent quizzes. If he was to keep on his toes, he would need at least eight hours.

Mathematics turned out to be more difficult than he had foreseen, so during the first six weeks of the semester he spent an additional thirty minutes a night reading his textbook. The habit of using his last half hour each night on a troublesome course was a good one, so he used it periodically during the semester on one course or another.

Fortunately, John was able to sample both subjects that interested him as possible majors—English and history. It is wise to find out, as early as you can, what is really involved in subjects you are considering as a major. In this way, you can clear up any misunderstanding you may have about what particular fields concern themselves with. Many students have romantic notions about the content of certain subjects. Another advantage in sampling possible major courses early in college is that you can discover whether you have the special ability they require.

Get started on your own study plan

If effective study is important in your scheme, adequate planning is the first step. The time you take in thinking through a realistic study program will pay off in many ways. Your grades will improve. You will learn more than you now can. You will reduce the worry that is a common student complaint. Does this seem attractive to you? Then here is the way to start:

- 1. Find out what each course demands.
- 2. Prepare a tentative study plan.
- 3. Modify your plan as needed.
- 4. Lay out the final plan and *use it.*

CHAPTER 2

HOW TO BECOME THE BEST
READER YOU CAN BE

IF you are going to make the best grades you can, you will have to be the best reader you can. College study is reading. No matter how well you read now, you would do well to take a look at the kind of reading you will have to do in college and make certain that you can handle it. Consider the range of reading you will have:

- Textbooks in all subjects—history, literature, art, science, sociology, psychology, economics
- Auxiliary readings—original source materials in many fields, commentary on the writing of others
- Reference materials—encyclopedias, periodicals, dictionaries
- Book reviews, your own notes on lectures and readings, research notes, laboratory notes, and, of course, poetry and fiction

—reading, reading, reading. Surely college success depends on your ability to read well.

This chapter can help you in two ways. First it will test your reading, and then it will show you how to go about improving it.

Check your reading comprehension

The two important characteristics of reading are how *much* you comprehend and how *fast* you comprehend. The first tests you will take answer the first question.

Below are three paragraphs chosen to test your ability to find ideas as you read. These paragraphs are not particularly difficult for a good college reader, yet they present interesting and important ideas. Being able to spot a significant idea at first reading is a skill you must cultivate. When you read for your college courses, you will constantly be on the look-out for the gist of the material you are covering. While not every paragraph will add a great deal to the main ideas an author is trying to develop, you must still understand just what he is telling you. As a good reader, you evaluate every thought you encounter, making notes on the most important, seeing the others in relation to central ideas.

The first paragraph in the test was written by a biologist, the second by a mathematician, the last by a social critic. It is interesting to note that the books these paragraphs were taken from all enjoyed wide distribution beyond university campuses.

■ READING COMPREHENSION TEST I

Julian Huxley, in his *Evolution in Action*,[1] shows us in nontechnical language how evolution works. Here is one paragraph from that book. The author states his main idea and elaborates by means of an example.

Read through the paragraph only *once* to find the main idea. When you have finished reading, go back to select the *one sentence* within the paragraph that contains that idea.

> The dominant beliefs of a community may have decisive effects on the lives of its members or on its own development. Thus the erroneous belief that death is never natural but is always attributable to some kind of witchcraft has led to the witch-smelling ordeals of Africa and has resulted in suffering or death for count-less thousands of her people. The ancient Egyptians believed that kings and important personages could be made to live on in an afterlife, but that their continued survival there could only be ensured by continuing to provide them with real or symbolic nourishment. This belief eventually changed the economic life of the country, by transferring an increasing proportion of the land from more efficient exploitation under the kings to less efficient exploitation by colleges of priests.

Which sentence contains the main idea? See the answer in the Footnote below.

[1] Harper & Brothers, 1953.

Surely the first sentence of the paragraph. The discussion of the Egyptians serves only as an example of what Huxley is trying to tell us.

■   READING COMPREHENSION TEST II

Here is an example of the kind of paragraph many students find hard to read. Why should this be so? You will not find the vocabulary difficult. The sentence structure is not awkward. The subject matter is not foreign to us. Why then should some students be fazed by it?

Because they come to their reading unprepared—often unwilling—to follow the logic of the discussion. Yet this is typical of much of the material to be read in college.

The paragraph is from a book called *The Human Use of Human Beings* [2] by Norbert Wiener. The author is known as one of the developers of cybernetics, the science of electronic computers. See how well you can do with this paragraph. Read it through only *once* with the single purpose of understanding the main idea of the paragraph. At the end, you will find three statements. Which best represents the main idea?

The idea that information can be stored in a changing world without an overwhelming depreciation in its value is false. It is scarcely less false than the more plausible claim, that after a war we may take our existing weapons, fill their barrels with cylinder oil, and coat their outsides with sprayed rubber film, and let them statically await the next emergency. Now, in view of the changes in the techniques of war, rifles store fairly well, tanks poorly, and battleships and submarines not at all. The fact is that the efficacy of a weapon depends on precisely what other weapons there are to meet it at a given time, and on the whole idea of war at that time. This results—as has been proved more than once—in the existence of excessive stockpiles of stored weapons which are likely to stereotype the military policy in a wrong form, so that there is a very appreciable advantage to approaching a new emergency with the freedom of choosing exactly the right tools to meet it.

Without looking back, select the best statement of the main idea of what you have read:

- *a.* Ideas, like weapons, cannot be kept in mothballs if they are to be useful.
- *b.* Information, like weapons of war, must constantly be expanded and improved, if it is going to be useful in the modern world.

[2] Houghton Mifflin Company, 1954.

   ● *c.* There is considerable advantage to starting fresh in
      attempting to meet each new military emergency in-
      stead of relying on old weapons.

Which answer do you select, *a, b, or c?* Check your selection
with the answer in the footnote below.

■   READING COMPREHENSION TEST III

Lewis Mumford tried in his recent book, *In the Name of
Sanity,*[3] to alert America to the necessity of doing something
about the cold war. The approach he suggested is far different from that we often encounter. In the part of his book
from which this paragraph is taken, Mumford called for cor-
recting "the succession of military and political blunders we
have perpetrated" since World War II.

In this test, you will be reading once more for the main
idea. You will have no choice of answers this time, nor will
you be asked to go back to the paragraph to find the sentence
containing the main idea. The situation will be closer to the
kind of reading you will be doing all through college. Just
as though you were taking notes on the paragraph, *state the
main idea in your own words.*

> With the invention of the atom bomb, the United States stepped
> into a role on the international stage not unlike that of the Em-
> peror Jones in Eugene O'Neill's play. We believed, officially, that
> the atom bomb made us invulnerable; but as we stumbled through
> the jungle of the postwar world, secure in this self-imposed delu-
> sion, we gradually lost our own sense of direction; presently, as
> night overtook us, menacing fears and specters arose in our own
> minds, making ever louder the ominous beat of the distant Russian
> war drums. None of our wild random shots has caused these fright-
> ening images to disappear; and at the end, we find that we have
> nothing left by way of an effective answer to our fears except the
> magic of a silver bullet: the atom bomb. Perhaps the figure would
> be a little more accurate if one said that we have a whole cartridge
> belt full of silver bullets; but like so many of the magic gifts in
> ancient fairy stories, there is an un expected penalty attached to
> their use: the result of using all of them might be to wipe out
> our friends and allies as well as our enemy. In O'Neill's play, you
> will remember, silver bullets killed the Emperor Jones. They were
> fired by savages who had copied his magic.

[3] Harcourt, Brace & World, Inc., 1954.

The best answer is *b.* Of course, *a* might have fooled you. But the author did not
discuss ideas, did he? If you thought *c* was the answer, go back to the paragraph
once more and observe how the author used military weapons only as an analogy,
a comparison of the new thought with something well-known in order to convince
or explain.

What is the main idea of the paragraph? Write it in one sentence without looking back.

. . . .

. . . .

Check your response with the one supplied in the footnote below.

Evaluate your reading comprehension

A good college reader would have no trouble answering all three tests correctly. How did you do?

These informal tests, administered by yourself, can tell you whether you read as well as you should.

- Did you feel the need to look back and reread the paragraphs in the second and third tests? (If so, you are not as confident about your ability as you should be.)
- Did you have difficulty in making up your mind about how to answer the tests? (You are not used to being questioned directly on your reading, and you will need to become accustomed to it.)
- Did you find it difficult to phrase your answer to the third test? (Being able to say and write the gist of material you are reading is essential to college success.)
- Did you find the vocabulary difficult? (This is an indication that your grasp of words is not what it should be.)
- Did you find the three paragraphs so different from your ordinary reading that you felt as though you were on foreign territory? (You can see that you will have to expand your reading horizons if you are to do college reading.)

How many trouble spots have you located in your reading comprehension? Let us go on to one more test. The paragraphs you were tested on may have been too short to get your teeth into.

■   READING COMPREHENSION TEST IV

The reading comprehension test you will take was selected from a book entitled *Memory: Facts and Fallacies*, written for

Possession of the atom bomb no longer means national security; it is a source of self-destruction.

the general reading public by a Scottish psychologist, I.M.L. Hunter.[4] No prior knowledge of psychology is necessary to understand the material. It concerns memory, specifically the unusual memory that we find in certain individuals. (Memory is also one of the central subjects of the present book.)

In taking this test, read as though the selection were an article found in a good magazine. Do not hurry, but read the selection only *once*. If, while reading, you feel that you must stop for a moment to ponder what you are reading, by all means do so. But do not *study* the selection. When you have finished reading, you will analyze some brief statements about the article. While doing that part of the exercise, *do not look back* at the selection. This is a test of how well you understand what you read.

Note the exact time you begin so you can tell how long the reading takes, but do not hurry.

From time to time we hear people refer to "photographic memory" and say wistfully how useful the gift must be. By this term is meant, presumably, the ability to image an absent scene with all the vividness, distinctness, and detail of a photographic print. Since many people suppose such an ability to exist, this section is devoted to an examination of the evidence for such a proposition. What approximates most closely to the popular notion of "photographic memory" is a remarkable form of visual imaging which has been estimated to occur in something like 1 to 10 per cent of the adult population and 50 to 60 per cent of children under the age of 12 years. This form of imaging was first investigated by the German psychologist, E. R. Jaensch, and found to have so many unique characteristics that it was given the name "eidetic" (virtually, identical or duplicative).

The observations of Jaensch and others on eidetic imaging have been summarized by G. W. Allport in an article published in 1942 in the *British Journal of Psychology*. Allport himself worked in Cambridge with some sixty eleven-year-old children, and his procedure may be mentioned because it is typical. At a normal reading distance from the child, he propped up a two-foot square dark gray mat on which he placed, one at a time, pictures cut from an ordinary picture book. The pictures were rich in detail and action, the principal features being in silhouette and the background objects in delicate tints. A picture was left on the mat for thirty-five seconds, during which time the child scrutinized it carefully. It was then removed and the child was simply asked to look at the gray mat and report what he saw. Thirty of the children then behaved in a most striking manner. It was as though they were still actually seeing the picture. Their imaging was unusually vivid and contained details of the absent picture with an almost photographic fidelity. This is eidetic imaging, and it differs

[4] Penguin Books, 1957.

from the more usual form of imaging in a number of respects, the chief of which concern its localization, its intensity, and its richness of detail.

As regards localization, the eidetic image is seen as situated in outer space. It is never localized "within the head," as the usual memory image so often is, but "out there," attached to the mat or a wall or some other surface. It is as though the child were looking at a picture on this surface and, indeed, if the surface is folded or bent then the "picture" too is likewise folded or bent. However, despite this "outer" character of the image, the subject always recognizes that it is a purely subjective phenomenon, that it is an effect which he is voluntarily producing, and that it has no outer, objective existence. As regards vividness, the image is so clear and strong that it tends to obscure the background against which it is projected. In this respect again, it is as though there were a filmy but almost opaque picture on the projection surface. In always appearing as projected on a surface in outer space, the eidetic image closely resembles the negative after-image. However, the two phenomena are by no means identical. For one thing, the negative after-image occurs only after the prolonged fixation of a relatively simple object, whereas the eidetic image occurs after the very different activity of letting the eyes rove hither and thither over an object rich in complex detail. For another thing, the eidetic image differs from both the positive and negative after-image in being more persistent: not only does it last longer, but it can be voluntarily revived some hours, weeks, or even months later. A further difference is that the eidetic image does not, like the negative after-image, vary its size with the distance between the subject and the projection surface: it does not obey Emmert's Law, for, while undergoing some slight change in size with distance, it is roughly constant for positions of the projection surface, at least between 25 and 100 cm. A final difference between the eidetic and the after-image is that, as we shall shortly see, the former is subject to qualitative distortions of a kind which never occur in the latter.

The most striking characteristic of the eidetic image is the wealth of detail it contains. Details are reported from the image such as the number of buttons on the jacket of a passer-by, the length and direction of the lines of shading in a stretch of roadway, and the number of whiskers on a cat's lip. The individual appears to be able to focus upon any detail and make it become gradually clearer so that the rest of the "picture" becomes obscure. It is this richness of detail which sets the eidetic image apart from the usual memory image, and this difference between the two can be demonstrated directly. When, after the picture is removed, the children are not asked to look at the gray mat but are asked merely to describe the picture, they do this without recourse to eidetic imaging. If they are then asked to turn their eyes to the gray mat, they supplement their account with what they "see" there. Allport found that, with scarcely a single exception, the eidetic imaging supplied detail lacking in conventional recalling, and it sometime happened that a child, on the evidence of his eidetic image, would spontaneously correct a misstatement which he made in his previous account "from memory." We may give just one example of the amazing details which may be "read off" the image. One of the pictures used by Allport depicted a street scene and contained, among other details, the German word *Gartenwirthschaft* written above the door of an inn in the background. The word was quite meaningless for the English children and was not usually reported at first, the subjects starting with descriptions of the more outstanding and dramatic features of the image. But on being pressed to observe more closely, each of the thirty children whose eidetic imaging was strong saw, often to his surprise, the small letters above the door. Three of these children spelled out the word without error, seven got no more than two of the letters wrong, and only five failed to give at least five letters correctly. In all cases, the letters were given with equal accuracy whether "read off" from left to right or in the reverse order. There was, of course, no question of the word having been memorized. The exposure of thirty-five seconds was insufficient for this, especially since the picture itself was filled with incident and details of lively interest which the child was likewise able to describe from his imaging.

From what has been said, it might well be supposed that eidetic imaging is photographic in its accuracy. Such, however, is not the case. The child cannot see each and every detail of the original, as witness the fact that the majority of Allport's "eidetic children" were unable to "read off" every letter in the long German word. Thus, the imaging, although truly remarkable in its detail, is not to be compared with a photographic reproducing of the original. Those parts of the picture which proved most interesting are likely to be seen in the image, while the less interesting parts tend to be either faint or absent altogether. For example, one investigator found that, of a group of children who gave a vivid eidetic image of the picture depicting a monkey, half failed to image an uninteresting picture of an ordinary house. In addition to the tendency to omit uninteresting details, there are also qualitative distortions. The child may change the position or character of some of the details or even add an item entirely lacking in the original. These distortions and added details are also vividly seen in the image, and there is nothing to distinguish them as innovations. Such changes are especially frequent when the picture is imaged after a considerable lapse of time. But this is not all. Many pictures portraying action result in an image where the action is carried to completion. On occasion, this movement in the image is voluntarily produced: a carriage is made to drive away, turn a corner in the road, and so disappear altogether from the image; people are made to enter and leave a "scene" and perform various normal actions. Sometimes this movement may also be produced at the suggestion of the experimenter. In an investigation reported in 1926 by the American psychologist H. Kluver, both voluntary and spontaneous movements appeared in the eidetic images of animal pictures. In imaging a picture containing a donkey standing some distance from the manger, the donkey crossed over to the manger, moved his ears, bent his neck, and began to eat. Suggestions from Kluver to the effect that the donkey was hungry sometimes served to set in motion a series of changes which surprised the subjects themselves. It was as if they were not looking at a static picture but at a living scene, for, as soon as the suggestion was given, the donkey would "spontaneously" race over to the manger. It is noteworthy that all these distortions, additions, and movements which occur in eidetic imaging are, like the qualitative changes which occur in recalling generally, in full accordance with the subject's framework of expectations. They are always consistent with the child's normal experiences, and he is definitely unable to introduce into his imaging features which are ridiculous or unnatural.

Thus, for all its rich detail, eidetic imaging is neither literally reproductive nor static, and the larger the interval between the original seeing and the imaging, the greater the likelihood of distortion and change. Even in the eidetic image—the nearest approximation which psychology has found to "photographic memory"—there are additions, omissions, and distortions and, as in recalling generally, the role of selective interests and accumulated past experiences is evident. The same is true of eidetic imaging in adults. Some remarkable examples of this have been recorded but, wherever these have been adequately investigated, it has been found that the imaging is far from being photographic.

Note the time again. How many minutes did the reading take you?

We found that photographic memory has not yet been demonstrated to the satisfaction of psychologists. But eidetic imaging is common. Let us see whether you can pass a short test on what you have read. Here are ten statements about memory. Without looking back at the text, mark each statement as true or false on the basis of what you have just read.

> FOR EXAMPLE: Allport recognized that earlier research had not properly studied the question of photographic memory. TRUE OR FALSE?
>
> THIS IS FALSE. Allport summarized a good deal of early research in this area. See paragraph two of the selection.

Without looking back at the selection, then, and relying only on what you read, mark each of these statements either true or false.

1. TRUE   FALSE   Eidetic imaging is more common among children than among adults.
2. TRUE   FALSE   To merit the name "photographic," memory must be complete in every detail.
3. TRUE   FALSE   Specific eidetic images soon fade from the memory of the subject.

4. TRUE FALSE Allport found evidence of imaging of al--
              most photographic fidelity among his sixty
              child subjects.

5. TRUE FALSE Interest in the picture shown will influence
              the amount of detail the eidetic imagist
              can repeat.

6. TRUE FALSE In eidetic imaging, the subject, after some
              time has passed, cannot summon more than
              a small fraction of the detail he has been
              shown.

7. TRUE FALSE The suggestions of the psychologist can in-
              fluence the response of the subject.

8. TRUE FALSE Obedient children are good subjects for
              experiments in memory.

9. TRUE FALSE If Allport had used photographs in his ex-
              periments, he might have received different
              responses.

10. TRUE FALSE By reporting movement within the image,
               the subject shows that his recall is not
               photographic.

When you are satisfied with your answers, compare them with
those given below in the footnote.

A score of least 80 per cent on this test would indicate
that you comprehend well. Taking into account your speed
of reading, if you were able to make a score at least as good
as 80 per cent and your reading of the selection took only
seven minutes, you are a good reader.

Are you satisfied with your results? If you are not, you
will want to read the latter half of this chapter very carefully. It will help you further to identify your reading difficulties and show you how to go about improving your reading. Now let us go on to discuss the second aspect of reading
ability: speed of reading.

How fast should you read?

While your ability to comprehend what you read must be
considered first in evaluating your reading, the question of
how fast you read cannot be overlooked. It is obvious that
speed of reading is important when you think of the quantity
of reading you will have to do in college. If you cannot get

You should have marked statements 1, 2, 4, 5, 7, and 10 True, because they are
supported in the selection. Each correct answer is worth 10 per cent. What is your
score?

through your assignments in good time, you cannot expect to pass your courses, let alone make top grades.

You are going to test your speed of reading with a few paragraphs taken from books you may read in college. Note the time before you begin each test. If you can, use a watch with a second hand. Note the time that you start in the space at the beginning of the selection. Then record your time *in seconds*.

You are the sole judge of how well you read in these tests; there will be no test of comprehension. As you read, make certain that you are really reading and not merely sweeping your eyes back and forth across lines of print.

■   SPEED TEST I

This selection is from a biography of two great English scientists, Thomas Huxley and Charles Darwin. Imagine that you have been asked to write a term paper on the great thinkers of the nineteenth century and you have chosen Thomas Huxley. The following excerpt from *Apes, Angels, and Victorians*, by William Irvine [5] describes the man. You want to determine whether you can use this material for your paper. Your job is to read quickly to see whether this information is going to be helpful.

The time now is ....

In his "Autobiography," Huxley notes with a biologist's interest in heredity that he inherited a quick temper, tenacity, and artistic aptitude from his father, and from his mother, swiftness of apprehension, which he seems to have valued most—and rightly, for, joined with the clarity which he later made a test both for truth and style, it lies at the very basis of his mind and character. He had the coolness, the sureness, the self-confidence which clarity and swiftness bestow. He was always mobilized for action. He never hesitated, was never less than himself. In fact, he was not so much the patient solver of problems as the prodigious performer—the rapid and voluminous reader, the ready and eloquent speaker, the facile and felicitous writer. He possessed the obvious virtues in nearly as much splendor as Macaulay and was almost as magnificently adequate to his age. Like Macaulay also, he remained personally modest but gratified his self-esteem by taking his duties and his world very seriously. In fact, he had some of Macaulay's faults, but he had them in less extreme degree. He was less inclined to formularize himself and his goods for mass production. He felt somewhat less, one suspects, the need of having

[5] McGraw-Hill Book Company, 1955.

a stream of ready-made thoughts going through his head at all times like a Fourth-of-July parade. He was probably more patient in groping for an idea or in grappling with a problem. He certainly did not retreat from difficult subjects. Metaphysics was one of his natural elements. Here he differed from Macaulay and resembled Voltaire. He had Voltaire's combativeness, his eager curiosity about facts and theories, his heroic but often negative and incredulous common sense, which sometimes closes the mind to large and daring conceptions.

At any rate, the obvious virtues turned his youth into a rather obvious Victorian success story. He was born in 1825 at Ealing near London, and went to Ealing School, of which his father was an assistant master. But the school had fallen upon evil days, and he gained little from it but a practical demonstration of the struggle for survival and a post-bellum friendship with a boy who turned up years after as a transported convict in Australia. When he was ten years old, the family moved to Coventry, where his father became manager of a small bank. After that time Tom had very little formal schooling.

The time now is . . . . Elapsed time (in seconds) . . . .

■   SPEED TEST II

One of the world's greatest problems is providing food and fuel for a rapidly expanding population. In your courses in geography, economics, chemistry, and biology, you will study the natural resources of the earth and concern yourself with the question of how man can make more efficient use of his endowment. This selection from *Where Winter Never Comes,* by Marston Bates,[6] deals with tropical disease and its control. If you were doing a paper on the possibilities of increasing cultivation of available land, you might need information on disease. Read this selection, then, with the thought of being able to give a résumé. See how long it takes you to read the selection.

The time now is . . . .

I sometimes wonder how anyone ever gets malaria, because the odds seem to be all against it. A particular kind of mosquito (an anopheles) must bite a man at a time when gametocytes are circulating in his blood. This mosquito must survive the hazards of nature for at least ten days while the parasite completes the cycle in his body; and the hazards of nature for a mosquito are considerable, so that the great majority surely die before the ten days have passed. Then the mosquito, when it bites again, must bite a

[6] Charles Scribner's Sons, 1951.

susceptible man—not a horse or a sparrow or man who already has that kind of malaria. It takes infinite pains to keep mosquitoes and malaria going in the laboratory; and out in nature, with no one to look after them, I don't see how the mosquitoes and parasites get along at all. Yet millions of people get infected every year, and the whole method of getting from man to man must be considered a great success from the parasite's point of view.

Of course, this very complexity helps in designing control measures. There are more than two hundred different kinds of anopheles mosquitoes in the world, and all of them could transmit malaria, but only a few do. Many are too rare to be important; others never live long enough; some rarely bite man, preferring other animals. The important malaria vectors are a few species that live in close association with man. These can be avoided by house screening, or their breeding places destroyed by drainage or treatment with insecticides. The most dramatic results of all have been obtained by spraying the houses with D.D.T. This does not kill all of the mosquitoes in the neighborhood, but it kills those individuals that have bitten or would bite man, thus cutting out malaria transmission. By systematic and thorough treatment of this sort, malaria can sometimes be completely eliminated from an area in a few years. Also the old standby of quinine has now been replaced by more efficient drugs, so that where medical attention is available, infected people can be cured, leaving nothing for the mosquitoes to transmit. This is the least hopeful method of control, because in most malarious areas, medical attention is simply not available for most of the population. It is far more economical to attack the disease through the mosquitoes than through the human host.

The time now is .... Elapsed time (in seconds) ....

■   SPEED TEST III

In your psychology courses, you will study how personality develops and how certain factors contribute to that development. One area of knowledge that many have explored is fear—its effects on people, its origins, and its control. This selection from *The Direction of Human Development*, by Ashley Montagu [v] gives some insight into how soldiers live with fear. You are reading for information, not to learn thoroughly. Try to get the central idea of the selection. See how quickly you can accomplish your goal.

The time now is ....

The recognition of the importance of this dependence, this precarious dependence, of one person upon another has recently, perhaps, been best illustrated in the findings concerning what used to

[v] Harper & Brothers, 1955.

be called "shell shock" and is today known as combat exhaustion. It has been known to military observers for some time that some combat units suffer fewer psychiatric casualties than others, and this in spite of an equal or greater degree of battle stress. In the battle situation there is an omnipresent conscious or unconscious fear of death. This fear, it has been discovered, exists in direct proportion to the confidence that his comrades are "all in there together" with him and will support him in his need. During the training period the soldier gains this confidence in the prospective functioning of his unit, his group. Colonel Albert J. Glass of the United States Army Medical Corps who reports these findings, writes, "Even the timid soldier comes to feel secure by being in a powerful group and often assumes the aggressive attitude of the organization. . . ." "In brief, the group offers protection against fear to the soldier and provides for his emotional needs, but demands that he give up personal desires and selfish considerations. In its simplest form, group identification is a matter of "united we stand, divided we fall.'"

Glass points out that "when men fight together and share common tribulations, they become bound by the closest of emotional ties. This affection, which is akin to love, serves to lessen concern for one's own life, thereby decreasing the crippling subjective sensation of fear." The commonness of such an emotional bond has been demonstrated by numerous instances in which soldiers have unhesitatingly performed dangerous and heroic deeds to save their friends, while the close kinship of men forged in battle is responsible for instances in which soldiers prematurely leave the hospital or a rear assignment to join their comrades. Glass concludes, "A member of an adequately led combat unit has increased resistance to mental breakdown because of the emotional and actual support provided by the group. The failure of such an environmental support is the major cause of combat exhaustion."

The time now is .... Elapsed time (in seconds) ....

■   SPEED TEST IV

In an English course, you may be assigned the reading of *Daisy Miller*, by Henry James,[8] a short novel of the experiences of an American girl in Europe. After reading it, you will have the task of reviewing it in a short paper. The excerpt reproduced here comes at the very end of the novel. Daisy is dead, and the story must conclude. Your purpose in reading is to determine how the narrative is resolved, how certain loose ends are tied together. How quickly can you read?

The time now is ....

But, as Winterbourne had said, it mattered very little. A week after this the poor girl died; it had been a terrible case of the

[8] Harper & Brothers, 1920.

fever. Daisy's grave was in the little Protestant cemetery, in an angle of the wall of imperial Rome, beneath the cypresses and the thick spring-flowers. Winterbourne stood there beside it, with a number of other mourners—a number larger than the scandal excited by the young lady's career would have led you to expect. Near him stood Giovanelli, who came nearer still before Winterbourne turned away. Giovanelli was very pale: on this occasion he had no flower in his buttonhole; he seemed to wish to say something. At last he said, "She was the most beautiful young lady I ever saw, and the most amiable"; and then he added in a moment, "and she was the most innocent."

Winterbourne looked at him, and presently repeated his words, "And the most innocent?"

"The most innocent!"

Winterbourne felt sore and angry. "Why the devil," he asked, "did you take her to that fatal place?"

Mr. Giovanelli's urbanity was apparently imperturbable. He looked on the ground for a moment, and then he said, "For myself I had no fear; and she wanted to go."

"That was no reason!" Winterbourne declared.

The subtle Roman again dropped his eyes. "If she had lived, I should have got nothing. She would never have married me, I am sure."

"She would never have married you?"

"For a moment I hoped so. But no. I am sure."

Winterbourne listened to him: he stood staring at the raw protuberances among the April daisies. When he turned away again, Mr. Giovanelli with his light, slow step, had retired.

Winterbourne almost immediately left Rome; but the following summer he again met his aunt, Mrs. Costello, at Vevay. Mrs. Costello was fond of Vevay. In the interval Winterbourne had often thought of Daisy Miller and her mystifying manners. One day he spoke of her to his aunt—said it was on his conscience that he had done her an injustice.

"I am sure I don't know," said Mrs. Costello. "How did your injustice affect her?"

"She sent me a message before her death which I didn't understand at the time; but I have understood it since. She would have appreciated one's esteem."

"Is that a modest way," asked Mrs. Costello, "of saying that she would have reciprocated one's affection?"

Winterbourne offered no answer to this question; but he presently said, "You were right in that remark you made last summer. I was booked to make a mistake. I have lived too long in foreign parts."

Nevertheless, he went back to live at Geneva, whence there continue to come the most contradictory accounts of his motives of sojourn: a report that he is "studying" hard—an intimation that he is much interested in a very clever foreign lady.

The time now is .... Elapsed time (in seconds) ....
Now let us look at the results of the four tests. Here is a chart

that will help you see at a glance how your speed of reading compares with the performance of a good college reader. Follow the instructions below in filling it out.

SELECTION	AUTHOR	NUMBER OF WORDS	YOUR TIME	YOUR SPEED	GOOD SPEED
I	Irvine	405			325 wpm
II	Bates	405			385 wpm
III	Montagu	370			405 wpm
IV	James	482			525 wpm

Instructions

- 1. In the appropriate column, enter your elapsed time for each selection.

- 2. Compute your reading speeds. To do this, divide the number of *seconds* you needed for each selection into the number of words in the selection. Multiply the result by 60.

  For example, a good college reader can get what he wants from Selection I (405 words) in 75 seconds. Dividing 75 into 405, we get 5.4; and 5.4 × 60 = 324 words per minute (wpm).

- 3. Enter your reading speed for each selection in the appropriate column.

How do your speeds compare with those made by a good reader?

A specific pattern should appear in your reading speed scores: you should have made your slowest speed on the first test and increased on each test, making your best time on the final test.

If your speed did not vary significantly, you apparently have not learned that reading speed can vary from one text to another. Indeed, you should read at varying speeds even within a single selection. The change in vocabulary, the change in purpose, the change in difficulty of a piece of writing of any length at all should produce a corresponding change in your reading technique.

Were your reading speeds significantly lower than those made by the good reader? The selections were chosen because they are from the kinds of books you can expect to find on college reading lists. If you had a great deal of trouble in learning what the authors were trying to tell you and therefore had to reread parts of the selections, your speed probably fell close to the 200 words per minute level. This speed is not adequate for college study. Though you will have many reading assignments in college that will force you to read at speeds even lower than 200 words per minute, most courses require a much higher reading speed if you want to do well in them and make your best grades.

Now we have measured how well you read and how fast. It is time to lay some plans for improvement.

Examine your reading habits

Regardless of what you may hear about the causes of poor reading, the majority of those who read poorly do so because they do not really read. And there is no reason why they should bother to improve their reading. Their reading habits consist of skimming the newspapers and reading here and there in popular magazines. They seldom tackle anything as consistently demanding as the day-to-day reading of the college student.

Take a look at your reading habits with the help of a questionnaire that has been prepared to cover reading problems most frequently encountered among college students. The items listed are all stumbling blocks to competent reading. They affect both speed and comprehension, and can make the difference between passing and failing your college courses. Any *yes* answer will reveal an area of difficulty.

■   YOUR READING PROFILE

1. I dislike reading.
2. I read everything at approximately the same rate.
3. I have to read many things at least twice in order to understand them.
4. I have read few books in my lifetime that were not assigned in school.
5. I almost never bother to notice the author's name or the title before getting into a book.
6. I cannot read if there is any noise about me.
7. I must have music while I read.
8. I ignore the preface to a book.
9. I ignore chapter titles and section headings within chapters.
10. When I complete a reading assignment, I remember little of what I have read.

11. Except for an occasional mark in a book, I write nothing while I am reading.

12. I try to underscore important parts of a book, but everything looks important to me.

13. I never bother to read footnotes.

14. I cannot be bothered with charts and graphs or other illustrations.

15. I read everything in a book, beginning with the first word and continuing right on through to the end, never bothering to reflect on what I am reading—except perhaps to look ahead to the end of the book to see how many pages are left.

16. I hear myself saying the words as I read.

17. I do not look up new or troublesome words in a dictionary.

18. I never read until the night before an examination because I do not remember for very long things I have read.

19. I often skip lines in reading without noticing the omission for quite a while; in fact, I occasionally skip whole pages without catching my mistake until well along in the wrong page.

20. I cannot concentrate on reading for more than half an hour.

21. I have to fight sleep when I read.

22. I cannot put the author's ideas into my own words.

23. Once I have finished reading, I cannot recall the points the author made.

24. I have difficulty in distinguishing between what is most important in a book and what is less important; I seem to come up with something entirely different from what my teachers find.

25. I am so afraid I do not understand what an author is saying that I go back and forth over the same material.

Fortunately, no one can have all the troubles listed here. But having even a few of them means that the rest of this chapter should be particularly helpful to you.

Points of attack in improving reading

Some courses in reading improvement emphasize most the role of the eyes in good reading. The student is told that he must take advantage of the great speeds at which his eyes can travel. He is shown how, after a bit of practice, he is able to move his eyes over thousands of words in a minute. Further, he is told that his visual span can be widened, his eyes trained to take in several words at a time, thereby speeding his reading even more. This is *not* improvement of reading. There is *no important difference* between how fast the eyes of the good reader and the poor reader can move. There is no difference between how wide a visual span the two kinds of readers have. The aim of reading improvement is not to strengthen your eyes.

What is important in reading is how effectively the brain grasps what the eyes see. Thus, two readers are shown the word *apothegm*. One knows what the word means, and the other does not. Have they seen equally well? Yes. Have they read equally well? Of course not. Without understanding, reading does not take place.

YOUR VOCABULARY IS YOUR FIRST POINT OF ATTACK

Good comprehension is not only a matter of your vocabulary. It depends on other factors as well, and we shall get to them soon. But knowledge of words is surely an important building block.

Unfortunately, vocabulary development is not an easy matter. By determined effort, you can help yourself greatly, but that effort must continue over a long period of time. Yet see how necessary such a program can be. Read this paragraph to see how your vocabulary is challenged by an author at work:

> One has called in doubt the type quality of Hamlet, Literary fashion takes him to be the antithesis of Don Quixote—as dreamer to knight errant; as man of thought to man of action. Does the text really bear out this convenient apposition? Hamlet is rather another illustration of a dramatist's surrender to the novelist's introspective and luxurious method, almost wholly controlled by the subconscious mind ministering to the creator's dominant mood at the moment. So subtle, so varied and elastic is the figure of Hamlet, that no one seems able to make a failure in the part. The great Hamlet, indeed, may be rare; the good Hamlet is a matter of course.
> —JOHN GALSWORTHY, *The Creation of Character in Literature*

Antithesis, knight errant, apposition, introspective, ministering —are all these words familiar to you? Unless they are, this passage—not difficult really—brings you up sharply. In fact, you would have a difficult time giving the gist of what Galsworthy said.

Every student must work at building his vocabulary in

college: education depends on it. In Chapter 5 of this book, you will find a method for learning foreign language vocabulary which you can adapt to learning the vocabulary of your own language.

EXPAND YOUR BACKGROUND OF KNOWLEDGE

Just as you had to know all the words in the paragraph from Galsworthy, you had to know who Don Quixote is and what his qualities are. If you did not, then the point of the paragraph could have escaped you. Your general knowledge affects your ability to read. Try this next paragraph, taken from a prominent work in anthropology. It will illustrate this point.

> The diversity of culture results not only from the ease with which societies elaborate or reject possible aspects of existence. It is due even more to a complex interweaving of cultural traits. The final form of any traditional institution, as we have just said, goes far beyond the original human impulse. In great measure this final form depends upon the way in which the trait has merged with other traits from different fields of experience.
> —Ruth Benedict, *Patterns of Culture*[9]

You can see that the vocabulary is not particularly difficult here, but if you do not have some experience in reading and thinking about the subject under discussion, you cannot come to grips with the idea being advanced.

If, on the other hand, you have some familiarity with what might be called the topography of the subject, you can more easily find your way through the particular area the author is concerned with.

Your college reading and lectures will of course open many such areas to you, but they will have twice the meaning for you if your own reading has to some extent prepared you for them. The broader your range of interests and knowledge, the greater your skill and pleasure in every facet of your college work, especially reading.

A good beginning for broadening your background of knowledge is a book entitled *Good Reading*, prepared by the Committee on College Reading, and published by New American Library. In it are listed titles in every area of interest—history, literature, the humanities, and science. If you will get a copy right away, you can begin immediately to

[9] Houghton Mifflin Company, 1934.

select your reading. Each title is accompanied by a description of contents that will help you in choosing books that appeal to your tastes and interests. Consistent reading based on this list is sure to enlarge and deepen your familiarity with a variety of subjects—and if you use your dictionary, you cannot fail to build up your vocabulary at the same time.

BECOME A READER

The habit of reading can be your most important ally during your college years and for the rest of your life. Through continuing contact with the images and ideas and information found in books, your own thinking will take on richness and depth that cannot possibly be stimulated by other media of communication—television and the like. There is no better way to converse with the minds of great men than to develop the habit of reading. It will not only broaden your knowledge but will expand your horizon of interests.

WORK WITH THE AUTHOR AS YOU READ

Effective reading means much more than simply viewing an author's words and then committing his ideas to memory. It means working along with him—thinking with him, putting yourself in his place, experiencing his ideas, debating his point of view. It means considering the relative importance of the ideas and facts he has assembled, their implications, and their relationship to other things you know. It means placing his principles and theories alongside your own and judging their relative values.

To the author, his book represents something that is finished; to you it is a project that is just beginning. If you approach your reading in this way, the time you spend with each book will double in value. You will know what you have read and you will remember it. And you will steadily improve your reading ability.

But you must be interested in what you are reading about if you are to work well with an author. It is easy to give up on a subject by proclaiming that you are not interested in it. Yet you can develop interest. It is a good bet that consistent and intensive effort in subjects that you initially find unappealing will ultimately pay off in growth of interest.

More often than not, lack of interest and boredom develop from the mind-wandering that bewilderment causes. When understanding is achieved by real effort—as it inevitably is—boredom disappears. Interest and understanding feed upon one another. When a subject that has drawn a blank suddenly appears meaningful, the reading process becomes less difficult. Certainly it is worth the hard work it takes to create real interest.

LEARN TO USE BOOKS SKILLFULLY

The reader who does not know how to use a book skillfully makes extra work for himself, while the reader who does and uses his skill gets the most out of reading in the shortest time. He knows where he is going, knows what to look for, and knows where he has been when he has finished.

Watch a skilled reader sometimes as he opens a book for the first time. He does not begin reading on page one, plowing through right to the end. He charts his way, just as the author charted his course before he began to write. Speaking now of nonfiction alone, consider the work an author does in organizing his thoughts and his material before he sets down a single word of his book. The reader can himself take advantage of that organization before he begins to read.

How is this done? There are various signposts throughout a book to help you do it.

First of all, there is the *preface,* in which an author may explain the title he has chosen for the book. He may tell you why he wrote the book. He shows what he was trying to accomplish. This is valuable information, for it shows where you are heading in your reading.

In some cases, you may even find an explanation of the main argument of the book. Or you may find a synopsis of the book. Finally, you may be treated to a more comprehensive look at the structure of the book than is given in many a table of contents. At any rate, cultivate the preface of a book. Do not skip over it, as so many do.

If the preface tells you where you are heading in a book, the *table of contents* tells you the intermediate steps toward that goal. Reading a table of contents will show you the grand plan of what you must read. You may find that the chapters of a book are grouped under several larger headings. So you know why the chapters are arranged as they are, and you can see the relationships between the various elements that make up a book. Sometimes your author will provide an outline of each chapter in the small print that follows chapter titles in a table of contents. This small print is the outline of the book. As you read it, you become familiar with the entire book. You begin to think with the author.

The *index* is one more help you must use. Before starting the book, pick out a couple of topics that are of special interest to you. Find them in the index and go to the pages referred to. You will read what the author has to say about these topics and can judge for yourself his method of treatment, his completness, and his point of view. Looking over the entire index, you find all the specific topics covered in the book. You can see in a few minutes the range of material covered. You know how to look ahead in the book for any information you may desire as a semester goes on, as your teacher mentions topics you have not yet read, as your author mentions topics he has not dealt with thoroughly up to that point. Without reading a book, you can find out a great deal about it in fifteen minutes.

HIT THAT FIRST CHAPTER ESPECIALLY HARD

The first is the most important chapter in any book. It gives you your most important clues about the writer. You find out how important the subject of the book is, how it relates to other subjects you are studying, what the subject includes, how it is going to be discussed. The subject matter of the book is defined, and new terms are introduced. If you bother to learn all these terms when you meet them in the first chapter of a book, your chances of reading that book effectively are greatly increased. If you do not, you will find yourself floundering all the way through.

To be at your best in reading a first chapter, you must follow this routine:

- 1. Look through the chapter to see whether your author has given you any *section headings.* These headings are the outline of the chapter, just as chapter titles are the outline of the book.
- 2. Inspect charts, graphs, and other *illustrations.* They may be the focal points of the chapter, presenting a résumé of the information you get from the chapter.

- 3. Read the *opening section* of the chapter and the *closing section*.

This is the way to find out whether your author has summarized in a special position the gist of the chapter. If he does this in the first chapter, the chances are that he will do it all the way through the rest of the book. If you read the summary of a chapter before reading the chapter itself, you are able to think along with an author. Keeping his main ideas in front of your mind as you read helps you understand a discussion and helps you learn effectively what a chapter is trying to teach you. If you know what a chapter is trying to do for you, then you can take part in the effort.

GO AFTER MEANING AS YOU READ

It would be easy to say, "Well, you are familar with how to size up a book. You know how to spend a few minutes looking through a chapter to discover its purpose and the points it will make. All you have to do now is sit back in your chair and read." This would be poor advice. The sitting-back-in-your-chair kind of reading is inadequate for college work.

Go after meaning as you read. Don't sit back and let the words flow over you.

Direct your attention toward finding the answers to the questions an author raises. As you find each answer, pause and think about what it means—in light of what has been said before and the topics that are about to be discussed. Think back and think ahead. This is real work. It is also real reading.

How long it will take to think about each point you encounter cannot be predicted. But only when you are content that you have understood exactly what has been said can you afford to go on ahead. You proceed from idea to idea until you come to the end of a chapter. At that point, you stop and think some more: what does it all add up to? Can you remember the entire line of reasoning? Do you understand how it all relates to what you have read before?

Does this sound difficult and time-consuming? Practice will make it easier for you, and such lists as the ones found in *Good Reading* can provide you with some first-rate practice material. Actually, these techniques *save* you time. You will find that the amount of time you have to spend in organizing your notes, papers, book reviews, quizzes, and so on, will be tremendously shortened. You will know the books you have read. You will know the questions they raise and the ideas they set forth. And you will know your way around in your books, so you can locate details quickly when you need to.

In exercising this skill, all you need to remember as you read is to *look for ideas,* for *answers to questions.* Here is a paragraph for you to practice on. It is taken from *An Introduction to Logic and Scientific Method,* by Morris R. Cohen and Ernest Nagel,[10] a book read by many college students before you. As you read it, keep in mind that you are after the main idea.

> The *fallacy of the argumentum ad hominem,* a very ancient but still popular device to deny the logical force of an argument (and thus to seem to prove the opposite), is to abuse the one who advances the argument. Thus the fact that a man is rich or poor, married or single, old or young, is frequently used as an argument to disprove the truth of the proposition he affirms, or to lend force to its contradictory. This has received a great impetus in recent times from popular psychoanalysis. Any argument whatsoever can be refuted in this way by inventing some unfavorable psychogenetic account of how or why the proponent of the argument came to hold that view. Thus attempts have been made to refute some of Spinoza's arguments as to the nature of substance, or as to the relation of individual modes to that substance, on the ground that they were advanced by a man who had separated himself from his people, a man who lived alone, was intellectualist in temper, and so on. Now it is true that certain motives weaken our competence and our readiness to observe certain facts or to state them fairly. Hence the existence of such motives, if such existence can be proved in any given case, is relevant to determine the credibility of a witness *when he testifies to what he himself has observed.* But the individual motives of a writer are altogether irrelevant in determining the logical force of his argument, that is, whether certain premises are or are not sufficient to demonstrate a certain conclusion. If the premises are sufficient, they are so no matter by whom stated. The personal history of Gauss is entirely irrelevant to the question of adequacy of his proof that every equation has a root; and the inadequacy of Galileo's theory of the tides is independent of the personal motives which led Galileo to hold it. The evidences for a physical theory are in the physical facts relevant to it, and not in the personal motives which led anyone to take an interest in such questions.

What was the main idea of the paragraph? Simply that we cannot refute an argument by calling our opponent names. Most of the paragraph is given over to illustrations of the

[10] Harcourt, Brace & World, Inc., 1934.

fallacy of the argumentum ad hominem. The opening sentence stated the main idea. Midway through the paragraph, you came upon a second italicized expression that stated that a person's character may be considered when he testifies to something he *himself has observed.* Otherwise his character is irrelevant. The main idea is yours now in convenient, nutshell size—and with practice you can soon develop the habit of extracting the essence of every paragraph in the same way.

IS CONCENTRATION YOUR PROBLEM?

In *Your Reading Profile* on pages 32–33, did you find that your problems seemed more like problems of concentration than of actual reading? All that you have read of how to improve your reading will help to solve the problem of concentration.

It is understandable that a college student cannot operate constantly at 100 per cent efficiency. One reason why this is so is that our minds are complex, our needs varied. At any given moment, our attention is attracted to several directions. Work competes with play, study with daydreams, attention with hunger. When distractions arise, we are sure to find it difficult to keep working on our studies. This trouble can arise in lectures, in the library, even in the examination hall. Therefore, do not be surprised or upset when this happens.

Whether your concentration suffers because you are uninterested in what you are reading or because you have a tendency to daydream, you can take certain steps toward helping the situation:

- 1. Read while sitting in a straight chair, rather than in a comfortable bed or armchair. Sitting in an attitude of attention will help you sustain attention.
- 2. Use all the techniques for active reading, in which you go after the author's ideas, working hard with him. The attention this demands will help you focus on your reading, while half-attention invites distraction.
- 3. Set your sights on many successive short goals rather than on reading straight through a long assignment without a break. As you attain each goal, make certain you understand what you have read, then take a short rest before starting out again. Incidentally, the best

kind of rest is a bit of calisthenics or deep-breathing. Your body gets more from improved circulation than it does from complete collapse.

HOW TO IMPROVE YOUR SPEED OF READING

What you have read thus far in this chapter has been directed toward helping you read faster than you now do. More needs to be said, however, about the wisdom of speeding your reading.

In many schools, students are permitted to waste a good deal of energy pursuing the will-o'-the-wisp of reading at fantastic speeds. Instead of concentrating on the kinds of reading matter they encounter in their courses and the reading techniques necessary to cope with them, they learn to fly along in such things as the weekly magazines. But this skill, in itself, is of no importance for you as a college student. For one thing, you can already do it, if you try. For another, you should devote yourself to learning how to read faster those things you *must* read.

A word should be said now about how *not* to accomplish this.

In many reading improvement courses, a student spends hours in front of devices like the "Reading Rate Accelerator," learning to stay ahead of a window shade that comes down over a book he is trying to read. As the student develops the knack of staying ahead of the shade, he steps up the speed of the machine so that it works faster and faster. But the window shade does not know whether all the lines on a given page should be read the same rate of speed—and presumably does not care. The fact is that no page of print has even been published that should be read at a constant rate of speed. Thus the machine asks you to read unrealistically—in fact, encourages you to read badly.

There are motion picture devices that are supposed to speed your reading. Their greatest drawback is that they run at a single speed while the viewers in a group read at many different rates. These machines have other handicaps that need not concern us now.

Such devices owe their popularity to novelty. The student is attracted to them because he likes gadgets. He enjoys them. But they do not teach him to read in the way college readers must read. You are better advised to forget about gadgets and work directly on your reading speed.

A flexible reading rate is your goal. You must have at your command several rates of reading that you can employ to meet the demands of any situation. Thus, you will read difficult books slowly and easy books quickly, with the range between these extremes also accommodated.

Being able to speed up and then slow down and then crawl and then repeat the entire process whenever understanding demands it is one of the miracles of your brain. The good reader slows down for material that is difficult to grasp. (He may cover only one page of physics in one hour.) The good reader speeds up for something that is easy to read. (He may read one hundred pages of light fiction in one hour.) He is constantly concerned with whether or not he is getting what he should from what he is reading, with whether there is a subtlety in the material being read that requires especially close attention, with whether there is some inconsistency or ambiguity in a text, with whether there is some vocabulary that is strange to the reader or that is being used in a novel way. When the signals are clear, the reader is able automatically to adjust his rate to what he is trying to accomplish.

Your goal in reading must be to extract meaning from what you read. One chapter in a book you are reading may survey a field and establish several important concepts. Succeeding chapters may develop each one in turn. Your familiarity with individual chapters will vary, as will your ability to grasp them. Therefore, your rate of reading must vary. One chapter may be crammed with important data that will have to be read carefully if you aim for complete mastery of that book. On the other hand, if you want only to survey the data and not study them, then your reading of the chapter will be different.

In order to be able to achieve the flexibility of reading rate that is implied here, you should spend a short time—all it really takes—on extending the upper limit of your reading speed. It is simple to do and worth your while.

The first step is to pull out all the stops and find out just how fast you can read now. For this experiment, use the easiest book you can find. A detective story or a light novel will do. The kind of book does not matter as long as it is easy. Without following detailed advice on how to speed your reading, time yourself on half a dozen pages. If you can let yourself go on this test and score something over five hundred words a minute, you will have the feel of what it means to read fast. From then on you ought to practice this speeding every now and then.

In the author's classes at Columbia University, many students want to speed their reading. They are given a selection to read and are told that when they finish they will have to take a test to show that they understand what they have read. Their speeds are always slow, well below two hundred words a minute on the average. Then they are told that they will have another selection to read that is taken from the same book as the first selection. The test they will take will also be similar to the first test. On this reading their speeds go up to an average of two hundred and fifty words a minute. The gain they have made from one test to the other is better than 30 per cent without loss of comprehension.

They have not learned to read faster. They have merely found something out about the kind of reading they will have to do on a test. They have also found that the test is not as terrible as they originally thought it would be.

After a few more tests and some discussion covering the same points being made in this chapter, they read at an average rate of higher than three hundred words a minute. Have they learned to read faster? Or is their increasing confidence at work, encouraging them to read at rates they already could handle? Most people, through lack of confidence, habitually read more slowly than they have to.

Here is a *ten-hour program to improve your reading speed.* If you want to get up to the astronomical speeds you read about, or if you want to read fast enough so that you can handle all your college assignments at a decent rate, try this simple routine. All you will need is a watch, pencil, and supply of books as easy to read as detective stories.

First, circle the page number on every tenth page of the first book. Then turn to page one, note the time, and read as quickly as you can. Remember, comprehension is not a problem. See how fast you can go. You know you will never read your course work in the same way, but you want to get the feel of speeded reading so that you can extend the upper limit of your reading speed.

When you get to page ten, stop, note the elapsed time and say to yourself, "I am going to cut that time down on the next ten pages." Away you go, stopping at every tenth page, noting the time, and then going on full of resolve to beat your previous record.

Do this one hour a day for ten days. It is best to do it

every day at the same time of the day. If you miss an occasional day, it does not matter, but do not let the practice extend more than two weeks.

You will be amazed at the results. It is common to see students double their speed in this time.

To satisfy your curiosity about how many words you can read in a minute, count the number of words on two or three pages to estimate the average number of words on a page. When you get your speed up to four hundred or five hundred words a minute on easy material, you read fast enough.

If your speed gets up this high before the ten hours are up, change to more challenging books—but don't plunge into Gibbon or Carlyle. Move gradually. A Dickens novel, or one by Hemingway, is more appropriate. Your speed will immediately drop, but not markedly. In a few hours of practice, you should be able to approach the same heights.

If you can do so, concern yourself no longer with your reading speed. Concentrate instead on developing the ability to read widely and well in all kinds of reading matter. Your college courses demand it.

CHAPTER 3

HOW TO LISTEN TO
A LECTURE

MUCH of the most important material and information for your college studies will be provided in lectures. You will know what to listen for when you are taking notes if you remember that a lecture has three main purposes:

- 1. To explain difficult subjects.

- 2. To present material you would have difficulty in locating without help.

- 3. To develop ideas incompletely discussed in your textbooks.

Although it is obvious that lectures are extremely important, they are no better than the notes you take in class. Here are two sets of lecture notes on the same lecture in a psychology course. The words that both employ are identical. The first notes are cramped, unattractive, unemphatic, and difficult to use. Compare them with the second notes. See how much more useful the same words become when they are set up properly.

Which notes would you prefer to study? Can you picture page after page of notes written in the first form?

Defense techniques - reaction against an obstacle or its cause, toward gaining help or getting out of trouble. Identification - borrows success or qualities of others to satisfy individual - child gets prestige from family wealth or status, membership in gang. Adults from club membership, neighborhood, reading hero stories. Attention getting - makes individual object of attention by others to satisfy individual. - Child crying. Adults hypochondria - Compensation - substitutes satisfying activity for difficult one. Child - who has trouble in school spends his time at sports in which he can excel. Adult excessive eating to forget failure in job. Rationalizing - thinking up valid reasons for socially unacceptable behavior - sour grapes - child who wasn't "really" trying to make "A" in school. Adult who didn't want to be president of his company because he would lose private life. Projection - seeing own characteristics or motives in others - Child calls another "bully". Adult accuses others of dishonesty.

Good lecture notes have to be written with an eye to their future use. This chapter will show you how to listen to a lecture so that you get out of it what you should and how to take the kind of notes that lead to top grades.

You will hear students say there is no use in attending lectures, that all you need to learn is found in textbooks. Not true. At a lecture, you have the chance to hear ideas and interpretations original with your teachers, you have the chance to think through problems with them. Above all, you have the sense of personal participation that is sometimes difficult to achieve through reading. This contact of mind with mind is extremely important in learning.

Defense Techniques

Definition:	reaction against an obstacle or its cause, toward gaining help or getting out of trouble.

I Identification.
def.	borrows success or qualities of others to satisfy individual.
ex.	Child gets prestige from family wealth or status, membership in gang.
	Adults from club membership, neighborhood, reading heroic stories.

II Attention getting
def.	makes individual object of attention by others to satisfy individual.
ex.	Child crying
	Adults hypochondria

III Compensation
def.	substitutes satisfying activity for difficult one.
ex.	Child who has trouble in school spends his time at sports in which he can excel
	Adult excessive eating to forget failure in job

IV Rationalizing
def.	thinking up "valid" reasons for socially unacceptable behavior — sour grapes
ex.	Child who wasn't really trying to make "A" in school.
	Adult who didn't want to be president of his company because he would lose private life.

V Projection
def.	seeing own characteristics or motives in others
ex.	Child calls another "bully"
	Adult accuses others of dishonesty.

How good a listener are you?

We take for granted the ability to listen. After all, twelve years of schooling before college certainly provides ample practice. Yet, in the author's classes in improvement of study habits, more than 70 per cent of the students report difficulty in taking notes. This is the more disturbing when we consider that many colleges rely heavily on the lecture in the freshman year.

Students who feel they are not doing an adequate listening job complain:

"I'm never sure that I am getting the most important points in a lecture."

"When I finish taking notes, I cannot read them. I cannot listen and write carefully at the same time."

"My mind is blank as I sit there. At best I am a stenographer, at worst a sleeper."

"I write so much that I find myself missing most of what is going on."

"The lecturer goes too fast for me."

"Taking notes is a waste of time for me, because I don't use them afterward. I guess I don't take very good notes."

What is the reason for these complaints? The handicap these students share is *inexperience* in the kind of listening needed in college.

Do you have a clear picture of how to listen? Effective listening is much like effective reading. In listening, you are at your best only when you share with the lecturer the search for ideas and understanding, just as you work along with an author in first-class reading. It is easy to work along with a teacher in a question-and-answer session. But when you are listening to a lecture, your responsibility increases. Just as in reading, the amount of effort you put in will determine whether you can keep up with the ideas being presented.

The notebook page in front of you as you listen to a lecture helps you participate in the lecture. Look upon it as a chance to outline answers you will one day supply on an examination. Rephrased, the lecture title can be an essay question. Main entries in your notes can be the backbones of the paragraphs of your answers. Each item under those main entries can be a detail to support your answer. Surely if you use note-taking as preparation for an examination, you will see the direction your notes must take.

Knowing how lectures are organized will help you listen and work effectively.

Unlike books, which can be read again and again, lectures can never be heard again.[1] Knowing this, your teachers generally tailor the nature and the amount of material they cover to what you should be able to handle. If you find yourself racing to keep up with a lecture, or unable to select material for your notes, *you do not know how to listen.*

A lecturer prepares an outline of the lecture he will give. Besides enumerating the main ideas he will present, he lists supporting arguments and information. In class, he may work from this outline or he may merely keep it available near him. But he works from his plan whether he appears to consult it or not. It is your job to listen for that plan in the spoken words of the lecture. If you train yourself to do this, the notes you take down will approach the form of the lecturer's own notes. While the lecturer will help you somewhat by emphasizing the most important elements of his talk, your own skill will count for a great deal. This is why so much is being made of the ability to listen.

The essentials of good listening

1. PREPARE YOURSELF TO LISTEN

How would you like to sit down now at a lecture for senior college students on the geological history of Outer Mongolia? How much would you learn from it—assuming you have had no previous study? How could you possibly take notes on everything the lecturer says that is new for you? Of what use would your notebook be in preparing for an examination? But let us dismiss this horrible picture from our minds right now.

You cannot hope to get anything from a lecture if you know nothing at all about the subject your lecturer will discuss. If you are up to date in your readings, you will have the necessary

[1] We have become used to the sight of an occasional student taking a lecture down on a tape recorder so that he can hear it again. This practice is an extraordinary waste of time. Listen properly and take effective notes rather than look for some "gimmick." The skill that you develop as a result of applying the principles of this chapter will do far more for you than buying a tape recorder.

vocabulary to understand your lecturer, you will understand the general *principles* of the subject, you will have your own *ideas* in mind. Thus, the outline of the lecture prepared by the lecturer will be easy to grasp and will be reflected in the notes you take yourself.

Without preparation, you flounder uncomfortably, wondering just what the lecturer is working toward, indeed what he means at all.

What can *you* do to prepare for a lecture?

- A. Read your textbook assignment *before* going to class, not afterward.
- B. Read over the notes you have made on your reading *before* the lecture.
- C. Read your notes on previous lectures *before* the lecture.

2. LISTEN AND THINK BEFORE YOU WRITE

Observation of skilled note-takers shows that they listen about 90 per cent of the time, write for the remaining 10 per cent. They do not rush into furious scribbling to make sure they miss nothing important. Rather they weigh the merits of what they hear, think back to what they have read, and finally compress the material they want to record into brief, accurate statements. The poor note-taker, in his desire to get everything, has no time left for listening.

Do *not* sit over your notebook with your pen poised like a knife to stab the first word the lecturer utters.[2] Your pen must not interfere with your listening. Keep it on your desk. Do not write until you hear something worth reporting.

Books supply chapter titles, but lecture titles ordinarily are not given. Finding the *title* for a lecture is one of your first tasks. That title will help you in your studying, just as a chapter title helps you in your reading. As was mentioned previously, the title of a set of lecture notes can well become an essay test question.

Under ideal conditions, you will have little trouble finding the title of a lecture. Don't be surprised, however, if you sometimes have to listen for a great while to find it. The style of your lecturer and your preparation for the lecture will determine how soon you understand just what a lecture is all about.

[2] A common campus joke has it that the teacher can tell the difference between undergraduates and graduate students by saying, "Good morning." Undergraduates return the greeting, while graduate students write it down in their notebooks.

Books supply subheadings within chapters to call your attention to main ideas, but lectures ordinarily do not. In a lecture, your awareness of the mannerisms of the lecturer and, again, your preparation for the lecture will show the way to main ideas.

When you have the first *main idea* of a lecture clearly in mind, *write it in your own words,* remembering:

• Parroting a lecturer does not indicate that you understand him, merely that you have heard him. Note-taking done well is part of learning. It is your first recitation of new material. It is not an exercise in writing.

• Your words will be fewer than those of the lecturer, because brevity in note-taking is essential. The less you write, the more time you will have for listening. The less you write, the easier will be your studying. Thus, a phrase will do better than a sentence, a word better than a phrase.

Remember the ratio 90-to-10. If you seriously upset that proportion of listening to writing, you are probably mistaking details and minor ideas for the main ideas that are your primary goal.

3. MAKE YOUR NOTES EASY TO STUDY

Good notes are written in outline form because relationships between ideas are best shown in that form. So use all the symbols commonly used in outlines. Assign your first main idea a Roman numeral and make the entry flush with the left-hand margin of your page. When you next write, it will be either to note the next main idea or the first subordinate idea under that main idea. Use letters of the alphabet to tag subordinate ideas. Or, as in the case of the psychology notes on page 48, label lesser entries with their function: *definition, example, reference,* etc. Don't forget to indent several spaces to show even more strongly the subordinate status of the entry.

When you have finished writing a note, concentrate again on listening, to guarantee that your notes will contain no more than what you will need for studying and no less. Remember that you are preparing a study source, not a permanent verbatim record of the lecture.

When a lecturer covers material you have already read in

a textbook, he is giving you a chance to review that material. You will see later in this chapter how important repeated reviews are in achieving high grades.

To see how well you have absorbed the points made so far on note-taking, here is the transcribed opening section of a lecture. It will give you a chance to practice note-taking. Assume that you are a student in a freshman English course, that the topic is *propaganda techniques*. If possible, have someone read this brief excerpt aloud to you, or read it aloud yourself, listening to it as though you were in class.

> As a responsible citizen and intelligent consumer, you must be able to recognize and understand propaganda. You will encounter forms of propaganda in almost every medium of communication. While the results of propaganda are not always important, you must be ready to see it for what it is.
>
> One way to begin a study of propaganda is to recognize the forms it takes most often: glittering generalities, name-calling, card-stacking, bandwagon methods, and the plain folks approach.

Can you see that the lecture is already cast in a form that will be easy to outline? The title will surely be *Propaganda Techniques*. Each technique will be a major section of your notes, introduced by a Roman numeral. Under each technique will come a description of it, and your notes will have to catch the gist of each description, just as was done in the psychology notes on page 48. Finally, you will probably be given examples of each technique, and your notes will show the outstanding ones. Knowing that the lecture will deal with all five techniques, write down the first one, *glittering generalities*. Underscore it and wait for its definitions and examples.

While many lectures you will hear are not as easy to organize in your notes, sufficient preparation on a topic combined with careful thinking and listening will give you the form your notes should take for maximum usefulness in study.

There are different kinds of lectures, and each will demand different note-taking techniques. Thus far, we have been concerned with the most predictable of all—the one we may call "carefully structured." The outline of the lecture is clear; our notes on page 54 reflect it:

You will also encounter the rambling lecture. This can take the form of an entertaining string of stories more like a performance than a straightforward lecture. While this kind of lecture makes special demands on your ability to prepare

Propaganda Techniques

I. glittering personalities
    A. (definition)
    B. (examples)

II. name-calling
    A. (definition)
    B. (examples)

III. card-stacking
    A. (definition)
    B. (examples)

IV. bandwagon methods
    A. (definition)
    B. (examples)

V. plain folks approach
    A. (definition)
    B. (examples)

notes for effective study, it is not without merit. It may be that the material covered in the lecture lends itself to this kind of treatment and, in fact, points may be made so effectively that they literally are never forgotten. The rambling lecture may occur because a student's question has tapped a subject of special interest to the lecturer. Rather than go ahead with the plan he had in mind for the hour, the lecturer will present material he knows well but has not organized especially for that particular time. The fact that the form of the lecture will present difficulties for the student is unfortunate, but it is outweighed by the opportunity it affords to listen to information and ideas close to the heart of the lecturer.

Whatever the reason for the rambling lecture, when you encounter one, at the least try to keep your notes legible. Get the important points down as you see them in short paragraphs composed of words and phrases rather than sentences. When the lecture has come to an end, read through what you have written to see whether, by *underscoring, deleting,* and *numbering,* you can impose some order on the material.

Often the point of the rambling lecture is not the information it presents, but the spirit, tone, or scholarly wisdom of the presentation. It is better in such a case to spend your time listening intently without trying to take any notes whatsoever.

Another kind of lecture may direct itself toward the "close examination" of a work of literature or other document. Have the poem or other writing in front of you during the lecture. Number the lines or the paragraphs to help you take notes. As you move along through the text, mark the notes in your notebook with the number of the corresponding sections of the text. When you come to use your notes, study them alongside the text itself.

4. THINK AHEAD TO EXAMINATION TIME

Every page in a good notebook outlines the answer to an essay test question. Each item on every page is a potential short-answer question. As you write your notes, keep in mind the tests for which they will prepare you.

Underscore with colored pencil words and phrases you want particularly to emphasize because the lecturer has done so. But do so sparingly. Some students make the mistake of letting themselves be carried away by inexperience and misguided enthusiasm. When they have finished a page of notes, everything is underscored, and nothing is emphasized.

Abbreviate to save time, but use forms you will understand tomorrow, next week, and next month. Nothing is more frustrating than wondering what the devil it was you meant to say when you wrote *LMD* or *gu/bef/destr.*

Use asterisks or exclamation marks or any other attention-getting symbols you want. But use them sparingly.

Place a question mark in the margin of your notes when you want to tell yourself that a point needs clarification after the lecture. Be sure to check the entry as soon as possible. If you wait a week, you may not even understand what the trouble was. One day, on a test, you will suddenly find that you should have done something about a certain word or phrase.

There is no substitute for a loose-leaf notebook. This makes it possible to shift pages around at will, and rearrangement is often necessary as a term goes by. You may find that information from a lecture given early in a semester is best studied along with notes made much later. You find that placing reading notes with lecture notes made on the same topic is a time-saver. You want to discard notes you have mastered so well that you do not need them any longer.

Use only one side of page to help make notes legible.

On the blank sheet opposite the page you are using for notes, write special entries specifically geared to study needs. See how the technique is used on the following page from a student notebook.

If some of these entries concern dictionary definitions, you have ample space for writing the definitions in your notes. If an entry sends you to a portion of a book or to an article for

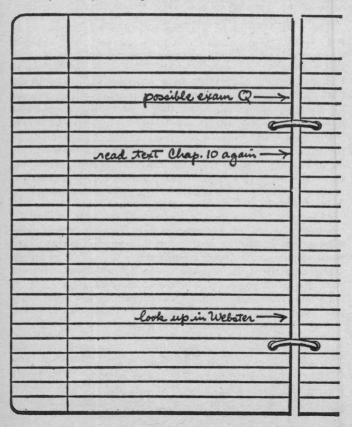

further reading, you have space for writing a brief summary of what you find there.

Before going on to how to use your notes in making top grades, let us sum up the four steps in note-taking:

- 1. Prepare yourself to listen.
- 2. Listen and think before you write.
- 3. Make your notes easy to study.
- 4. Think ahead to examination time.

How to use your lecture notes

There is no point in learning how to take good notes if you are not going to use them properly. Yet many students make a great effort to take conscientious notes during lectures and then use them badly, if at all. They seem to feel that as long as the notes are there in a notebook, they should do nothing further about them until the chips are down, on the night before a test. Notes that have not been looked at in months usually mean nothing to their authors on that fateful night.

Proper use of lecture notes involves three main steps:

- 1. Initial reading right after the lecture is over.
- 2. Second reading just before the next lecture.
- 3. Periodic review.

Let us examine these three steps in detail and see *how using a few minutes of time well before an examination* can save you many hours of frantic boning and can pay off in higher grades.

1. INITIAL READING

The sight of students scrambling to get out of a classroom when the hour is over can make your blood run cold. You would think someone had released tear gas. Lecturers usually do not bother to look at their watches to see whether an hour is drawing to a close. The audience begins to get restless. Pens are put back in pockets with the greatest show of finality. Books are arranged neatly for carrying. Notebooks are closed with the solemnity and formality of Big Ben striking the hour.

Unless your schedule calls for a quick dash to a classroom far across campus, never rush away from a lecture. Investing a few minutes after a lecture ends can pay big dividends. It is then that you can best check your notes for completeness, clarity, and usefulness.

The lecturer's words are still fresh in your mind, and a quick reading of your notes will show whether you have left any pertinent material out of them. You may also find unnecessary repetition. Examine the flow of ideas from one page to the next to see whether everything holds together as it should. Check the titles you have written for accuracy.

Highlight those parts of your notes that merit special attention. Perhaps you will find it best not to underscore during the lecture, so you will do that now. See whether the numbers you have used to mark main ideas are in proper sequence, whether some of the main ideas are really as important as you thought they were while writing. Take this chance to correct mistakes. An abbreviation you invented during the hour may already have lost its meaning and is bound to give you trouble next time you read your notes. Spell the word out or devise a better abbreviation that you can use the next time you need it.

So your first reading job is primarily that of editor. But in the *three minutes* you spend in editing, you will learn an amazing amount.

2. SECOND READING

In the first part of this chapter, you were told that it is important to read your notes of a previous lecture before listening to the next. You will recall that this is part of your preparation for a lecture, making the lecture easier to understand and organize in your notes.

It has another purpose. In the second reading of your notes, which comes just before you listen to the succeeding lecture, you have your first chance to see how much you learned in the class just gone by. This self-test is your first attempt to quiz yourself in advance of the day when your teacher will test you. As much as possible, look only at the main ideas in your notes and *try to recite from memory the supporting detail or evidence for the main ideas.*

Study right from the start as though you were taking the test you will take one day.

This second reading is advisable because you learn most effectively through repeated exposures to the material you are studying. And, for best results, the exposures must not be crowded together, but must be spaced widely and regularly over a period of time.

Do not delay this second reading until you have accumulated notes from several lectures. If you do it just before each lecture, you will be surprised at how much you remember from the lecture itself and your first reading of your notes. If you delay, you lose this recollection. At that point, the material might just as well be brand new.

As with the first reading, you spend only a few minutes in this recitation or test. Surely the minutes before class are habitually wasted by most students. Using these *minutes* during the weeks and months before your tests will save you *hours* later on.

3. PERIODIC REVIEW

In an experiment, the author had twenty students learn a ten-word nonsense vocabulary. A few days later, a five-minute review of the words was given to half the group. One week after the initial learning period, only one of the ten students who had not reviewed was able to write more than half the words. Of the group who reviewed, seven were able to write more than half the words.

This observation is in line with the claim frequently made by psychologists that students forget about 80 per cent of what they learn within two weeks after they have learned it *unless they review during that period*. The second reading of your notes is your first effort to defeat that discouraging statistic. And it is effective because it comes so soon after learning took place.

But there is need for much more than one review.

In the lower grades, your teachers provided all the review you needed to prevent forgetting by giving you frequent tests of material they had taught. Those tests, combined with home-work assignments, forced you to go over and over your material. In college, except for a few subjects in which you will have regular homework, the responsibility for review is entirely yours.

Your history professor, for example, will proceed through

the course material he has laid out whether you are keeping up with him or not. For the student who wants to shirk his work, the college system is perfect. He will not have to pay the piper until the very end of the semester. The student who wants to make good grades and learn all he can feels ill at ease through all the semester if he is not doing his reading and using his lecture notes.

Make review automatic. Use part of the regular study time allocated to each course.

How often should you review yor notes? As often as necessary for you to learn them—*but with a breathing space between sessions.*

In general, if a course meets three times a week, you should inspect all your notes at least once each week. If the course meets less often, you can stretch the review period out to once every ten days or two weeks.

Each time you review, read through your notes completely and then go back to test yourself by looking at major headings and trying to recall the information under them. Begin with the earliest notes and go right through to the end.

At the beginning of a semester, you will have few notes to review, and the work will take but a few minutes. Do not wait until you have a sizable amount to study. The object is to learn the material as it is presented so that you can always have time for the current material as it comes into your notebook.

Periodic review sharply reduces the amount of time you will need for final review. With the writing, initial reading, reading before your next lecture, and at least seven reviews, you will have gone over your notes ten times. Even the lectures that come just before the end of a semester will be reviewed at least three times.

How about the student who has not reviewed periodically? On the night before the Big Day, he is in hot water.

CHAPTER 4

HOW TO IMPROVE YOUR WRITING

HOW well can you express yourself in writing? Thousands of college teachers claim that incoming college freshmen cannot write a decent sentence. Unfortunately there is a good deal of truth in this sweeping generalization. Even though it may not apply to you, *you should work hard at becoming the best writer you can be.*

Don't be concerned now with the question of how much talent you possess. Whatever natural ability is yours exists to be used. So regardless of how great it is, regardless of how small it is, develop it further.

In this chapter you will find practical suggestions for improving your writing, and while the focus of the discussion will be upon the demands of freshman English, everything you read will prove useful for whatever writing you do both during college days and afterward.

Choose theme topics you can handle

In the fifteen weeks of a one-semester course in composition, you will be called upon to write anywhere from ten to fifteen themes of two kinds: *impromptu* and *prepared.* Students usually think of impromptu themes as requiring no advance work, not preparation. Actually this is far from the truth. Well done, the impromptu theme reflects the greatest amount of preparation—a lifetime of study and thought. You prepare for impromptu themes by reading the newspaper every day for as many years as you have been able to read, by reading magazines that are worth reading, by listening to good music and good conversation, by going to the theater and art museums, by reading good books. You prepare by thinking about things worth thinking about. You prepare by being interested in the world around you.

Our concern now is with the prepared theme, which is usually done outside class, although it is sometimes written in class from notes made outside. A prepared theme is written only after careful choice of a topic, consideration of just what should be said about it, preparation of a plan for treating the topic adequately, research in the topic when necessary, and a careful outline. You will notice that the first responsibility is the choice of topic. This is no small matter, but it is one that is often treated lightly by students.

Care in choosing a topic will prevent a great deal of trouble. Students make the mistake of jumping at the first idea that comes to mind. They may end up with a topic about which they have nothing to say—result, no paper. Worse, they may come up with a topic that can be handled only in book length. The average college theme is apt to run about five hundred words. (Don't expect this to be the case in every classroom. Some teachers would rather have much less, some more.) If you tackle all the world's problems in one theme, you cannot do a good job. It is far better to develop a limited topic completely than to try to do justice to a grand scheme in few words. Make certain that you do not underestimate the scope of a problem you are going to discuss.

Choose theme topics that involve no more research than you can complete in the time at your disposal. When you think of how many themes will be required in your composition course, you will realize that you cannot write papers week after week that demand many hours in the library without neglecting your other courses. There just is not enough time to do all your work properly if you succumb to choices of topics that get you in over your head. Even more trying than topics that demand library research are topics requiring research in sources hard to locate. How frustrating it is to spend hours trying to find information not available to you. Before embarking on any paper that requires research, check your resources to find out whether you can find what you are after. It is exciting and valuable to search out information, but freshman English does not always provide the time you need.

Thus far, you have been told to choose topics you can

- Treat adequately in the time you have for preparation.
- Treat adequately in the assigned theme length.
- Research without excessive difficulty.

These recommendations will help make life livable at college and help you improve your writing. Now for a word on planning.

Don't be caught by deadlines

New theme assignments are generally made by your teacher each time you turn in a completed assignment. If you are going to do your best work and make the best grades you can, you must manage your time so that you can handle the flow of work.

Whenever an idea for a theme comes to mind (it may be while your teacher is making an assignment), *write it down* so that you will have a record of it. A special section of your notebook is advisable for recording these ideas. A separate page or half-page for each idea is a good investment, because you will have space under each entry for recording subsequent thoughts concerning each topic.

Look at your theme topics from time to time to see whether outlines for the papers come to mind. This frequent consultation will also help you see whether you will have to have some time in the library for a topic you will undertake.

When you find that some source material is needed, make a place in your weekly schedule for a trip to the library. An orderly procedure such as this is far better than discovering that some last-minute work is vital before you can write a paper on the night before it is due. What you need may be some significant data to support an argument you will advance. It may be that you will want to verify some claims you are going to make. Or you may want to find out what someone else has said in regard to a question you are going to treat.

Make careful notes on your research. Relying on your memory is dangerous. It can result in duplication of work if you find that you have to go back to your source, or it may cause slipshol reporting of what you have found. Use your notebook idea pages for whatever research notes you have to make.

Record ideas even for papers that have not yet been assigned. Sooner or later, every theme you ever thing is worth writing will have its chance to be written. If you can keep a supply of theme topics on hand, they will never go to waste.

The writing itself

How does the student go about learning to write well? How much can books teach him on the subject? Writing is itself a difficult subject to write about. Some experts like to speak generally of the characteristics of good writing as if there were just a few attributes of good writing that need only be defined and illustrated in order to tell the student all he has to know about writing. Obviously this is not enough. Others like to dwell on the mistakes of writers, thinking that if you avoid stylistic errors you will improve your writing. Finally there are the experts who list rules of grammar and usage, with the idea that if you learn the rules you will become a good writer.

The remainder of this chapter draws on all three methods. Yet you must understand that careful reading of this chapter will only help you make a start toward becoming a good writer. Criticism by your teachers will be even more helpful. Practice —thousands of hours of it—will help you further. And one day you will feel that you can write; perhaps you will be correct in your judgment. Even if you are, you will then want to read more about how to write, be criticized further, and practice for additional thousands of hours. The process is endless but worthwhile. Good writers are universally admired and needed.

Clarity

If you are not understood, you have not written. Never mind the poet whose meaning *you* cannot grasp. Never mind the novelist *you* cannot cope with. Never mind the theoretical physicist whose meaning is far beyond *you* now. We are speaking of you and what you will write in college. English themes, term papers, examination answers, senior essays, research papers, laboratory reports, short stories, poetry, plays—whatever *you* write must be understood. Of course not by everybody, just as the poet or novelist is not understood by everybody.

Consider your audience. When you write a theme, you are writing for your teacher and perhaps for your classmates. In the English class, unless your teacher specifies otherwise, your audience is limited to the English class members. You will soon discover by listening to comments of your classmates and reading your teacher's remarks that your writing must display good sense, accuracy, convincing argument, evidence, direction, precision, and respect for the intelligence of the reader. Above all, it must be clear.

CLARITY OF THOUGHT

How is clarity achieved? First of all, by being clear in your own mind as to what it is you are trying to convey. Your thesis, your main idea, the attitude you are trying to produce in your audience—whatever your purpose in writing—should be before you always as you write. "I want to tell them that things are all wrong in our times, that the values I respect are gone from modern life. I want them to feel as I do that revival of the religious spirit is essential." "I think that politics is an honorable profession and that we all ought to be in politics to a greater extent than we now are." "I want them to know things about me they do not know, things about themselves they do not know." "I want them to see that modern literature misses out because it looks at us wrongly."

Write your purpose on a large sheet of paper and keep that paper before you as you write. Consult it frequently as you write. Consult it before you begin, between paragraphs, before editing your work. Every word you put down should be justified on the basis of whether it helps achieve the goal you have set for your paper.

OUTLINING AND CLARITY

Your purpose in writing will influence your plan of writing or outline. In the process of outlining, ask yourself what is the best possible arrangement of elements in a paper for clear understanding by your audience. Is your reader barely able to hang on to the thread of argument, or is he helped by the arrangement you are setting up for him? You are trying to work from some initial point toward a final point. That goal may be a state of mind, an attitude, a reasoned conclusion firmly held, a mental picture, an emotion. The best outline for a paper guides the reader inexorably toward the goal you have set for him.

Suppose you were assigned the task of commenting on some

phase of modern communications, television, radio, or the press. One title that comes to mind is *Comics Are Not Funny*. You could take the position that children are being harmed by exposure to horror comics. Such a paper could be written in these steps:

- 1. State your position.
- 2. Describe a fair sample of the comics you have in mind.
- 3. Cite figures to show their wide distribution among the young.
- 4. Quote authorities showing that such comics harm the young.
- 5. Draw conclusions and recommendations you feel are merited.

Incidentally, in writing on this topic, you might well take a point of view opposed to the one just presented. A skillful job could be done by comparing horror comics with the fairy tales of Grimm.

Perhaps you can see that a good paper might also be written as a comparison of today's comics with those of an earlier day A good paper could be constructed along these lines:

- 1. Describe modern comics.
- 2. Describe older comics.
- 3. Discuss the values of each.
- 4. Conclude that today's comics are not what they might be.

Another theme developed from the same topic could present the ambitious argument that comics are not funny today because our society is humorless, that the publications under attack in many places merely reflect how we feel and act, that they thrive because of this and will change only when we change.

Whatever direction you choose to follow, go steadily and logically from your reader's present state of mind or understanding to where you want him to be when you have finished. Are the intermediate steps in the plan as clear as they should be? Are there gaps in the presentation? Do you gloss over important aspects of the problem? Are you giving your reader all the information he needs in order to grasp your point clearly?

TOPIC SENTENCES AND CLARITY

Once the outline satisfies you in regard to clarity of direction, write the topic sentence for each step in the development of the paper. You will not know how long your paragraphs are going to be, but you know the major sections of the paper. Develop the topic sentence of each individual section as a signpost showing the way to the end of the paper. Think of the sentences you write as a short summary of the entire paper. If you have really thought through your topic, you will not find it hard to write the topic sentences, and you will reap great benefits.[1]

You help yourself considerably by writing your leading sentences first and then working from them: For example, in a paper dealing with the contrast between the comics of today and yesterday:

- 1. Analysis of the story lines of the five leading modern comics reveals that they are not comic at all.
    A.
    B.
    C.
    D.
    E.

- 2. The five leading comic strips of 1934 were quite different.
    A.
    B.
    C.
    D.
    E.

- 3. Let us examine the response of the young reader to these stories and situations.
    A. The modern comics may appeal to a youngster's love of adventure, but he finds not one joke to laugh at. (examples)

[1] It is common to hear writers complain that they have trouble in starting a paper, and once they have finished the first page they can write easily from then on. Thinking ahead to all the topic sentences in a paper puts off for a while the actual writing but makes writing easier by showing you just where you are going in the paper. It is much easier to write from topic sentence to topic sentence than to start out with a vague conception of where you are going but no idea of how you are going to get there. That first fresh sheet staring at you can be pretty menacing when you are not sure of what you are going to say.

    B. Laughter appears to be the chief aim of the older comic strip. (examples)
- 4. Of interest also are the drawings presented.
    A. style and content of modern drawings
    B. style and content of older drawings
- 5. Surely there is justification for calling most of today's comic strips by some other name.

Developing your outline one step further in this manner, to include topic sentences at critical places in the development of the ideas, will help make your paper clear.

PARAGRAPHING FOR CLARITY

Clear paragraphs each contain only one important idea or major portion of an idea. When you have laid out the topic sentences of a paper, logical paragraphing will be no problem. It is hard for the reader to miss what you are trying to say when the divisions between ideas are clear.

As you write, you may find out that the topic sentences you have set up will not always find their best position at the beginning of a paragraph. Consider this paragraph from the writing of Abraham Lincoln:

Fishes, birds, beasts, and creeping things are not miners, but *feeders* and *lodgers* merely. Beavers build houses; but they build them in no wise differently or better now than they did five thousand years ago; but just in the *same way* they did when Solomon referred the sluggard to them as patterns of prudence. Man is not the only animal who labors; but *he is the only one who improves his workmanship*. This improvement he effects by discoveries and inventions.

Surely Lincoln built up *to* his main idea rather than down *from* it as Mrs. Eleanor Roosevelt does in this paragraph:

The flow of water has, in fact, been a source of friction between the two countries from the beginning. On partition, India gained with the East Punjab only three of the original sixteen canal systems. This is an area in which extensive irrigation is essential, for millions of refugees poured in here and they depend on the land for a living. Pakistan claims that by diverting the water for her own irrigation schemes, India has reduced the flow into Pakistan, and that her vital canals are drying up. India attributes the reduced volume to drought on both sides of the border, and insists she is continuing the supply of water as before.[2]

[2] *India and the Awakening East.* Harper & Brothers, 1953.

Depending upon what you are trying to accomplish in a paragraph, what was said in the preceding paragraph, and the kind of paragraph that will follow, *your topic sentence can fall in almost any position.* The beginning and the end are favored positions only because your reader likes them best, and the logic of the development of your argument will demand those positions most frequently. You must decide how clarity is best served in each paragraph you write.

SENTENCING FOR CLARITY

Every sentence you write must meet the test of clarity. Read each of your sentences with these questions in mind:

- 1. Can it be made any clearer?
- 2. How far is its *grammatical subject* from its *predicate?* The closer the better.
- 3. Will your reader have to work hard to understand what its pronouns stand for?
- 4. Does each sentence take the reader further along the lines you are developing or does it retard him?
- 5. Does the length of the sentence clarify or obscure meaning?
- 6. Do you have any sentences that are so fogbound that the reader will have to grope his way through them?
- 7. Does each sentence you have written belong just where you have placed it within its paragraph? Perhaps it belongs in an adjacent paragraph, perhaps nowhere in the paper.
- 8. Can some of your sentences be improved by reducing them to clauses and attaching them to adjacent sentences?

As you examine your sentences for clarity in this manner, bear in mind that the reader is the person who is to be considered.

CLARITY AND THE PRECISE WORD

We have considered how your outline, paragraphs, and sentences affect clarity. The final consideration is your choice of individual words. In your first draft of a paper, don't spend time worrying over individual words. Too much care in select-

ing words during your first writing will make the writing
process torture. But after the first draft is complete, take another look at what you have written. Is each word you have
used going to be clear to your reader? Will your reader immediately understand the precise meaning you intend?

G. M. Trevelyan was one of the best historians of our time.
The college student despairing of understanding some other
historical works turns to Trevelyan for clear, direct prose. See
how the following paragraph stirs no uneasiness in the reader,
but conveys meaning in as direct a manner as possible. Yet
there is a charm and attraction in the lines.

> If the England of the Eighteenth Century, under aristocratic
> leadership, was a land of art and elegance, its social and economic
> structure was assistant thereto. As yet there was no great develop-
> ment of factories, producing goods wholesale, ruining craftsman-
> ship and taste, and rigidly dividing employers from employed.
> A large proportion of wage-earners were fine handicraftsmen, often
> as well-educated, as well-to-do and socially as well considered as
> the small employer and shopkeeper.[8]

Clarity is surely the achievement of this paragraph. No word
in it need send you to the dictionary, nor should you have to
wonder precisely what each word means in its context.

Student conversation and student writing, unfortunately,
are sprinkled with words that add nothing to meaning and
serve only to get in the way of ideas. Take the loose use of the
word *thing,* for one example. What is the specific object intended by it? Is there not an exact word for it? When young-
sters say a book or movie or play is *cool* or *keen,* do they mean
exciting, absorbing, interesting, beautiful, meaningful, funny,
sad, detached, perceptive, or a thousand other words?

Use words that clarify rather than obscure, pad, or approximate. Your vocabulary must be up to your ideas if you are to
write well. Your examination papers, your themes, all the
writing you do will suffer if you do not pay attention to the
words you use.

A THREE-PART TEST OF CLARITY

Before you decide to hand in any paper you have written,
try this:

[8] *English Social History.* Longmans, Green and Company, Inc., 1942. Don't wait
for an assignment from your history professor to enjoy the pure pleasure of this
work.

- 1. Read the paper aloud to yourself so that you can hear each word and judge its value. Oral reading forces you to focus on each word of a paper, puts a spotlight on obscurity.
- 2. Outline the paper as you read. Forget that you were the writer. Imagine yourself the teacher reading the paper for the first time. When you have finished, the outline should be well constructed. If it is, your readers will accept the paper.
- 3. Have a classmate read the paper to see whether he can grasp your ideas easily. If he has to ask questions about your theme, then you have not been as clear as you should have been. Get back to work.

Emphasis

Any paper you ever write will contain ideas and information varying widely in importance. One of your main aims in writing must be to stress what you consider to be the most important points in your papers. There are many techniques that are helpful in achieving emphasis, and it is worthwhile to review them.

1. EMPHASIZE YOUR MAIN IDEAS

While you are outlining a paper, think about the relative values of the ideas you are going to describe. Which one is most outstanding? What evidence in support of that idea is most attractive? When you have decided these questions, you have the proper focus for your paper, and you know where your greatest emphasis should be placed. You will not want to paint an untrue picture by telling your reader only what supports your thesis, but you certainly will give *most* and *best* space to material that supports your point.

Loudly acclaiming everything you have to say will muddy the waters. "The greatest show on earth," "dazzling spectacle," "brilliant display"—these superlatives make the intelligent person shudder, because experience has taught him that advertising of this kind is usually untrue. Use words as powerful as your ideas and convictions warrant.

2. CONCENTRATE YOUR ATTACK

Too often, the impact of a piece of writing is diluted because the writer skips hither and thither through his theme, touching on ideas briefly, whetting the reader's appetite, and going off merrily on something else, leaving us unconvinced and unmoved. How can a reader see the relative importance of ideas in such a paper? Build support carefully for a prominent idea before going on to something else. Dealing with one point at a time will help your reader keep his attention on the important point you are making.

Do you want to convince your reader that United States membership in the United Nations is vital to world peace? Do not entertain him with stories of Mussolini's adventures in Africa or Woodrow Wilson's gallant campaign for the League of Nations—both interesting but digressing from the point you want to make. Proof of any idea rests on specific elements. Group them together so that your reader can grasp their full impact. Then deal with each one separately in detail. When you have finished your detailed presentation, you may review your arguments as a final convincer, if you want. But direct everything toward moving your reader.

3. GET TO THE POINT FAST

We know too well how difficult it is to keep a reader's attention. Think of your own reading habits. How often have you started out bravely in a book, but had to wait so long for the author to say something worthwhile that you put the book down? Your reader's needs are the same as your own. Don't slowly and furtively creep up on your subject. The *beginning* of a paper, the *beginning* of a section, the *beginning* of a paragraph, the *beginning* of a sentence—every beginning point where the reader starts out fresh with you is the place where you must capitalize on his willingness to work with you. Don't disappoint him. Say something worth reading.

See how Henry Steele Commager gets right to the point in the opening paragraph of his essay, "The Necessity of Freedom":[4]

Freedom of speech and the press—that is, freedom of inquiry, criticism, and dissent—are guaranteed in state and federal con-

[4] In *Freedom, Loyalty, Dissent*, Oxford University Press, 1954.

stitutions now over a century and a half old. It is a sobering fact, however, that each generation has to vindicate these freedoms anew, and for itself. Yet this is not wholly a misfortune; one might almost see in it Providential wisdom. For there are risks in taking things for granted, risks not only of failure to appreciate them but of failure to understand them. Freedoms vindicated anew are more precious than those achieved without effort, and only those who are required to justify freedom can fully understand it.

After a beginning like this, the thoughtful reader is sitting straight in his chair, ready to come to grips with the argument. Do you try to do the same in your own writing?

If the opening position in every unit of your paper is attractive to your reader, he will be able to follow your reasoning. The author who leads up too slowly is playing solitaire. His reader has left him long before the main idea is at hand.

Newspapers know that the first paragraph of a story is the one that will either persuade a reader to go onto all the facts of a story or lose him altogether. That is why the *newspaper lead* was invented. Look at these three examples from the first page of *The New York Times* of June 17, 1959:

> The Western powers presented a final draft of proposals for a Berlin settlement to the Soviet Union tonight.

> President Eisenhower's request to increase the national debt limit to $295,000,000,000 for one year was approved today by the House Ways and Means Committee.

> The Defense Department reported today that two MIG jet fighters with Communist markings had attacked a United States Navy patrol plane over international waters of the Sea of Japan.

The reader of each of these stories knows the gist of the event. In the last two examples, he has enough information so that he need read no further unless he wants to know the entire story. In the first account, he might want to go on to read the details of the proposal, but even there he has a good grasp of the tone of the event described.

Examine the stories on the front page of your newspaper today to see how the editors insist on getting to the point fast. In your writing, don't let your reader's interest die waiting for your first significant statement.

4. USE A VARIETY OF SENTENCES AND PARAGRAPHS

Sentences and paragraphs should reflect the importance of what you have to say. Long sentences sometimes point up an idea you want to impress on a reader, but short sentences usually do it better. A steady diet of either short or long, however, makes everything you say seem of equal importance. Choose sentence length and sentence construction for the effects you want to achieve. Do you want to pile fact upon fact upon fact? You can do it in one long sentence loaded with punctuation. You can do it in a series of staccato sentences, short and piercing. How about a question to make a point? Or a fragment? Variety is available, as you will see later in this chapter. Use variety carefully to gain prominence for the ideas you are proposing in any paper you write.

Paragraph length and construction can also be used to achieve emphasis. Say something worth saying in each paragraph you write and, when you have completed the thought, *stop*. After you have finished the entire paper, read it through to see whether your paragraphing has helped your purpose. Here are the questions you must seek to answer as you read:

• Are all your paragraphs of the same length? They should not be if your ideas are not of equal importance—and they are surely not.

• Are they all cut from the same pattern—main ideas followed by evidence, or explanations leading up to main idea, or introduction building up to main idea and then details? All your ideas do not lend themselves equally well to any single form of paragraph construction.

• Which paragraphs should be shortened, which lengthened, which eliminated?

• Do your paragraphs move logically from idea to idea?

• Does each paragraph belong exactly where it is placed? Good paragraphing reflects the emphasis you want to give main ideas, the subordination minor ideas must have.

5. SOME STYLISTIC DEVICES FOR ACHIEVING EMPHASIS

As your writing improves with practice, study, and criticism, you will begin to use language in striking ways. You will find yourself inspecting everything you write for emphatic expression. Read the remainder of this section in order to become familiar with common devices used by writers to punch home what they are trying to say. When you write your next paper, read through this section again. You will find yourself awakening to opportunities for effective communication.

THE SHORT PARAGRAPH

How much more remarkable than many hours of sunshine is the first ray of the sun after a thoroughly gloomy morning. Nature calls our attention to the warmth and brilliance of the sun dramatically and *emphatically* by giving us this contrast. The short paragraph standing between long paragraphs has the same property. Here are three uses to which the short paragraph can be put.

To introduce a new topic. Emerson, in *The American Scholar:*

> I read with some joy of the auspicious signs of the coming days, as they glimmer already through poetry and art, through philosophy and science, through church and state.

(The next paragraph begins to enumerate the signs.)

To call attention to an outstanding idea. James Madison, in *The Federalist, No. 10:*

> The inference to which we are brought is that the *causes* of faction cannot be removed, and that relief is only to be sought in the means of controlling its *effects.*

To repeat and highlight the gist of the preceding paragraph. William James, in *What Makes a Life Significant?:*

> All this is to tell us, in effect, that our lives are hard, barren, hopeless lives.

All these exceedingly short paragraphs were carefully and effectively placed between longer ones. Otherwise they would not have the emphasis they do have.

UNDERSCORING

Modern printing makes accessible to the writer many devices for achieving emphasis that were not possible for the writer of

an earlier day. Two most frequently used are the *italicized* and
bold-face word or group of words. As a student writer, you
do not often have the services of a printing press offered to
you. Your press is the typewriter or the pen. But you can
underscore to achieve the same emphasis.

You can easily find thousands of examples of the uses of
typographical devices for calling attention to particular parts
of a sentence and to entire sentences. Here are but two from
American Politics in a Revolutionary World, by Chester
Bowles.[5] See how Bowles selects certain words for spotlighting:

> In the absence of some *massive shock* to our sense of security ...

> In other democracies—Germany, India, Israel, Burma—where
> there is basic agreement upon a worthy national purpose *yet to
> be achieved,* there is no failure to mobilize . . .

The italics are used as the printed counterpart of a speaker
rapping the table or raising his voice to give special emphasis
to certain words. In another section of the same book, Bowles
lists many questions that depict the scope of the challenge
facing modern man. He *italicizes* all the questions and makes
each a *separate paragraph,* thus using two devices simultane-
ously to give emphasis.

But would emphasis have been served if Bowles had italicized
his entire book?

Colorful Language

Thoughts can be expressed in many different ways, and the
form of the expression used determines whether your reader
is going to react in the way you want him to. Do you want to
move him emotionally? Convince him intellectually? Influence
him politically? The first requirement for the words you use
in your writing, as we have said, is that they say exactly what
you mean and that your reader will interpret them in the way
you intend. How much your words move, how quickly and
thoroughly they convince, how directly they influence—this is
the second requirement placed on the words you use. In short,
how emphatic are they? We call this special attribute of language *color.*

Read these few sentences from *The Causes of World War*

[5] Harvard University Press, 1956.

Three, by C. Wright Mills.[6] I have underscored certain words to call attention to outstanding examples of colorful language. Words chosen less carefully would soften the impact of the ideas.

Oil is a key industry in the making of U.S. foreign policies and of U.S. foreign obstinacies.

The monolithic assumptions of the military metaphysics and the thrust toward war which follows from it . . .

Historically, the professional military have been uneasy and poor relations of the elite; now they are demanding first cousins and soon, many competent observers feel, they may well become elder brothers.

In your own writing, search for the exact word to liven a dull, unemphatic statement.

REPETITION

One of the oldest and best devices for achieving emphasis is repetition. A word, a phrase, or a sentence can be repeated to direct attention to important thoughts. For example, notice how the indefinite article "a" was repeated in the sentence you just read. If it had been omitted after its first use (a word, phrase, or sentence), the rhythm of the sentence would have changed. Would the reader's attention have been as strongly captured? Repetition does not have to be restricted to words; grammatical forms and sentence structure can be repeated also. You have probably noticed already that the author of this book is fond of this device and uses it now and then. Look for it as you read ahead and see whether it improves emphasis.

Now read these examples taken from Mills' *The Causes of World War Three.* As in the preceding section, I have made underscorings to call your attention to the device of repetition.

The doctrine of Massive Retaliation has become massive nonsense.

Acheson and Dulles are in continuity; bipartisan foreign policy has become bipartisan default of policy.

[6] Simon and Schuster, 1958.

The causes of this war are not inherent in some vague, historical context of drift and maneuver called "international relations." The causes are seated mainly in the U.S.A. and the U.S.S.R. The immediate cause of World War III is the preparation of it.

Politicians, hiding behind the supposed expertise of testifying and of advising warlords, have abdicated their proper job of debating and deciding policies. Political administrators have abdicated their proper job of creating and maintaining a really civilian and a really professional senior civil service. It is in the vacuum created by such political abdications and hesitations that the military ascendancy has occurred. It is because of this political vacuum that the warlords have been drawn—often unwillingly—into the higher political decisions.

In many of the examples cited, an editor could easily rewrite sentences to eliminate duplication of words. But would he be increasing the effectiveness of the argument or would he be robbing it of vigor? [7]

QUESTIONS

Good teachers ask questions and see that they are answered —by the student, if the student can, by the teacher, if the teacher must. Many books are designed to teach, and so are many of the papers you will write in college. You have gone out to make yourself an expert in some corner of learning by examining what the library can tell you and by thinking about the subject a good deal. When the times comes for you to write, you want to instruct your reader in what you have studied and learned yourself.

It is not surprising, therefore, that you should ask your reader questions as you go along in an essay. Sometimes you let him supply the answers—either when the answers are implicit in an earlier paragraph of yours or when the answers should be self-evident. In other cases, you supply the answers in sentences that follow the question. In all cases, you ask questions to give emphasis to ideas.

What better example of the question as a device for giving emphasis than the *Dialogues* of Plato? If the questions and

[7] You should observe, of course, that Mills resorts to familiar devices of propaganda in some of the language he employs. The word *warlord* is not one that you

answers are read carefully, the reader is in no doubt of what it is the philosopher is trying to teach.

Gilbert Highet, in *The Art of Teaching*,[8] gives us this example of the effectiveness of the question as a device for achieving emphasis:

> But what kind of man or woman will the good teacher be? Are there any abilities which are absolutely essential?

Of course there are. And the reader would not even need the second question to understand the argument. But Highet takes no chances. He helps the reader by supplying the second question; he makes sure that the reader will be ready for the answer that is about to be given.

CITING AUTHORITY

Of the many ways to achieve emphasis, appeal to authority is one of the best. This technique will be dealt with more fully in Chapter 11, when the research paper will be discussed.

Citing authority can be accomplished in several ways, and while it is not a substitute for your own thinking, it is a powerful weapon for the writer. We may mention four techniques, with examples of their use taken from Harold Laski, *The American Democracy*.[9]

Quote an official source or the work of a respected authority:

> "A majority," said Lincoln, ". . . is the only true sovereign of a free people. Whoever rejects it, does, of necessity, fly into anarchy or despotism. Unanimity is impossible; the rule of a minority, as a permanent arrangement, is wholly inadmissible; so that, rejecting the majority principle, anarchy or despotism in some form is all that is left."

Paraphrase and cite the source:

> The Reverend Russell H. Conwell, one of the half-dozen most popular preachers of his time, told scores of thousands of citizens all over the United States that it is a duty to secure wealth and an

---

would find in the work of an author defending the military. There are many good books on propaganda and on semantics that you will find valuable reading. If you have not given much thought to propaganda, you should read Hummel, William and Keith Huntress, *The Analysis of Propaganda* (William Sloane Associates, 1949). Read especially the section *Affective Language* in Chapter 4.

[8] Alfred A. Knopf, Inc., 1950.
[9] Viking Press, 1948.

important test of a man's usefulness to his community. He urged men to enrich themselves and not be diverted from their purpose by the foolish envy of the unsuccessful.

Quote directly and paraphrase, giving the source:

Professor Brogan long ago pointed out the need of such a party. Not since the days of the Federalists, as he has said, has America had a party "opposed to aggression against property rights, denying the egalitarian thesis of their opponents, and attempting to hold up the American Revolution at the point most convenient to the upper middle classes."

Mention a name or conclusion without referring directly to a work:

If it is found in Socrates, it is found in Albert Schweitzer; it is unmistakable in the last supreme utterance of Vanzetti, it is a light that gleams in the controlled, yet impressive, emotions the careful observer can find in many of the writings of Mr. Justice Brandeis.

In the first three examples, Laski cites the source of the quoted and paraphrased material so that the reader can verify the author's use of the material. In Chapter 11 of this book you will find a full discussion of bibliographical form, so that you will be able to cite sources in proper manner. In the case of the last quotation, you have only Laski's word that the point of view represented is found in the authors he mentioned, with the exception of Vanzetti.

Yet all these uses of authority add strength to the argument of an author, and you must not overlook this device in your writing.

NUMBERING SCHEMES

The use of numbers to designate chapters of a book is quite well known. But in recent times we have seen numbers coming into greater use to separate sections of a chapter or paper. Why are they employed?

Used properly, numbers or other signals catch the reader's attention, showing him that "these units belong together, being all parts of one whole." The reader can usually see this without having numbers to guide him, but he is helped just a bit more by their presence. They are another effective aid for him as he sifts, understands, and learns the important features of a discussion. It is as though the writer were saying, "Mark this well. This is the logic of the argument." The writer knows his reader will be able to remember better what he has read if the writer has said, "These are the facts, and they are *five*." See how this device is used in a book about the modern civic university in England. In *Red Brick University*,[10] Bruce Truscot writes:

> It [charter of student rights and responsibilities] had five points, each asserting a student's right:
> (1) To the free expressions of opinion by speech and Press.
> (2) To organize meetings, discussion and study on all subjects within the University and College precincts.
> (3) To belong to any organization, whether cultural, political or religious.
> (4) To participate to the full in all activities outside the universities, and to collaborate with extra-university organizations.
> (5) To share in the government and administration of the universities.

Truscot first gives the reader the key by saying, "It had five points. . . ." Then he ticks them off one by one, driving them home as individual thoughts and as a group of five.

Use numbers, then, to arrest the reader's attention. Use letters of the alphabet. Use asterisks, check marks, or any other signal you can find that will help you. But do not use these devices so often in a paper that your reader will feel like saying, "Oh, just another list! This writer lists everything." Save the device for times when it is most needed, when your information is most striking.

FRAGMENTS

After all you have been told over the years about the construction of a sentence (by definition consisting of a subject and predicate), now you must be told that emphatic writing will employ fragments—or nonsentences, as they sometimes are called.[11]

While nothing advances an argument in the way that a full-fashioned sentence can, since it and only it makes a statement, the fragment has its uses too. If it is the logical tail

---

[10] Penguin Books, 1951.

[11] See John H. Middendorf and Ernest G. Griffin, *Manual of English Prose Composition*, Holt, Rinehart and Winston, Inc., 1956, for a brief and excellent discussion of the use of the nonsentence.

of a thought that wants emphasis, or the subject, or what would be the predicate, then the writer might detach any of these from a sentence and set it up all by itself. But you must do it artfully.

There are many examples of the fragment to be found. One interesting illustration is seen in a book on linguistics by Eric Partridge, *Here, There and Everywhere*.[12] See how the fragment coming at the end of a paragraph serves as a conclusion:

> The fourth and last part of the book *Gulliver's Travels* is 'A Voyage to the Country of the Houyhnhnms'. The Houyhnhnms, horses both intelligent and high-principled, are what the name, pronounced *Whinnims*, proclaims: the Whinniers', from *whinny*. Swift makes them the rulers of the Yahoos, whom he describes as having the form, partly of men and partly of chimpanzees, and all the vices, none of the virtues, of men; disposed to 'nastiness and dirt'. Hence our *yahoo*, with small, not capital *y*.

The last sentence, which begins with *hence,* emphatically concludes the discussion. How wasteful, how pedantic it would have been to write a complete sentence: From all of this it can be concluded that Yahoo etc.

Of course, you will find the fragment exploited most often in modern fiction. The novelist who translates fragmentary speech into formal sentences robs his prose of emphasis. Listen to the speech of your contemporaries and see how frequently they speak in incomplete sentences. Read transscriptions of the press interviews of public figures, and you will see the same.

As a writer, you have the opportunity and the responsibility to find new and attractive forms with which to achieve emphasis. In all the reading you do, be on the lookout for the devices other writers are using. Become adept at writing eye-arresting titles and subtitles for your papers. Always keep in mind that you must catch and hold the reader's attention, and your writing will improve in vigor and conviction.

Importance of economy in writing

Economy in writing does not mean brevity alone. It means careful development of a theme in as forceful a manner as possible in as few words as necessary. It means careful control of your topic and precision in the use of language. Poor writing goes over the same ground several times when once

[12] London, Hamish Hamilton, 1950.

around would be better. At the other end of the spectrum, putting brevity before clarity is also poor writing.

In reviewing a paper you have written, always ask yourself whether you have said the same things more often than they have to be said, whether you have used more words than you have to in order to say them, whether you have said them clearly. Every statement should be pertinent, every explanation justifiable, every proof necessary.

When an assignment is made for a paper of specified length, your first task is to choose a topic that is suitable for that length. Of course, you will not be able to estimate precisely how many words will be necessary to deal with any topic. To be safe, therefore, select a topic containing subtopics that can be developed if necessary.

For example, if you are discussing dictatorship in the twentieth century, you may have a general section in your paper dealing with characteristics that all dictatorships in the period possessed in common. In addition, you may find it necessary to choose some specific examples of the points you want to make. You cannot hope to deal with all aspects of these dictatorships in detail, but you should plan a greater number of topics to be dealt with than you think you will use. This gives you a backlog of discussion material and makes your paper expandable to the required length.

This is far different from merciless padding of a manuscript through unnecessary repetition, endless circumlocution, and lengthy quotation—all favorite devices of writers who say nothing in many words.

Ten common faults in writing

In many freshman English classes, a theme is unacceptable if it contains a single mistake in spelling or sentence structure. This rule is sensible since such errors cannot be condoned in the writing of an educated person. If you are a poor speller, you have a long and tiresome journey ahead of you, for you can solve your problem only by drilling yourself on the words that give you trouble. Write the offending words on a sheet of paper several times until you are certain you know how to spell them. Then have someone quiz you on the words you have learned. A few days later, repeat the test. If some of the words still give you trouble, repeat the procedure.

Sentence structure, on the other hand, can be improved with less difficulty, because it depends less on memory and has a logical foundation. If you have been plagued by sentence structure errors, effort at this time will correct the situation. Here is a list of ten common errors in sentence structure. See how many you are guilty of and try to eliminate them now. Undoubtedly you will have to check yourself from time to time, so go back as often as necessary to these pages.

1. THE RUN-ON SENTENCE

The McIntosh is one of the best eating apples, it is remarkably sweet and firm.

Can you see that two independent clauses have been inadequately joined? A comma will not do. What is needed? A semicolon, a period, or a conjunction.

The end of the term had come all had passed.

Here two independent clauses have been run together willy-nilly. The reader has the feeling that the sentence might have gone on even further if the writer had more to say. How would you correct it?

2. THE SENTENCE FRAGMENT

In spite of all the preparation for the trip.

This group of words says nothing about anything. It does not communciate with the reader. To correct it, you would have to attach it to an independent clause. Used carefully and purposefully, fragmentary sentences are valuable. Before trying them, however, you will have to prove to your teachers that you know what you are doing.

3. PRONOUN TROUBLES

Robert and Andrew found that no one was interested in the monologue even though he had rehearsed it adequately.

He? Separate a pronoun from its antecedent, and you ask for trouble. A general rule of sentence structure is that related sentence elements should be kept together. If the writer had followed the rule, he might not have made this boner.

Do you know whom is going to be chosen for this job?

The *whom* mistake is encountered so often in the public statements of politicians who put on grammatical airs and then fall on their faces. Somewhere in the dim past, these people were told to use *whom* rather than *who*. They never recovered from the brainwashing they suffered and now use *whom* indiscriminately in every formal statement. Of course, the form of the pronoun is dictated by its function in a sentence.

4. AGREEMENT OF SUBJECT AND PREDICATE

Cooperation of all three parties—labor, management, and government—are necessary if we are going to have labor peace.

Everybody knows that subject and predicate must agree in number. The writer of this sentence knew, too. Then why the trouble? Another case of separating sentence elements that should have been kept together. *Cooperation are necessary* would never appear in any freshman theme, but you will see how many times students will be tripped up when they begin putting modifiers between the noun and a verb.

Rising above the buildings in front of them is the new tower and gymnasium.

Turn the sentence around if you have not seen what is wrong with this sentence. An inverted sentence is a welcome sight if it does not cause you to forget the grammatical subject of the sentence.

5. COMMAS AND MODIFIERS

The house, on the hill, is for sale.

The student, who came to my office, was sent by his classmates.

The two modifiers should not have been enclosed in commas, because without the modifiers we would not know which house or student was intended. Essential modifiers are those which restrict and identify the nouns they modify. Restrictive modifiers are *not* set off by commas. On the other hand, nonrestrictive modifiers which describe an already identified noun are set off by commas.

Our house, which should have been torn down years ago, is for sale.

Television, despite all its shortcomings, is useful because it keeps small children quiet while their fathers nap.

Whether the house should have been torn down years ago is not essential in identifying the home for sale. The shortcomings of television are not essential either. Both modifiers, therefore, are non-restrictive and require commas.

6. COMMAS SEPARATING RELATED SENTENCE ELEMENTS

Student writers have a tendency to feel uncomfortable if their sentences do not contain a sprinkling of commas. But before you use a comma in a sentence, make certain that you can justify its presence. In fact, before using a comma, you should feel certain that the sentence cannot get along without it.

Unrestrained use of commas makes your writing hard to read. Consider these two sentences.

Thinking along the lines suggested by the teacher, failed to produce any clues that might help in solving the problem.

The music that met our ears, was all that anyone could expect, from musicians playing on borrowed instruments.

The punctuation of these two sentences seems to be based on rhythm rather than on meaning. There is no justification for separating grammatical subjects from their predicates in this way, or predicates from their complements.

7. QUOTATION MARKS COMBINED WITH TERMINAL PUNCTUATION

A period or comma occurring at the end of a quotation is placed *inside* the quotation marks; colons and semicolons *outside;* exclamation marks and question marks *inside or out,* depending upon whether they are part of the quotation or part of the sentence that contains the quotation. The British do not agree with our custom, but never mind. The rule is arbitray. Learn it.

"Quick, Henry, the *Flit!*"

Did he really say, "I came, I saw, I conquered"?

Notice that there is no period after *conquered.*

8. Dangling Modifiers

A modifier must have something within reach that it truly modifies. The *beautiful* girl, to skate *easily*, a record *I would like to have.* The concern of these modifiers is clear in each case. But how about these modifiers.

Standing in water up to his knees, the temperature was obviously inappropriate for swimming.

Unable to take another step up the mountainside, the expedition seemed about to fail.

Surely there were people *standing* and *unable,* but who were they? From the construction of the sentences, the reader might worry over whether the temperature was standing and the expedition was unable. Your reader will quickly spot a dangling modifier.

9. Misplaced Modifiers

Sometimes, writers will make certain that modifier and that which is modified are both present in a sentence, but will place them so far apart that the reader is not certain of their relationship.

Teachers do their best work with children only when they like their work.

Who should like to work—teachers or children?

Wearing a sari, she saw an Indian woman on Fifth Avenue.

Who was wearing the sari?

Place your modifiers as close as possible to what they modify. Remember that you are perfectly aware of your intended meaning in any sentence you write, but your reader may have trouble in deciphering it.

10. Faulty Parallelism

Parallel ideas should be expressed in parallel form. This requirement rules out such things as *to be or not being; swimming, boating, and to fish; politics, literature, and to argue.* Correct the faulty parallelism in the following:

The most acceptable aspects of the work were its color, form, and exciting the emotions.

The State Department was interested in how the Russians would react and the attitude of England.

Many of the common errors can be avoided by putting ourselves in the place of the reader and examining our writing from his point of view. In other cases, we must learn arbitrary rules and follow them. If you have difficulties of the kinds mentioned, get to work now and do something about them. A few hours' work will pay off.

Here are several books you can consult for full explanations of writing practices. Buy one of them and get started on a program of helping yourself become the best writer you can be.

Kierzek, John M., *The Practice of Composition*. The Macmillan Company, 1951.

Middendorf, John H., and Griffin, Ernest G., *Manual of English Prose Composition*. Holt, Rinehart and Winston, Inc., 1956.

Wooley, Edwin C., Scott, Franklin W., and Bracher, Frederick, *College Handbook of Composition*. D. C. Heath and Company, 1958.

CHAPTER 5

HOW TO LEARN A FOREIGN LANGUAGE

DESPITE the fact that almost every college freshman has already had two or more years' experience in foreign language study, no single area of college work is subject to more haphazard, ineffective, and wasteful study techniques. In fact, it can be said that foreign language study is too often characterized by complete absence of study techniques. The typical student treats language courses as a necessary nuisance to be disposed of as quickly as possible. The opportunity to really learn a foreign language seldom seems to enter into the picture. The results are useful to no one. Most of our college students can do little more than translate a bit of another language. A few years after college, even this skill disappears.

Yet ability in languages is needed if you want to go on to graduate studies. Business is becoming more international in character than ever. Opportunities abroad are increasing. Travel overseas is becoming almost commonplace. While colleges have for years required work in foreign languages, today more than ever before, the requirement becomes meaningful.

One result of the interest in languages is that high schools and colleges are increasing their language offerings. We are growing accustomed to seeing Russian added to courses of study. But if you want to appreciate the range of languages studied in a university, read this list taken from a recent Bulletin of the School of General Studies, Columbia University: Albanian, Arabic, Armenian, Azeri-Turkic, Bengali, Bulgarian, Chinese, Czech, Estonian, Finnish, French, Georgian, German, Greek, Hebrew, Hindu, Hungarian, Irish, Italian, Japanese, Kalmyk-Mongolian, Kazan-Turkic, Korean, Latin, Lithuanian, Persian, Polish, Portuguese, Provençal, Romanian, Russian, Serbocroation, Slovak, Spanish, Swedish, Tibetan, Turkish, Ukrainian, Urdu, Uzbek, Yiddish.

Language study has its own special problems and techniques.

This chapter is designed to help you learn languages effectively and make your top marks while doing it.

The first thing you will notice in our discussion of foreign language study techniques is the emphasis on repetition. If you have not studied a language in high school, you will find out soon enough that learning the vocabulary and grammar of a language is mainly an exercise of your memory. It is through the *principle of overlearning* that we make our memories work for us. Simply expressed, overlearning makes use of meaningful repetition beyond the point of initial understanding. Thus when you encounter new words and new rules, it is suggested that you repeat them fifteen times; not until you merely understand them but until they have become stamped on your memory.

In the following sections on homework, classroom work, translation, and examinations you will find that the more often you expose yourself to new material, the better you will learn it.

The will to learn a foreign language

Regardless of how important languages are and how much influence your knowledge of them will have upon your career, if you do not *want* to learn a foreign language, you are going to be miserable in college language courses. Maybe you have already found out how unhappy Latin or German can make the unwilling student.

No one can convince you that you want to learn a language if you do not. Countless essays can list all the reasons for studying French. Popular magazines can supply all the charming anecdotes anyone would ever want to read about "three words of Polish and how they saved a man's life." The virtue of being able to say *please* and *thank you* in all the languages of the world can be repeated a thousand times. Yet, somehow or other, the taste for speaking or writing a language cannot be taught. You either have it right now or you do not.

Children take to languages because they like sound, because they enjoy learning. Indeed, children can even be talked into wanting to learn a new language. But you cannot. What are you going to do about it? You must do something, because here are some requirements typical of those you will meet in American colleges:

Two years of a modern foreign language

Three years of a classical language and two years of a modern foreign language

Candidates for a degree must demonstate speaking knowledge of at least one modern language other than their own

Students must be able to read and translate the scientific literature of at least one language other than their own

The only thing that will help you master these demands is true interest. For those who do not naturally like languages, there is one ray of hope. *Success breeds interest; interest returns success.*

If you can experience some success in your study of languages, you will discover interest you have not experienced before. The French proverb, *rein ne réussit comme le succès,* cannot be denied. Nothing succeeds like success.

If you have had persistent lack of interest in languages and have failed to do as well in them as you should, the best thing you can do for yourself right now is to *find out just how to study a language for maximum results and make a fresh start toward proficiency*. The fact is that language study has all the fascination of science and social studies, and the thrill of being able to converse in another language is unique.

Let us now lay our plans for successful study. In most of the discussion that follows, French is the language used for illustration. The choice of French is for the author's convenience; you are not being advised to choose French as your language.

How to do your homework

Learning languages is more an exercise of memory than is any other subject you will study in college. While there is system in foreign grammar and spelling that enables you to think many things out, in order to become truly proficient in a language, your memory must serve you well. In reading, speaking, or writing a language, you must be able instantly to call the right expression to your mind. Although this does not sound easy, you will find it within your power if you work intelligently toward mastery.

Memory depends on

• *Selecting* what you want to remember,

- *Organizing* the material to be learned in a form that lends itself to easy learning.
- *Spacing* your learning effort.

Your foreign language textbooks help you in all three respects: selecting, organizing, and spacing. They *select* for you short, varied exercises, each designed to teach you one specific fact, bit of information, or principle. They *organize* the material in a general way, but you will have to organize it further so that it is in the form easiest for you to learn. Finally, the textbooks *space* the learning effort for you if you keep up with your assignments. An assignment in a history textbook, by contrast, demands that you select the material to be learned, organize it completely on your own, and space the learning effort yourself.

There are four steps involved in doing your homework in a manner guaranteed to produce results:

- 1. Read through the pages assigned.
- 2. Learn new vocabulary.
- 3. Study grammar section.
- 4. Practice and review.

Let us discuss each one in turn and find the best procedures for accomplishing them.

STEP 1—READ THROUGH THE PAGES ASSIGNED

The emphasis is upon the word *read*. Read the new vocabulary and its meanings, read the grammatical principles exactly as stated, read the English sentences you are going to translate later on, read the French sentences in French, and read whatever other review sections appear.[1] The few minutes you spend in this way previews your next class session. It is customary for many language teachers to give written and oral quizzes almost daily. You can expect any part of the lesson to form the subject matter of the quiz.

There are many advantages in reading through your lesson in this manner. For one thing, many of the items in a lesson

---

[1] If you are doing your work in your own room, where you cannot disturb others, *read the lesson aloud*. Trying to sound out the French words will help you become accustomed to their sounds. Reading the rest of the lesson aloud will force you to pronounce every word.

are quite easy to learn. There are cognate words, for example, that are learned immediately upon recognition. There are rules of grammar that appear so logical you are able to grasp them at once. There are idiomatic constructions that stick in one reading.

In this reading, then, you are finding out which parts of the lesson are going to make the greatest problems for you. When you come to the thorough studying of the lesson, you will know what will have to be emphasized and what will take little time. The repetition from one part of the lesson to another actually gives you several exposures to the same material, and so you learn just by reading alone.

Step 2—Learn New Vocabulary

What is the best way to learn vocabulary? Regardless of whether your primary objective is to read, speak, or write a language,

> *read new vocabulary*
> *speak new vocabulary, and*
> *write new vocabulary.*

- Read the first new word aloud *five* times.
- Look away from your text and say the word *five* times, pronouncing it as well as you can.
- Read the English equivalent, *but do not say it.*
- Write the new word *five* times. The first time on an index

le chapeau

card, the others on any sheet of paper. This paper will be discarded at the end of the lesson, but the card will be saved for later review. When you write a *noun*, always include the definite article so that you will learn the gender of the noun at the same time. When you write an *adjective*, give both masculine and feminine forms.

• Repeat the process for every word in the list. After you have finished, you will have *one card for each word*.

WARNING: *As you say each French word, do not say its English equivalent. Your object is not to learn the words Frenchmen have for English words. You want to learn French.*

• After you have finished the last word in the list, go back to each word card. On its reverse side, write a short sentence *in French* using the word on the face. If you are studying the first lesson in an elementary French text, you will have trouble finding enough words to make a sentence. Try. Look at the other words in the lesson for what you need. The object of writing

> Le chapeau de mon
> frère est noir.

this sentence is to help you learn a new word without having to think of its English equivalent. Avoiding English will help you establish the habit of thinking in French, which is essential for mastery.

The extra time you take in learning your first words of French in this way will pay off.[2]

Why all these techniques to avoid writing English words? You are steering clear of the greatest pitfall to mastery of a foreign language: the easiest and most damaging thing for you to do when you are approaching a new language is to learn it as a translation. Of course translating is easier, faster, more immediately satisfying than any other technique. Who cannot learn *je* = I, *tu* = you, *il* = he, *elle* = she, by merely repeating the list over and over again? Countless thousands of American students have done this, have passed their French courses, and *have not learned French.* Every time they have to think of a pronoun, they run through the list they have learned until the right word pops out. Can you picture them conducting a conversation in this manner? They have learned French words and their English equivalents.

Contrast the kind of rote learning with the manner in which the same students learned their first *sentences* in French:

"Bonjour, monsieur. Comment allez-vous?"

"Très bien, merci, et vous?"

From the first day in almost every beginning French class, the teacher drills his students in this greeting. No attempt is made to translate word by word. There is no bothering with English. And every student learns these French sentences.

Everything you study in French should be studied the same way. Study French, not new foreign synonyms for English words.

The sooner you are able to write sentences, the sooner you will be using all of your language ability. Even if some of your sentences sound childish to you, they are sentences and they have meaning. And you will not need to translate them when you study them, for you will know what they mean as soon as you see them in studying. Every time you go over them, you will be *reading a foreign language.* What is more, you will be

---

[2] Until French pronunciation no longer gives you trouble, you will find it helpful to mark the pronunciation of a new word on the face of its card. This can be done either in phonetics, if you can handle this useful tool, or in the English alphabet, *Il* = eel, *elle* = ell, *moi* = mwah. By listening carefully in class as your teacher explains and demonstrates correct pronunciation, you will soon be able to omit pronunciation entries on your cards.

Your biggest barrier to good pronunciation of a foreign language is the self-consciousness that hits most of us when we tackle something new and strange. The sounds of French are not difficult if you are willing to pitch in and sound silly for a while until you catch on. When your teacher enunciates a new word, say the word to yourself. This will help fasten the new sound to the word itself. Every time you see the word from then on, you will hear it also until you become fluent.

reading something you have *written*. When you can say the
sentence aloud without looking at your card, you will be *speaking* the language. And reading, writing, and speaking are the
key to vocabulary building.[8] If your vocabulary is going to grow,
you must work at it, and the first time you meet an unfamiliar
word you want to learn is the best time to learn it. When you
put off learning the new vocabulary in a lesson you are doing,
you make succeeding lessons that much harder. Unfortunately,
you also make yourself more and more reluctant to go at vocabulary intelligently, because the number of words you must learn
increases rapidly with the passing weeks of a semester.

STEP 3—STUDY GRAMMAR SECTION

Grammar is not an end in itself for the college student. While
the scholar finds satisfaction in exploring the *system* of a language, you want to learn the *language*. Grammar is only a tool
to that end, necessary though often troublesome.

The modern language teacher asks his students to communicate first and then learn grammar. As communication gets
under way, grammar is introduced when needed. Your textbooks follow the same practice. You learn some words. You
learn to read them, write them, and speak them. Only when
you can communicate to some extent is it time to learn the
rules that govern language.

To learn grammar first is surely to put the cart before the
horse, but grammar must be learned eventually if you are to
master a second language as quickly as possible.

The grammar section in every lesson in your textbook will
state, explain, and illustrate one or more principles of grammar. Your job is to incorporate that rule into your thinking in
the language. The strategy is to *understand* the principle,
memorize its exact meaning, and *put it into practice* in the
language you are studying.

[8] Sets of vocabulary cards have been published for the foreign language student.
By putting down a few dollars, the student obtains some hundreds of drill cards all
made up and ready to study. Impressed by the fact that a lot of the work he would
have to do has already been done for him, the student uses the printed cards in
preference to working up his own.
These cards have limited value. For one thing, the words you will meet in them
may not be the same ones your teacher wants you to learn. For another, and this
is more important, *the work of making your vocabulary cards is part of the vocabulary building process.* You meet the words, you write them, you think of a sentence
and write it down. These several exposures to each word add up to a great deal of
the effort you will have to put out anyway, and as you work on your cards, you
are exposing yourself to the new words in the various ways you will want to practice
them. Reading a card someone else has printed robs you of valuable learning time.

Here is how to do it. First make sure you understand the terms it employs. In studying grammar, you will be learning abstractions that can be applied throughout all the years of study you will undertake, all the conversations you will have, all the books you will read, and all the letters and translations you will write.

When you understand what each term in a grammar lesson means, reach each rule aloud five times.

Now put the book aside and recite the rule aloud correctly from memory five times. Do so many recitations seem excessive? Repetition is essential if you are going to make each rule part of you. Once it is part of you, it will be unnecessary to think of it again. If you do not make it part of you, it will always be necessary to think about the form of what you want to express instead of thinking of the substance.

For some students, it is advisable to write out the more difficult rules of grammar. While the object of studying rules of grammar certainly is not to be able to quote them from memory, some students find rules easier to learn by writing rather than speaking them. If you find it helpful to write out rules, try putting them in your own words to test your understanding. You can remember better when you express a rule in your own words.

You may not know the terms of grammar as well as you should. But your language teachers will expect you to know them thoroughly.

Do you know the *parts of speech*?

	DEFINITION	EXAMPLE
noun	name of a person, place, thing, or idea	John, New Jersey, ball, democracy
article	used before nouns to limit their application	a, an, the
pronoun	word use in place of a noun	he, them, it
verb	word or words used to express an action, condition, or state	eat, go, grieve
adjective	word used to describe or limit meaning of a noun or word used as noun	happy, funny, sad, hopeful
adverb	word used to modify verb, adjective, or other adverb	happily, quickly
preposition	word used to show relationship between word in a sentence and a noun or word used as a noun	between, into, among
conjunction	word or words used to connect other words or groups of words	and, either . . . or, because, so
interjection	word or words used to express emotion, but having no grammatical relationship with the other words in a sentence	oh! golly! hurrah!

There are several dozen terms that are used in describing the functions of words within sentences. While some of them are not used widely in English, there art at least *ten* you will have to know in foreign language study.

	DEFINITION	EXAMPLE
active voice	verb is in active voice when its subject performs act	I *hit* the ball.
antecedent	word or expression to which a pronoun refers	I know the *man* who is going by.
auxiliary verb	verb that assists other verbs in forming their tenses, voices, and moods	It *was* heard no more. I *ought* to go home.
complement	word or phrase used to complete the meaning of a verb	He was called *Corky.* The dinner was *delicious.*
intransitive verb	verb that does not require an object to convey meaning	Anne *swims* beautifully. The tide *was running.*
number	changes in nouns, pronouns, and verb to designate singular or plural	boys, boys he, they eats, eat
object	*direct*—noun completing sense of transitive verb	Dick lifted the *cat.*
	indirect—noun indirectly affected by sense of verb	Johnny sent a gift to his *mother.*
passive voice	verb is in passive voice when its subject is acted on	The choice *was made* by me.
person	changes of verbs and pronouns to indicate speaker, person spoken to, person spoken of	I do. You go. He fights.
transitive verb	verb that requires object to convey meaning	We *found* gold. We *got* what we wanted.

How many of these terms do you already know? If you do not know them all, *learn them now,* before you meet them in your foreign language study. By learning these terms now, you remove one obstacle to successful study.

Step 4—Practice and Review

The practice exercises provided in a lesson are at least as important as the vocabulary and rules of grammar presented. If you use practice exercises properly, you reinforce the points made in the lessons.

- READ ILLUSTRATIVE MATERIAL ALOUD FIVE TIMES and get the point of every example supplied.

As you repeat the phrases and sentences your text supplies to show you how to use the rules of grammar being taught, see how the examples illustrate those rules. *Never work through an illustration of a principle without thinking of what it shows.*

- WRITE YOUR OWN ILLUSTRATIONS AND READ THEM ALOUD.

Besides teaching you a rule, your own example one day will be useful in compositions you write, when you find that idiomatic and grammatically correct expression comes easily to you.

- STUDY REVIEW EXERCISES.

Students generally fail to grasp the significance of the review exercises they do as part of each lesson. The function of the review exercise is to take you back and forth systematically across everything you have studied commencing with the beginning of a semester. Knowing that your classroom time is limited, the textbook writer makes sure that you get enough practice time in the language by forcing you to review.

- REVIEW THE DAY'S NEW VOCABULARY.

As the final part of each day's homework, go over once more the words you met in that lesson. The best way of accomplishing this is to use your vocabulary cards.

Look at the face of each card, say the word aloud, and then try to recall the sentence that is on the back of the card. If you can, you surely know the word. Do *not* think of its English meaning. By working only with your cards, you avoid contact with English and develop the habit of thinking in the foreign language.

As you look at each card, you are testing yourself to see how much you have learned. When you find that you know a word, mark the face of the card with a *check*. If you do not know the word, study the back of your card to refresh your memory, but do not mark the card. Go through all the cards for the day in this way.

As the days go by, you will be accumulating a large store of cards. *Review each card daily*. When you have checked a card three times, signifying that you have recognized its meaning on three separate occasions, put that card in an inactive alphabetical file. Keep that file on your desk. It is your glossary of terms you will meet again and again during your French studies. It will also serve as review material before tests. In time you will know some of the words so well that there will be no need for keeping cards on them. Eliminate them to keep your file within practical bounds.

The cards that do not have their quota of three checks are your active file. *They go with you wherever you go*. Keep them in your pocket, not hidden away in your briefcase. They are to be used whenever you have a spare moment on a bus, waiting for a class, just before you go to sleep at night. In addition, establish one time of the day for regular review. Some students find that they learn new words best if they study them just before breakfast. Others like to study before they go to language class. Find out when you learn them best and study them at the same time each day.

Whenever you do your studying, do not neglect vocabulary. It is easy to learn a few words a day, difficult to learn a week's backlog at one sitting.

We have seen how to attack your daily work in languages. The four steps in doing a lesson effectively will help you make top grades if you follow them. Now let us go on to further discussion of effective language study.

The art of translation

The most common expression in reviews of translated novels and plays is, "The work suffers in translation." This is understandable. Not only must a language be translated, but history, culture, and manners as well. In light of the trouble even professional translators have in preserving the flavor of an original text, the student might protest that as a beginner he cannot be expected to do well. Your teachers understand the problems inherent in translating. Yet even when you are translating for the first time, you must be concerned with the quality of your effort.

The most obvious requirement of a good translation is that it preserve the meaning of the original. A further requirement, and in this you cannot expect to be proficient for a long time, is that it preserve the *literary qualities* of the original.

The best example of how not to translate a French sentence comes happily in the satiric song, *La Plume de Ma Tante*. The song is based on the opening sentence in the typical old-fashioned French primer, in which everyday words are combined in sentences that unfortunately are not everyday. As difficult as it is to conceive of anyone ever uttering this particular sentence, many thousands, if not hundreds of thousands, of students learned French through studying it and others like it:

La plume de ma tante est sur le bureau de mon oncle.

The songwriter translates this ineptly as:

The pen of my aunt is on the bureau of my uncle.

What mistakes have been made in this translation? For one, the French word order has been taken over into English, so we automatically do not have an English sentence. The second is in the translation of *bureau*. We do have bureaus in English, but the French *bureau* means *desk*. The primer translated correctly for us, but the song has a little fun at the expense of those who teach French through such quaint sentences.

The word order of any language you study is different from ours. If you expect this, you will not be upset when you encounter it. There is no special logic in the word order of any language; there is only custom. Take the manner in which we address letters in this country. We give first the name of the person who is going to receive the letter, then his house number and street, and finally his city and state. What is the first information the post office needs in sorting mail? Surely not the name of the recipient. Europeans do a lot better by giving the state and town before the street address. But they list the name of the recipient first too.

Don't fall into the trap of using convenient but incorrect cognates. *Plume* in French is not *plume* in English. And *on parle français* means *French is spoken,* not *one speaks French,*

Translate meanings, not words. Read through material you are going to translate to get the flavor and intent of the original. Then read through the opening sentence once more before translating it. Do the same for the second sentence and all the rest. Students make the mistake of translating each word as they come to it. Keeping the unbroken thought unit of the sentence in front of you as you work will ensure that you come up with a translation of thoughts.

Observe the tone of the material to be translated so that you can capture it in your translation. Don't put the King's English in the mouth of a person who obviously would not use it.

As you acquire knowledge of vocabulary and sentence structure, you will find that translating from one language to another is an enjoyable art.

Making the most of class time

If you want to progress rapidly in language, make your time in class an integral part of your effort. You will have practice in vocabulary, explanations of points of grammar, review of your textbook. It is not necessary to make more than an occasional note in the French class. Rather you must consider class time as a help in learning material already covered in your study.

One of the main functions of your class sessions will be to help you acquire an "ear for French." The practice you get merely by listening to your teacher is invaluable. Pay attention to exactly how each sound is made and how words are grouped. When you recite in class—and later when you are practicing alone—imitate your teacher's speech as closely as possible. There is no reason why you must sound like an American in Paris when you attempt to speak French. But if you are very self-conscious about how you sound, that is exactly what will happen.

There is always the possibility of buying French records to develop a good accent, but they are not necessary. Records are excellent if you attempt to study a language on your own. As long as you are studying the language with a teacher who speaks well, you might just as well forget records. They are not as good practice as the classroom, where you have the opportunity to have your own speech criticized. Going to French movies is good for your speech after you have made some progress in the language, but movies are not a substitute for class practice.

French movies serve a more important function for you. They can become a link between you and the culture you explore when you undertake study of the French language. Reading a French newspaper can also help in this way. The most important activity of all for the serious student of French is to join La Maison Française or whatever other French club meets on your campus. Almost every modern language department on a campus will organize a club for its students to help them in their studies by providing an opportunity for conversation in the language. Teas, lectures, and discussions are scheduled that can do much to help you progress rapidly.

Examinations

Prepare for tests by reviewing all the study materials you have—your vocabulary cards, the review exercises in your textbook, the rules of grammar you have studied. Check over any returned quizzes. Look especially at the mistakes you have made to be certain that you will not make the same mistakes again.

Many language tests have an oral section, in which your teacher dictates a selection you have not seen before. Your job is to write it perfectly. It will test how well you have studied the spelling of vocabulary. As your teacher dictates, he will read through the entire selection first and then go back over it phrase by phrase at a pace slow enough for you to take dictation. During the first reading, concentrate on understanding what he is saying. During the second reading, listen without writing until he comes to the end of a phrase, and then put it down correctly. When the dictation is over, read it through for meaning.

The written language examination is perhaps the easiest kind of test for the student in the sense that he can predict almost exactly what will appear on it. In keeping up with your day-to-day work, you are taking the final examination over and over again. The sentences you translate in every lesson appear in almost the same form on tests. This is far different from other courses, such as the social sciences, in which the subject matter ranges far and wide. The student has to spend a good deal of his time in selecting the points of emphasis that he will concentrate on for examinations. Another advantage of the foreign language test is that it tests only your ability in the specific subject. In other tests, your ability in English composition is put to the test almost as much as your knowledge of subject matter. Your ability to reason is also on trial. Thus, language test preparation is not as difficult as preparation for other tests you will take.

When a test paper is returned to you, check it carefully to find out where you have missed your mark. Relearn the points you missed. Where mistakes are due to carelessness, you may want to write the corrected version of the answer a few times in order to get rid of the tendency to make the same mistake again.

The study of classical languages

Because so few students select Latin or Greek these days, no mention has been made up until now of the differences between studying modern and classical languages. Both can be studied in the same manner up to a certain point. The vocabulary and grammar can be tackled in the same way, but the grammar of the classical languages is more complex than that of most modern languages. Parsing a Latin sentence can approach the complexity of solving a difficult problem in mathematics.

The marked difference is in the orientation of the teaching of the two groups of languages. Practically no attempt is made in teaching Latin, for example, to help the student speak the language. The focus of attention is upon reading the great classical literature. The progress of the student is from Caesar to Cicero and on to Vergil and Ovid. Thus, translation is the main activity of the student once he gets on his feet in grammar.

Students sometimes use translations in studying classical texts, but they must be used with care. Word-for-word translations, called trots or ponies, can save time in a difficult translation, but they do not teach the grammatical interrelationships of a sentence. By all means, take advantage of the trot, but don't make the mistake of trying to memorize it. You will have no trot with you in class, so you must work through all your lines anyway.

The main thing to keep in mind as you approach a foreign language is that *repetition* is your greatest study aid in this field. The mastery of a foreign language is largely an exercise of the memory, and the best way to make your memory work for you is to repeat the material over and over again.

CHAPTER 6

HOW TO STUDY MATHEMATICS

YOU will probably have at least one year of college mathematics. If you are like many other students, it will be the greatest single obstacle standing between you and the bachelor's degree.

Why do so many students find mathematics difficult? It is hard to say. Yet somewhere along the line, probably at the point where arithmetic leaves off and algebra begins, a great many otherwise capable students lose their taste for the subject. Undoubtedly much of the difficulty comes from poor reading and listening habits. Also to blame is the student's inexperience in the kind of thinking required for mathematics. Mere counting skill is replaced by abstract reasoning of the highest order. The final explanation that comes to mind is that students approaching college mathematics find it strangely impractical in the sense that the problems considered are totally detached from their experience.

Yet the inherent interest of mathematics cannot be denied, and the need for mathematics is greater than ever before. Astronomy, engineering, chemistry, physics—all science and technology use mathematics, but it finds a place outside these fields as well. Economics, psychology, sociology, and demography use mathematical techniques. Of late they have joined the sciences in using electronic computers to speed their work and make available solutions of problems that never before could have been tackled. These computers require the attendance of trained mathematicians. Business uses the machines in making forecasts of needs, production, and sales. It can easily be seen that mathematics is no ivory-tower subject.

You will find that once you get into college math, both the theory and application are far more difficult and complicated than anything you met in high school. The learning techniques that worked for arithmetic and elementary algebra will not be much help to you when you come up against calculus and analytic geometry. This chapter will show you, first, how to understand and commit to memory the theoretical aspect of college math, and, second, how to apply these theories intelligently in your homework, classroom work, and examinations.

Are you sure of your fundamentals?

Mathematics is certainly one field in which it is unwise to run before you have learned to walk. Never mind the stories

---

ADD

(a)	369	(b)	6412	(c)	6	(d)	1
	856		7359		3		9
	492		1165		7		5
	771		4920		2		6
	182		8863		5		7
					9		2
					3		4
					1		3
					4		8
					5		6
					9		7
					8		8

MULTIPLY

(e) 68.417	(f) 21986	(g) 34972	(h) 8268
386.4	7.26	.0651	1.025

DIVIDE

(i) 26.509) 193.621736   (j) .0163) 62.94082

FIND THE SQUARE ROOT

(k) 4199.04

MULTIPLY

(l) $(x-3)$ $(x-3) =$

---

about Albert Einstein's youthful difficulties with arithmetic. If your arithmetic and algebra are weak, you cannot hope to do well in higher mathematics. Take this brief test devised to find out whether you are as strong as you should be.

Accuracy is most important, but time yourself to see whether you complete the test in a reasonable amount of time.

You should have used no more than ten or twelve minutes for this test without making a single mistake. If you took longer, or if you were uncertain about how to handle some parts of the test, now is the time to brush up on your fundamentals. If you still have your high school mathematics texts, use them. If you do not, or if you feel that you would profit from a good review and explanation of all the mathematics you have studied until now, consult Alfred Hooper, *A Mathematics Refresher* (Holt, Rinehart and Winston, Inc., 1942). You will find *arithmetic, algebra, geometry,* and *trigonometry* explained clearly. This book was written originally for men in the Royal Air Force who had been out of school for some time, so it is not a book for children. You will find it interesting as well as instructive.

As you review basic mathematics, remember that it is important to develop *speed* as well as *accuracy* in computing. As you work through your review, time yourself so that you can see whether you are developing the facility you must have.

Do you know how to read mathematics?

Have you ever seen students rocking back and forth in their seats trying to memorize a formula? They are committing it to memory as though it were some mysterious rite that would help them to a place among the chosen. Ask them what the formula means, and they are speechless.

It is a rare test that will ask you only to supply a formula. Formulas are methods for solving problems. Mathematics tests ask you to read a problem and work it through to an answer. While it is undeniable that you must know the proper formula to apply, indeed have it right at your fingertips, you must also understand it and be able to apply it. Thus it is not enough merely to memorize every formula you encounter in your studies. You must make certain of its meaning and know how to put it to work.

For example, it is all very well to know that "the area of the square erected on the hypotenuse of a right triangle equals the sum of the squares erected on the other two sides." It is also good to know this fact as $a^2 = b^2 + c^2$. But do you know how to use this equation? Can you picture it in your mind? Can you draw it? Can you take a square root? In short, can you apply the Pythagorean theorem to a typical problem, such as:

Find the length of the hypotenuse of a right triangle whose other sides are 6 and 8 inches long.

If you have only memorized a formula but have neglected to learn how to use it, you have not *really read* the theorem. And precise reading is 90 per cent of the battle in mathematics. Understanding a discussion in a mathematics text and being able to reproduce the discussion after you have finished reading are the results of precise reading.

The next few pages will show you a sure-fire technique for doing your mathematics homework. As you will see, the technique is simply a way of reading mathematics. This approach to the subject may be an eye-opener for you.

How to Do Your Math Homework—Step 1

Read the introductory section of the assignment to identify and understand the principle it teaches. Some students mistakenly try to do homework problems without bothering to read the introductory section of the assignment. They do this in order to save time. But does it work? As they attempt to solve each problem, they go back and forth between it and the sample problem the author solved for them. This kind of learning, in which the student in essence tries to deduce principles himself instead of relying on the author, is wasteful. First of all, it is hit or miss. And the misses often go uncaught. Secondly, the drill work that is built into the lesson is lost by the student because he is not aware of what is being drilled until well into the lesson *if at all*.

You certainly know by now that learning mathematics is a cumulative process. If you have not mastered what went before, you will always have difficulty. Let's take as an example the *point-slope form* of an equation which you should encounter about halfway through your first semester in college mathematics. You will not be able to do this lesson if you have failed to understand the equation for the slope of a line, which is one of the first things you learn in analytic geometry.

Here is an explanation of the point-slope form from *Analytic Geometry,* by John Wesley Young, Tomlinson Fort, and Frank Millet Morgan (Houghton Mifflin Company, 1936). It is a typical textbook for freshman mathematics:

> In the last chapter we stated that a very important problem of analytic geometry is to learn how to plot a curve when its equation is given. A second important problem is, given a curve, to find its equation with respect to a given set of coordinate axes. We shall now consider the simplest case of this problem, namely, where the given curve is a straight line.
>
> Let the given line pass through a fixed point P_1 (x_1, y_1) and have a given slope of m. Since the line has a slope we know it is not parallel to the y-axis. Let P (x, y) be a variable point on the given line. Then, equating slopes, we have

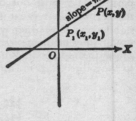

$$\frac{y - y_1}{x - x_1} = m \text{ or}$$

> (1) $y - y_1 = m (x - x_1)$.
>
> This equation is satisfied by the coordinates of every point on the line and by no other points, since the raito $\dfrac{y - y_1}{x - x_1}$ formed for a point (x, y) not on the line does note equal m.
>
> Equation (1) is called the *point-slope equation* of a straight line. It enables us to write the equation of the line passing through any given point and having any given slope.

Have you identified and understood the definition being taught? Do you understand the steps taken to arrive at the point-slope form? Can you repeat them without consulting the text? If the answers to all three questions are *yes,* then you have read precisely. If not, then you must go back and read again. This time, in reading, try this method:

- 1. Make certain you understand the meaning of every word in the discussion.
- 2. Visualize every step along the way. If you can see the action portrayed in the sentences, then you understand them.
- 3. If you find a particular sentence difficult to comprehend, repeat the discussion up to that point. When you are sure you know it well, try the difficult sentence again.

You will be able to see from this brief excerpt how the text-book authors have tried to teach carefully what they want the student to learn. How foolish to skip this introduction and try to do homework problems directly!

Exactly what have the authors done for you? They have provided a definition and justification for a concept that will be useful as you proceed further into the subject. To memorize the definition without understanding the reasoning behind it is very difficult. The term *point-slope form* must become second nature to you. And so must every other concept the book introduces. Page after page, lesson after lesson, you will find information introduced along with reasoning to support it. You must not try to skim the information and skip the reasoning. It is far easier to learn facts when you understand them than when you accept them blindly.

The next help you receive in the typical lesson is in the form of sample exercises.

How to Do Your Math Homework—Step 2

Do the sample exercises.

Sample exercises are an integral part of the lesson to be studied. How you use these exercises will determine how well you understand the principles being taught and whether you will be able to work problems based on those principles. Thus, these samples are the pivot around which the entire lesson turns. As you use them, one part of your mind is on the text you just finished reading, and one part of your mind is saying "Now this is the way I will be doing things shortly, so I had better pay attention."

- *Read* each step carefully.
- *Understand* every term used.
- *Follow* the reasoning behind each manipulation.
- *Solve the problem all over again on your own.*

Inspect the sample exercise that follows the discussion of *point-slope form* in Young, Fort, and Morgan. See whether the example adds to your understanding.

Example. Find the equation of the straight line passing through $(1, -2)$ and having a slope of -3.

Solution: $x_1 = 1$, $y_1 = -2$, $m = -3$.

Substituting in $y - y_1 = m\ (x - x_1)$, we have
$$y + 2 = -3\ (x - 1)$$
or $3x + y - 1 = 0$

It is a good idea to reserve a section of your loose-leaf notebook for working through the sample problems that your author gives you. As you do them, be sure to include in your proof every step that you require, even though the author has left some out. Writing out the steps in a problem in this way is far better than merely reading through what the author has written. It guarantees that you are working along with him. If you are to *learn* as effectively as possible and *remember* as long as necessary, that understanding is vital. If, as you work, you also think of the *why* and the *how*, your learning will be that much better.

The mathematics work sheets that accumulate in your notebook will be a handy review for you before examinations. If you work your sample problems on one side of the sheet only, then the blank sides can well be used for taking notes in class. If you are careful to take class notes on the sides opposite your homework for the same material, then your mathematics review material will be complete and well organized for study.

In your notebook or on index cards, you should keep a list of terms that you have come across in your studies so that you can drill yourself on them until you have mastered them.

How to Do Your Math Homework—Step 3

Recite the principle you have learned.

Once you have completed the sample problems in the lesson, repeat from memory the principle they illustrate. Do this either in your own words or the words of the textbook if you can. Be sure that you understand exactly what the words mean if you use the exact words of the textbook.

If you cannot repeat the principle, go back to the opening section of the lesson and read it through again. Only when you feel you know what it means should you go on. Indeed, unless you know what it has said, you cannot go on, because in the last section of the lesson you will have to demonstrate your understanding. Incidentally, in class you probably will be asked to recite the principle anyway. You may as well make certain you can recite creditably before going to class.

To test your alertness now, try to recall the expression the above lesson in analytic geometry has been trying to teach you. Think for a moment. What does it mean? Can you give the form of the equation that expresses it?

Further helps in homework

Homework problems are your tests of how well you have learned, your rehearsals for tests you will take one day, and your guarantee of *overlearning*. And the extent of your overlearning will determine *how long you remember*. Even if you feel you understand a principle on first reading, working an assortment of problems is beneficial. With their help, you retard the inevitable forgetting that begins to operate just as soon as we learn something. With their help, you learn to apply principles in all the ways you will be expected to use them. Homework problems are powerful aids to effective learning.

Students are tempted to use sample exercises as matrixes—forms in which to insert numbers—for the homework problems they have to solve. It seems so simple to save time by merely substituting numbers in the sample problems that textbooks have already worked out for you. Doing your homework in this way is a sure way to miss the entire point of doing homework. As a number-substituter, you can find solutions to problems all day long without learning a thing!

Mathematics textbooks are not written by newcomers to the art of teaching. The textbooks you will use are the result of years of careful observation of students and their needs. The tendency of students to borrow freely from sample solutions is well known. Thus your textbooks will make an effort to frustrate mere substitution. Problems will be inverted, and the kinds of answers required will be different from one problem to the next; in short, you will not find meaningless guesswork very satisfactory.

As you approach each problem in an assignment, *see it as an example of a principle being taught.* Then (1) you will understand the proper approach to the problem, and (2) you will help yourself drive the principle home at the same time.

USE DRAWINGS FREELY TO HELP IN SOLVING PROBLEMS

If you have ever seen a mathematician at work, you know that he can hardly think without a piece of chalk or a pencil in his hand. He always seems to want to draw a curve or diagram to help his thoughts.

Wherever possible, do the same. A drawing will often make clear an otherwise difficult formula or definition. In solving a problem, a drawing will help you find the direction you need. What is more, drawings will help you remember.

Here is an exercise from another part of the same textbook we have been using for our discussion in this chapter.[1] Perhaps you cannot do the work described, but you can surely follow the discussion. Read the problem carefully to see what is asked. What would your procedure be if you were asked to solve this problem?

Find the slopes of the sides of the triangle with vertices (5, 7), (6, 2), (3, 5) and prove the triangle is a right triangle.

There are actually four problems within this problem. Did you find them? The terms employed in the problem must be understood—slope, triangle, vertices, locations of points (5, 7) etc., right triangle. Do you know them all? If you do not, you cannot go on without help.

Now diagram the problem. You will see how the problem suddenly comes to life.

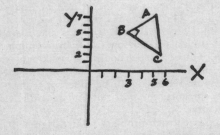

[1] Young *et al.*, *op. cit.*, p. 30.

If you do not know how to interpret such abbreviations as *et al.* or *op. cit.*, consult your freshman English manual. The ones used here mean "from the work already mentioned, by Young and other authors, page 30."

You can see that you need to find the slopes of AB, AC and BC. After you have determined the slopes, you can go on to prove that this triangle is a right triangle. Do you see how the drawing helped?

See how effective a drawing is in this problem taken from page 5 of *Calculus* by Lyman M. Kells (Prentice Hall, Inc., 1949).

Consider a block (see Figure 1) moving on a striaght smooth track *AB* inclined 18°6′ to the horizontal. If the block passes point *A* with a speed up the incline of 100 ft./sec. and reaches a point distance *s* from *A* in *t* seconds, then

$$s = 100t - 5t^2 \text{ approximately.}$$

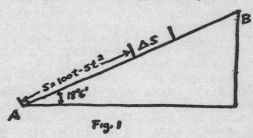

Fig. 1

With the description of the problem just beginning, the author has given us a drawing that will help the student understand the problem.

When you are working a problem, draw it so you can understand it as you go along. Pretty pictures are not necessary; the crudest kind of picture will do as long as it is *big enough to read easily* and as long as you *label clearly and correctly*.

High school *algebra* can be learned easily by most students because its concepts are not much different from arithmetic. You may have resorted to representing algebraic symbols by real objects to help yourself visualize a difficult problem, but by and large you felt little need for this practice. In *geometry* you surely used drawings as study helps. If you acquired the habit then, you know how helpful it is. Practice it whenever you can in college mathematics. It will save time, improve the quality of your learning, and help you remember.

DO YOUR HOMEWORK UNDER TEST CONDITIONS

Unfamiliar situations are apt to give us difficulties. Looking ahead to a test without knowing what sort of questions we will be asked, how much time we will have for answering, or how long it will take us to write the answers, can be uncomfortable. The tension that builds up inside us because of the strangeness of the situation can harm the quality of our work.

In one sense, homework problems are a test: you have read a statement and discussion of an idea or principle. You have worked through sample problems that further clarify the points being made. When you get to the assigned problems, you are ready to see how much you have learned. If you do these problems in the spirit of a test, they become the best possible preparation for the tests your teachers will give you.

Simulate test conditions. When you are ready to do your problems, set a time limit and do your best to observe it. If you cannot get through your work on time, you are either working too slowly or you have been too harsh with yourself in deciding the amount of time you should have. If you feel that you are working fast enough, ask your teacher how long he thinks you should have to work at your problems. Find out from him how much work he expects from you on an actual test.

While you can expect your homework assignments to vary in difficulty and so take varying amounts of time to complete, you should try to turn out more and more work in a given time. You will want to have time to check your computations during a test, so be sure to allow time for checking your homework tests, too. Careless errors reduce test grades.

Inspect the questions you are going to answer to make certain you know exactly what each word means. Make sure you do not overlook important words in the questions. Missing a single word can delay your understanding of a question and even set you off on the wrong track.

As you work, make certain that you use enough paper and write clearly enough so that you will be able to read your computations over easily.

If, when you read a question, you come up with a complete blank, *stop and think*. Just where does the difficulty lie? Perhaps your author has deliberately worded his question so that it looks totally different from the other problems you have been working. Read it through again and again until it becomes clear. Use drawings to see whether they can help in getting you started. If you have tried your best and cannot come up with the solution, leave that question and go on with the next problem. After you have worked that one or the one after it, you will usually find that you have discovered the approach needed for the problem that has given you trouble.

It is not uncommon for students to draw a blank on a question or two during a mathematics test. The worst thing they can do during the test is to sit there hopelessly. As time begins to slip away, they become more and more frantic. Not only do they fail to answer the one difficult question, they do not even attempt to answer later questions they may well be able to complete.

The opportunity in mathematics to rehearse directly for a test is not available in most other subjects. In such courses as literature and history, for example, you will not have the chance to write essays as rehearsal for examinations. For those courses, as you will find in a later chapter of this book, you will have to use considerable ingenuity if you want help in previewing an examination.

TAKE CARE IN COMPUTING

If you are going to make the highest grades you are capable of, you will have to be precise in computing the answers to homework and test problems. To develop the careful attitude you need during a test, work your homework problems with the same degree of care that you will want to display when you are taking a test.

The first consideration in working a problem is to make sure you are headed in the right direction before you begin to work. Just what are you after in a problem? Have you been asked to supply an equation? Supply it. The measurement of an angle? A line? A velocity? The location of a point?

What units will your answer be expressed in? Will you have a choice of degree of accuracy, such as is possible with decimals and degrees? Will you have to reduce fractions?

All this is well understood by students, of course, but in the heat of a test or their desire to get through homework problems as fast as possible, they frequently go astray.

One technique of which students are not always aware is that of predicting the range of possible answers to a problem before they set to work. If you can estimate in advance the reasonable upper and lower limits to the answer to a problem, you safeguard against having to work right through to the end of a problem before you know you have gone completely haywire. Careful reading of a problem will usually tell you what you need for a prediction. Drawing the problem in the form of a sketch or graph can also help. Measurement of an angle, a line, an area, or a volume lends itself to this technique. In a rate or speed problem, you usually have to resolve two extremes to find an answer. It is easy to see that the result must fall somewhere between the extremes. Have you ever watched a mathematics teacher go at a problem on the blackboard? He does not plunge right in. The few moments he spends inspecting the problem are devoted to estimating the range of answers. You will learn techniques for doing this in every mathematics course you take. Practice them until they are habitual.

Once you have begun to work on the problem, take care to *perform each step accurately.* If you do not, despite the fact that you have looked ahead in the problem and know where you are supposed to be heading, you will come up with an answer that will force you to retrace your steps completely.

In studying arithmetic, you were taught to check *addition* by adding the column of figures upward instead of down, *subtraction* by adding, *division* by multiplying, and *multiplication* by dividing. In *elementary algebra,* you checked your reasoning by substituting values found in the equation you started with. This is still good practice for arithmetic and algebra where the problems you encounter lend themselves to such methods.

College mathematics does not often give you the same opportunity to check your work so easily. The solution to a typical problem requires many steps of many different kinds. Thus, checking an entire problem is an arduous task for which you do not always have the time. There are two ways to overcome this. One is to become as proficient as you can at the basic computational skills so that you can rely on your ability. The other is to *check each step in a solution as you go.* There are definite check points you can look at to find the most frequent causes of errors.

Observe the restrictions of the *signs* associated with the values you are manipulating. Did you remember to change a negative value to positive when you moved it from one side of an equation to the other? Did you treat exponents properly in adding, subtracting, multiplying, and dividing values? There is plenty of room for careless error there.

Did you double check every *reading* you made in a table? Use a straight edge for taking numbers from a table. Read first from column and row headings to your value; then read from your value to columns and rows.

Use your *slide rule twice* for each reading you take. When you take the second reading, start right from the beginning in setting up the rule, as though you had not read it before.

Care in computation will minimize errors and save time.

REPEAT RULES AND PRINCIPLES FROM MEMORY

While you may think it impossible to memorize exactly the textbook formulations of all the principles you will encounter in a semester's work in mathematics, it is entirely possible to memorize them in your own words. And you will find it beneficial to do so. After you have completed a lesson—discussion, sample problems, and homework problems—go back to the *principle* you have learned and try to commit it to memory.

If you have done your work properly until that point, the chances are excellent that you will already know the principle by heart in your own terms. And that is the best way to know it, because that is the way you will always think of it anyway. But test your memory before you leave your homework. If you find that you cannot get anywhere near stating the principle, you have not been focusing your attention on what the lesson was trying to do for you.

If you have difficulty in committing a rule to memory, try these four techniques:

- *Read* the rule silently to understand every term in it,
- *Draw* a picture of what it represents or *write* a sample equation to show you understand,
- *Read* the definition aloud several times,
- *Write* the definition on a card so that you can drill it whenever you have time.[2]

All these techniques will help you memorize. The principle is the employment of as many senses as possible in learning. By following the above suggestion, you help understanding and memory by seeing, hearing, and touching the material to be learned.

Students are sometimes scornful of the help provided by writing out a statement they must learn. But what better way to prepare for a written test than by writing out what you must learn!

Another point must be made before leaving the subject of

---

[2] Here is another use of the index card. The definitions, principles, and rules must be learned just as much as the meanings of new vocabulary in a foreign language. If you have especial trouble in memorizing a principle of mathematics, consulting a pack of cards regularly throughout a semester will help you. The procedure is much the same as that used for vocabulary development. Look at the opening words of a principle or rule and try to give the rest from memory. Look at a term whose meaning you want to learn and see whether you can define it. The definition on the back of the card will serve as a reminder when you cannot remember the correct definition. Use a system of check marks to retire cards from your active study file. Your inactive file can be consulted before tests to make sure you remember all you should.

memorizing mathematical principles. In the case of extremely difficult concepts, students—even advanced students—no matter how hard they work, sometimes are not able to understand a principle they have to use. In this case, the student has no alternative but to memorize *verbatim* and seek understanding elsewhere. Perhaps it will come from his teacher, perhaps from working through the problems he will encounter in his homework. You can expect this dilemma to arise just as often in studying physics as in mathematics. This is understandable. Do not panic when you just cannot learn something the first time you try it. The technique of memorizing may help you over it.

ALWAYS HAVE ONE FOOT IN THE PAST

Because mathematics is a building subject with a foundation upon which are placed successive layers of knowledge, each process and principle you learn must be kept firmly in place while you are learning others. Overlearning, to retard forgetting, is especially important in mathematics because you have so much to remember through a semester. To keep everything constantly fresh in mind, work back regularly over every topic covered during a semester.

You may find that your teacher will give you a short test at the conclusion of each unit in a term's work, but that is not always so. Even if your teacher does test you regularly, do not think you have seen the last of a particular subject when you have been tested on it once. There are mid-semesters and finals to think about. Besides, you will have to know the content of each mathematics course you take in the courses you take afterwards.

In keeping up on material that accumulates during a course, you can use returned test papers. They will show you where you are weakest and they will also show you the kinds of problems you can expect on final examinations. Another technique is to go back to the sample problems you have worked in your loose-leaf notebook. You can also go to the problems in your textbook that your teacher did not give as homework assignments. Finally, there are other textbooks available in your college library that will give you further review.

Whatever technique you adopt for review of past topics in a mathematics course, be sure that you keep up with your review schedule. Make review a part of your calendar. It will eliminate last-minute cramming.

WORK HARDEST AT THE MOST DIFFICULT PROBLEMS

If you come up against a difficult concept in a mathematics course, don't give up on it. Memorizing the concept without understanding it has already been mentioned as one help. You know that you can ask your teacher for help. Other students can help you too, although you have to make sure that you get the right information. A student who has already taken the course you are taking can frequently be an excellent tutor because he has gone through the same difficulties you are experiencing.

Perhaps the best way to overcome a difficulty in learning by yourself is to consult another textbook. It may be that the words of another author will make you see the light when your own textbook could not.

Once you have understood the concept that gave you trouble, take plenty of time to fasten that new understanding in your mind. Do all the homework problems you have been assigned and do other problems as well. You can get these problems from your textbook and from the other textbooks you have consulted. Review the work more frequently than is your practice. When you finally have the knowledge securely, you can abandon the all-out effort just described.

You may say that you have enough trouble getting through your regular homework without digging up extra work for yourself. But your regular homework was not enough to teach you the work. Somewhere along the line—sometimes dangerously close to the end of a term—you will have to make the additional effort necessary to master every topic assigned. You may as well undertake it as soon as you discover the deficiency. If you put it off, you will make learning advanced topics that much more difficult. Putting off needed study is a trap for the unwary.

Making the most of class time

If you have ever wrestled for hours with a mathematics problem and then gone to class where your teacher resolved your problems in a matter of moments, you appreciate the tremendous importance of classroom work in mathematics. In fact, the ease with which you frequently get to the heart of a troublesome concept by listening to a teacher can be dangerous. The student in trouble in mathematics is sorely tempted to rely completely on class discussion instead of trying to work things out on his own.

Homework helps you remember what you learn in class. It also teaches you to think in mathematics.

Yet you can get much from your teacher and you must be ready to get as much as possible. The extent to which you will learn in the classroom depends on how well you do your independent work. The rules for good listening, explained in Chapter 3 of this book, apply completely to mathematics:

- (1) Do your homework before coming to class so that you will understand the discussion and be able to ask questions about anything that troubles you. A student who is unprepared sometimes does not know enough to ask a question or is too embarrassed to reveal his ignorance.

- (2) When your teacher goes over material you have already learned, use the opportunity he gives you for overlearning. Pay strict attention to him, thinking with him, trying to work one step ahead of him.

- (3) If your teacher presents a problem on the blackboard, do not struggle to copy it into your notes if one like it is already in your textbook or looseleaf notebook. As he works, think with him.

- (4) Focus your attention on the principle being taught and on the method of computation. What your teacher is working through for you is what you will have to do one day on a test.

- (5) If your teacher works ahead of your assigned problems, concentrate on the material being taught. The help he gives you will come in handy when you sit down later to study that material in your textbook. Do not bother with taking notes. Mathematics problems are worked too rapidly for you to learn very much from frantic note-taking.

- (6) Whatever notes you do take ought to be written in the same section of your notebook in which you write your solutions of sample problems. If you write the problems on one side of the sheet only, you can use the opposite side for classroom notes.

One final reminder: In all your work in mathematics, develop the habit of verbalizing equations so that they have meaning for you, and learn the exact meaning of every symbol you encounter. Learning mathematics is not unlike learning a foreign language. It is not enough for you just to pronounce it. You have to know what it means if you are going to use it properly.

CHAPTER 7

HOW TO STUDY SCIENCE

WHETHER in lecture hall, library, classroom, or laboratory, poor science students exhibit one common trait: They are so taken up with detail that they do not grasp the central theme or principle of a unit of study. Because they bog down in detail, they cannot hope to do well in their courses. In this chapter and Chapter 9, you will be shown how to go about your science studies so that you can make your best possible grades.

Surely the brightest academic star in the minds of the people of our country today is science. Never before have military success, economic strength, national health, and agricultural output so depended on it. The lion's share of student scholarship aid goes to science students. The competition among businesses for each year's crop of college graduates is keenest for science majors. Foundations and the government support scientific research at a level far beyond that of the social sciences and the arts. All the communications media leap eagerly on news of every scientific advance.

If science comes easily to you, look carefully at these fields —anatomy, astronomy, biochemistry, biology, botany, chemistry, geology, meteorology, microbiology, physics, zoology. These are some of the science offerings awaiting you in college.

If science has been something less than a joy to you, you probably are wondering how many courses will be required and how you can get through them painlessly.

Whether or not your major interest lies in science, you will surely take one or more years of science. And whether or not you ever make direct use of science, you will profit greatly from your training if you go about it correctly. Nothing is more important than learning the scientific method of either forming a theory from the facts or testing a hypothesis with the facts.

The study problems you will face in science are much like those in other courses. You must read and listen effectively, prepare for and write examinations. The principles of study are the same: careful identification of what is to be learned, frequent review, recitation to oneself, and testing.

Chapter 9 will deal with the proper approach to laboratory work. The present chapter shows you how to develop the vocabulary you will need to listen and read effectively, how to do a reading assignment, and how to learn from a science lecture. Finally, you will find special techniques for getting your best grades in science:

- 1. How to attack a problem that has you stumped;
- 2. How to adapt your studying to special situations;
- 3. How to identify and remove stumbling blocks to effective study;
- 4. How to profit from a science demonstration; and
- 5. How to apportion time strategically before an examination.

Build your science vocabulary

If you are going to read and listen with maximum effectiveness in the sciences, you will have to pay special attention to vocabulary building.

Read this paragraph from page 3 of an elementary geology textbook.[1] How many of its words are familiar to you?

Geology is a very broad science and therefore has a number of subdivisions, each of which emphasizes certain phases of the subject. One branch of the study (cosmology) treats of the early history of the earth and the relation of the earth to other heavenly bodies in the Universe, such as the sun, the other planets, and other stars; another (petrology) is devoted to the study of the character and origin of all types of rocks; still another (structural geology) deals with the arrangement or the structural relations of rocks and particularly with their relations to each other. Other branches are concerned with the forces and movements (dynamic geology) that have affected the rocks and the results of these movements and with the various land forms (geomorphology) or contour of the surface of the earth and the origin of the mountains, valleys, and plains. A biological branch (paleontology) is the study of the remains of ancient life that are found in the rocks and the evidences of the gradual development of that life

[1] William H. Emmons, George A. Thiel, Clinton R. Stauffer, and Ira S. Allison, *Geology Principles and Processes*, McGraw-Hill Book Company, 1955.

throughout the known eras of geologic time. It is closely related
to a study of the history of the earth (historical geology) as shown
by its rocks and particularly the record of events that is revealed
in the rocks. An economic branch (economic geology) treats of the
occurrence, origin, and distribution of the materials of the earth
that are valuable to man. It includes the study of the deposits of
the metals, coal, petroleum, and many other substances. The
extent of the uses of these materials is indicated by the fact that
mining and allied activities now represent one of the four basic
industries which furnish the raw materials needed in our modern
world, the other basic industries being agriculture, lumbering,
and fishing. According to the U. S. Bureau of Mines the total value
of the mineral production of the United States in 1951 was approximately 10 billion dollars.

Did you find that the names of the subdivisions of geology were
unfamiliar: cosmology, petrology, structural geology, dynamic
geology, geomorphology, paleontology, historical geology, economic geology?

If some of these words *are* familiar to you, unless you have
studied geology before, you probably know them in a sense
other than the one intended here. Cosmology, for example, is
also used in philosophy. Just because most of the words in
English have multiple uses and meanings, don't be fooled into
thinking you understand a scientific term when all you may
know of the term is a nonscientific definition quite useless in
your study.

Another pitfall must be avoided. The word *petrology* resembles *petroleum,* and you might think that petrology deals
with oil rather than the much broader "study of the character
and origin of all types of rocks," as your geology textbook
defines it.

So we see that almost at once—*on page 3 of an elementary
textbook*—your reading in geology meets the challenge of new
vocabulary that must be understood and committed to memory
if you are to be able to read real understanding. And *each page*
in such a book may introduce additional words you have never
before encountered.

How would you get along in biology if you did not learn
new words as you came to them? Here is an excerpt from
pages 403 and 404 of an elementary textbook in biology.[2]

The bryophyta in their morphological features occupy a position intermediate between the green thallophytes and the pteri-

[2] Edmund W. Sinnott and Katherine S. Wilson, *Botany: Principles and Problems,*
McGraw-Hill Book Company, 1955.

dophytes. Although undoubtedly derived from green algae, there is no evidence that they bridge the gap between these primitive forms and vascular plants and it seems best to conclude that they represent a side line of development which has not been ancestral to any higher types. The group consists of forms commonly known as mosses and liverworts, or anthocerotes, often placed with the liverworts. About 23,000 species of bryophytes are known, all of which are of relatively small size in comparison with other land plants, rarely exceeding a decimeter in length. They are essentially land plants and, for the most part, are restricted to moist and shaded situations, requiring an abundance of water for reproduction and successful growth. A few are aquatic, and this aquatic habit is thought to have been acquired secondarily and not to be primitive. A very few have adopted what appears to be a xerophytic habit, living in the shallow crevices of rocks, where they are exposed to extreme temperatures and drying winds. Such forms, however, grow only during wet weather and are remarkable for their ability to withstand long periods of drought. Although abundantly represented among the plants that make up the flora of the forests, ravines, and the north slopes of uplands in temperate regions, bryophytes seldom become a conspicuous part of the vegetation. Acid bogs of the north temperate regions, including certain types of tundra of the far north, may consist largely of bryophyte species. In tropical forests also, especially at high altitudes, bryophytes may make up a considerable part of the vegetation and often include epiphytic species which hang in festoons from the trees and shrubs. Although significant because of the role that they play in plant succession, bryophytes have in general very little economic importance. Within recent years, however, a number of the species of the genus *Sphagnum,* the peat mosses, have been used as a garden mulch, as a material to increase the water-retaining property of certain poor types of soil, and as a means of maintaining the relativity high soil acidity required by certain decorative and otherwise economically important plants.

The authors of the textbook assume you know the meanings of some pretty fancy words: bryophyte, morphological, thallophytes, pteridophytes, vascular, liverworts, hornworts, anthocerotes, xerophytic, tundra, and epiphytic. Indeed you must know them, for they are representative of the vocabulary of the sciences. Note that this selection was taken from a late section of the textbook, so you would probably have met all these words at least once before. But if you had not made the necessary effort to learn and remember their meanings when you met them for the first time, you would have a lot of dictionary-thumbing to do just to read one paragraph.

The best way to learn any new vocabulary is to use index

cards in the same way you study foreign language vocabulary and mathematical principles. The authors of science textbooks generally define specialized words when they use them for the first time, so you are spared the difficulty of looking all of them up. Of course, you can use the sentences you find the words in as examples for your cards.

---

tundra

---

undulating treeless plain of northern arctic region

Acid bogs of the north temperate regions, including certain types of tundra of the far north may consist largely of bryophyte species

---

It is important to get to work right away and stay with the job. You will meet so many new words in each chapter of a

Many teachers and writers emphasize the value of learning common Latin and Greek *roots* and *affixes* as an aid in learning English vocabulary. Perhaps their point would be better taken if more students had studied classical languages in high school. If Latin and Greek can help you anywhere, however, it is in studying the vocabulary of the sciences—particularly biology.

Bryophyte, thallophyte, pteridophyte, xerophyte, and epiphyte obviously share a common ancestor. It is the Greek word *phyton*, a plant.

Your desk dictionary will show

> **bryon,** moss
> **thallos,** young shoot
> **pteris,** fern
> **xeros,** dry
> **epi,** upon

so that we move quite easily to

bryophyte, any of the mosses or liverworts

thallophyte, and of a phylum of shootlike plant forms (e.g. fungi, lichens)

pteridophyte, any of a phylum of plants which includes the fern

xerophyte, a drought-resistant plant

epiphyte, a plant which grows upon other plants, but is not parasitic, deriving the moisture for its development chiefly from the air (e.g., moss).

Exercise extreme caution in guessing the definition of words containing parts you recognize! In the list just given, a student can easily confuse *pteris*, fern, with *pteron*, meaning feather or wing, which he may know from the word *pterodactyl*.

Knowledge of roots and affixes give no more than a clue to meaning. It is not a substitute for a dictionary or textbook definition combined with systematic study of the meaning and use of a scientific term. Rather than try to commit a long list of roots and affixes to memory, learn them in passing as you use your dictionary.

textbook that if you do not learn them as soon as you come to them, you will find yourself completely bogged down in difficult terminology after a semester has been under way just a short time.

The special demands of science readings

If there is one kind of study in which you must not even think about *speed* of reading, it is your first reading for a science course. You will not be burdened with vast amounts of reading, as you sometimes are in social science courses. Each reading assignment may run no more than several pages. Obviously the emphasis is upon *quality* of reading.

The ideas and information in a science textbook come thick and fast. If you are going to read well, you will have to keep three things in mind:

- 1. Determine what is to be learned.
- 2. Read for understanding.
- 3. Master it so that it becomes part of you.

Let us take each of these steps through typical reading assignments in a geology textbook.

1. DETERMINING WHAT IS TO BE LEARNED

Read very carefully the first section of the assignment. Your purpose is to find out whether the author uses that section to forecast what he is going to do in the chapter or part of one that you are going to read. If you are told what he is going to cover, then you have your *outline of the chapter* right in front of yourself. You know the main questions that are going to be dealt with, and you can easily set up your notebook. If you see that the writer does not habitually forecast the scope of a chapter in the early part of the book, the chances are that he will not do so in the remaining chapters. But find out. Some students do not wake up to the organization of a book until they have read more than half of it.

The opening section of a chapter has other purposes as well. Frequently it provides background knowledge that will be essential for understanding the rest of the chapter. It may give the central thought of the entire chapter. The most frequent use, of course, is to present the first of a series of ideas that make up the entire chapter.

Whatever the use to which an author puts chapter openings, learn to recognize it so that you can get right to work.

Read the last section of the assignment to see whether it summarizes the highlights of the chapter. In one form, this can be a *restatement* of what has been covered thoroughly in the chapter itself. As often as not, a chapter can end in a *series of questions and problems* designed to test your understanding and recollection of what has been covered. If the opening paragraphs of a chapter do not outline the chapter, and the headings of the individual sections are unsatisfactory, then the closing section of the chapter may do the job for you. If the help is in the form of questions, you should read them in advance to see whether they can be the precious outline that will be so useful to you in your reading. However a textbook outlines its chapters, recognize the outline and use it.

Let us put into action the principle of determining what is to be learned. We will use the geology textbook we used earlier.[8] Let's examine Chapter 4, less than fifteen pages in length and amply illustrated, to see what we can learn—in two minutes—of the job that faces us in reading that chapter. If you can use your imagination, it is not necessary for you to have a copy of the book in front of you now. A quick look shows that the chapter is divided into sections, the first untitled, the rest titled. Let us first examine the role of the opening section.

Chapter 4:

ATMOSPHERE, WEATHER, AND CLIMATE

The atmosphere is the blanket of air that covers the rocks and the waters of the earth. Its mass is less than a millionth part of that of the earth, but its activities and influences are far-reaching. Its presence is necessary to sustain the varied life of the earth, and it acts as a blanket to equalize the temperatures of the earth's surface. It serves as a medium for the transfer of water that is evaporated from lands and seas and that is precipitated as rain upon the earth, wearing away the rocks and trans-

[8] W. H. Emmons *et al.*, *op. cit.*, pp. 60–75.

porting them to the seas. It is one of the chief agents of weathering.

The weather of any one place is the temporary state of its atmospheric conditions—its temperature, air pressure, wind, humidity, cloudiness, and precipitation. Its climate is the composite of the weather over a long period of time. Climate is described in terms of mean annual temperature, temperature variations, humidity, amount and seasonal distribution of precipitation, storms, and winds. Meteorology (the study of the atmosphere) and climatology are separate branches of earth science, and so a detailed treatment of them is beyond the scope of this text, but some consideration of the atmosphere, of weather, and of climate is essential to an understanding and appreciation of the effects of the atmosphere upon geologic processes. Just as soils and vegetation are determined largely by climate, so geologic processes, especially the weathering of minerals and rocks and the erosion of the land, differ greatly from place to place in different climates.

What has this section done for us? Essentially, the chapter title has been expanded by showing us what the three terms, atmosphere, weather, and climate, *mean* and how they are *important* in studying geology. If you had not before now made the connection between geology and these terms, you should be aware now of why they must be considered in geology.

Have the authors outlined the chapter yet? No. Therefore we go on to the second step, inspecting section headings:

- Composition of the Air.
- Changes with Altitude.
- Atmospheric Stratification.
- The Aurora Borealis, or Northern Lights.
- Sources of Heat.
- Weight of the Air.
- Distributon of Air Pressures.
- Movements of the Atmosphere.
- Cyclonic Storms.
- Moisture of the Air.

Here are the *ten main topics* of the chapter. As you inspect them, you can imagine the examination questions that a teacher can ask. They might be:

What are the sources of the earth's heat?

How does air pressure vary with altitude?

How does the moisture of the air affect the weathering of rock?

Of course, many more come to mind. From the very beginning, as you read a chapter, think ahead to what you are expected to learn from it, to the examination questions that can be based on it. The more actively you think along these lines, the sharper your grasp of what you read, the longer your memory of it.

Inspection of the final section of the chapter reveals only that it is devoted to a bibliography that you will not find useful in the ordinary course of events. Should you want to read further on the topics of the chapter; should you have a term paper to write; should the chapter as written require further explanation before you understand it, then this bibliography is your guide. As for as immediate usefulness is concerned, you find nothing for you in the bibliography. You are ready to proceed to the second step in your reading of the chapter at hand.

2. READING FOR UNDERSTANDING

The first section heading in the chapter was *Composition of the Air*. Write the section heading in your notebook. Put the notebook aside. You are ready to read. What will you read *for?* To find the "composition of the air." All the way through this section, keep in mind that this is what you are after. When you have finished reading the section, you will be able to give a general answer to the question from memory: "What is the composition of the air?" Your mind and memory are ready.

Dry air is a mechanical mixture of gases consisting of about 78 per cent nitrogen, 21 per cent oxygen, and 0.94 per cent argon by volume. Additional constituents include carbon dioxide, hydrogen, and ozone in minute amounts and, locally, certain volatile organic substances, sulfurous gases, chlorine, etc., from volcanoes and other sources. Water vapor also is an important part of the air, probably averaging about 1.2 per cent of the total volume. Its abundance varies according to the temperature; it forms about 2.63 per cent at the equator, 0.92 per cent at Lat. 50°N., and 0.22 per cent at Lat. 70°N. Fine earthy matter, smoke, soot pollen, spores, bacteria, volcanic dust, meteoric dust, etc., may be spread as impurities through a considerable part of the atmosphere, sufficiently at times to darken the sun and reduce visibility. The obvious evidence of the presence of dust in the atmosphere is in the occurrence of the red colors at dawn and twilight. Dust particles have an important function in that certain types of particles serve as nuclei, or centers, around which water vapor condenses to produce cloud particles.[4]

[4] *Ibid.*, pp. 60–61.

Question: What is air composed of?
In your notebook:

> Composition of air.
> gases, water vapor, fine earthy matter

Can you go further from memory? Try to give the important details your textbook introduced to describe the three constituents. *Make your memory work.*

> gases – primarily nitrogen (78%)
>   oxygen (21%)
>   argon   (0.94%)
> water vapor – averages more than 1%
>   of total volume, presence
>   varies directly with
>   temperature
> fine earthy matter – smoke, soot,
>   pollens, dust serve as
>   nuclei for water vapor
>   that condenses to produce
>   cloud particles

Quite enough. Were you able to do most of this without looking back?

Of course, you have not completed your study of this section. You may have done well in the notes you just wrote, but will you remember the information, a week, a month, three months from now? That degree of learning will come about only through careful review.

But if you were able to read the section *once* and remember enough to write the notes supplied above, then you have made a good start. You are ready to go on to the remaining sections of the chapter. Let's read one more section for another look at how the technique works. Remember that you must read to find the main idea of the section. It is called *Changes with Altitude;* be ready, therefore, to answer the question: "What is the effect of changes in altitude upon the composition of the air?"

The air extends to great elevations above the land. Mountain climbers have reached elevations of more than 29,000 feet on Mount Everest, and observers in balloons and airplanes have reached elevations of more than 17 miles. Rockets carrying meteorological instruments have reached elevations of approximately 250 miles; meteors, white-hot from friction with the atmosphere, have been observed about 125 miles high; and auroral discharges are seen 375 miles above-ground.

Because the air is heated chiefly at the bottom, the temperature of the air decreases upward about 1°F. for every 300 feet of difference of vertical elevation to altitudes of 6 to 8 miles, above which a zone of nearly constant temperature (about −67°F.) is reached. Differences in altitude account for the pronounced differences in temperature and corresponding differences in climate, in vegetation, and in habitability of places having the same latitude. A change in altitude of 1 mile in general is about equal to a change in latitude of 800 miles.

The dust and other earthy material in the air are confined essentially to the lower layers of the atmosphere. As one ascends into the air, he leaves the smoke and coarser dust behind. The water vapor becomes less and less, until at 6 or 7 miles above sea level in the middle latitudes is it so cold that practically no moisture can remain in the air. Consequently no ordinary clouds exist. This altitude marks the lower limits of the *stratosphere,* a region of cold, clear, thin, dry air where there is nearly a constant temperature of about −67°F.

About one-half the mass of the atmosphere occurs in the lower 18,000 feet. Thus at an elevation of about 3½ miles one is above more than half of the atmosphere. *Explorer II,* a United States Army balloon, reached an altitude of 72,395 feet, or 13.71 miles, above sea level. It was above 96 per cent of the mass of the atmosphere.[5]

Question: What is the relationship between altitude and air? *In your notebook:*

Changes with Altitude

1. air exists far above earth
2. as you go up — temperature, earthy material, and water vapor decrease.
3. air thins rapidly with altitude

You will want more specific information than this in your notes. How much can you give from memory? When you have exhausted your recollection, go back to your notebook to pick up the remaining notes and check your memory on the details you remember.

Now your notes might look like those on the following page. Now you have the gist of the section, and you are ready to go on. But if you were not able to give at least the three general statements (air exists far above earth, etc.), then you have not read well enough. You need to work at strengthening your reading ability. Go back to Chapter 2 to see how.

The temptation is strong for students to sit with pen in hand, spearing each fact as they come to it in their reading. This stenographic procedure is not suitable for a college student. It teaches you almost nothing. It gives you a substitute textbook. From the start of your reading of an assignment, you must emphasize, "What do I understand of what I am reading?" "What can I remember of what I am reading?" "How much can I give back of what I am reading if someone were to stop me and ask me to recite?"

And when you finish a section of your reading, you must

[5] *Ibid.,* pp. 61–63.

1. Air exits far above earth

375 mi — Auroral discharges

250 mi — rockets

125 mi — meteors

17 mi — mountain climbers

EARTH

2. As you go up
   a. temp. decreases about 1°F every 300 feet up to 6-8 miles
   b. 6-8 miles on up — 67°F prevails
   c. earthy materials and water vapor decrease

3. Air thins rapidly as you go up
   a. beginning of stratosphere (6-7 miles) air is cold, clear, thin, dry
   b. about ½ mass of atmosphere occurs in lower 18,000 feet
   c. balloon 13.71 miles up is above 96% of atmosphere

ask yourself the questions your teachers will ask you. Only when you have answered these questions in your notebook *from memory* can you feel that you are reading properly.[6]

When you are satisfied that you have recorded all the material you need for effective study and review, you are ready to go on to the next section of the assignment.

After you have completed the assignment, you are ready to enter the final phase of the study process. Think of what you have accomplished thus far. First, you subdivided a reading

[6] While this attitude toward reading for study purposes can be applied to other kinds of reading as well as to science, there are certain characteristics of textbooks in other areas of study that require additional discussion. You will read a full explanation in Chapter 8.

assignment into its component parts and arranged them for efficient study. Then, one by one, you read each part, extracting the important information well enough so that as you completed each section, you were able to recite the gist of what you had read in the form of written notes. This combination of finding information and comprehending it well enough to recite it is your first step toward top grades.

3. Mastering the Material so that It Becomes Part of You

Periodic review and recitation reinforce learning. They are your organized effort to retard forgetting. If the review and recitation are performed in a manner closely resembling your final examination, then you cannot fail to perform well.

Step 1—Review

Read through the notes you have written after you complete the entire reading assignment. Can you understand everything you have written? Are your abbreviations clear? Can you improve readability by underscoring, using colored pencils, Roman numerals, letters of the alphabet, indentation? Are all the notes correct? Perhaps you misunderstood an early part of the chapter that further reading corrected for you. Has some of the material become so obvious to you that you should not waste space and study time on it? Is there unnecessary repetition? Have you omitted anything?

Step 2—Recitation

Looking only at the section headings in your notes, recite what you can recall of the notes themselves. When you falter in a section—and you surely will, for you have worked hard through the reading and are no longer as alert and fresh as when you began to work—look back at the notes.

Never leave your notes until you can pretty nearly recite them from memory. You may be quizzed on that material on the next morning. You may have to recite part of the material in class. Your understanding of the next day's lecture hinges on how well you know what you have been assigned to read.

Step 3—Periodic Recitation

Once each week throughout the semester, go over the material in your notes. At first, look only at section headings and try to recite the material under them. Read your notes over again only to check your recitation or to fill in information you cannot recall. As time goes by, the chapter titles themselves will suffice to recall all the notes to you.

This is quite different from the usual practice of students and it is far superior. What most students do is to read and reread all their notes many times. Periodic recitation in the manner described not only forces you to go over the material many times, but also shows you whether you are learning as you go. You will be tested sooner or later on whether you can *recite* the material, not on whether you have read it. Prepare yourself directly—by reciting.

As a term goes by, you will find that you know certain material so well that you will not have to keep on going over it. Don't waste your time on it. But be certain that you really know the material well before you leave off studying it. Go back to it for a final recitation just before tests.

Proper study of chemistry and physics entails some of the work described in Chapter 6. *How to Study Mathematics*. You will find, as you take up the sciences in college, that textbooks in chemistry and physics usually provide exercises and problems at the end of each chapter. You will be required to do most of these problems as part of your reading assignments. Thus they become a part of your review, a built-in guarantee of overlearning, like mathematics problems. Do them in the same way prescribed for homework problems in mathematics.

In writing your notes on readings in chemistry and physics, you will find that you do not need to write nearly as many notes as you will have to take in descriptive sciences, such as biology and geology. A chapter in a physics or chemistry text is broken down into a series of principles and techniques followed by proofs and illustrations. If you learn the principle, and understand and work through the proofs and illustrations, your notes will be brief. The important function of note-taking will be obscured if you substitute laborious copying in a notebook for real effort at understanding.

The notes you take on principles will be extremely valuable if you follow the procedure suggested for your notes in mathematics. Write only when you have understood. Write from memory as much as possible. This recitation marks a real step forward in mastery of your material. When you have completed a chapter, follow the same procedures for systematic review and recitation that were developed in the first portion of this chapter.

How to attack a problem that has you stumped

In the chapter on mathematics, you were told that you should devote the lion's share of your study time to the parts of a course you find most difficult. This is true in physics and the other sciences as well. In studying science, you can expect to come up against concepts that seem to be just too much for you to cope with.

It is important that you do not give up prematurely on a topic just because it is difficult. Study as best you can, trying all the techniques given for difficult mathematics problems. Use drawings freely. Read problems carefully for clues you may have overlooked. Go on to your next problem, because it may make the needed mental connection for solving the problem giving you trouble. Check your computations and reasoning. A silly slip may have thrown you off. Recite a difficult concept over and over again. Think back to preceding work. By building up once more to the concept that stumps you, the trouble may disappear.

Don't make the mistake, however, of staying up half the night on a homework difficulty. An hour of study while you are fresh is worth ten when you are exhausted.

Often, in the morning after a frustrating session with a difficult problem, you will find that you are able to go back at the topic and lick it quickly. What has happened is that you have assimilated the parts of the problem you understand well so that—with the freshness of the next day—you have the mental resources to overcome the trouble of the preceding night. But this does not mean that going to sleep on a difficult problem will automatically solve it the next morning. If you have already worked hard with the material, the various parts of a problem will fall into their proper places when your mind is rested.

If the trouble confronting you concerns a concept that just does not seem to make sense—and you inevitably will find some —try reading an explanation in another source. Your library will have copies of other textbooks, as will your campus bookstore and the second-hand bookstores that thrive in almost every campus town.

Don't run off to another source after a single reading. Go over the material two or three times before you give up. Then the change in writing style, the possibility of a different explanation, a happy choice of example, or a good illustration may do the trick.

Here are two discussions of a subject covered in most first-year physics courses. Neither discussion is superior to the other. They are different from one another, and because they are different, they may be helpful.

Polarization by crystals. If we have two pieces of tourmaline crystal (cut parallel to the axis and about 1 mm. thick) mounted in a framework (Fig. 36-1), we may rotate one crystal over the other by means of the worm gear. If the projection apparatus is set up as in Figure 36-2, we may project the image of the tourmaline crystals on the screen. When their axes

FIG. 36—1. Mounting for rotating a tourmaline crystal.

are parallel, considerable light will be transmitted; but when one crystal is rotated, the transmitted light through the center will gradually decrease. When the crystals are at right angles ("crossed"), the light through the center is extinguished.

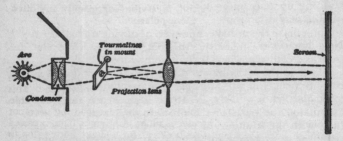

FIG. 36.—2. Apparatus for projection of a beam through tourmaline crystals.

The foregoing experiment shows that the tourmaline crystal can transmit light only when the light is vibrating in one plane. We can visualize this fact by a crude mechanical analogue. Suppose we set up transverse waves in a rubber tube. If the tube is vibrating up and down, we may erect two grids of vertical slats without interfering with the vibratory motion of the tube. But if we turn one of the grids at right angles to the other as in Figure These grids represent the tourmaline crystals.

The experiment with the tourmaline crystals leads one to suppose that light is a transverse rather than a longitudinal vibration since a grid would not stop longitudinal vibrations. The light which strikes the crystal is vibrating in a plane at right angles to the beam, or line, of propagation, but in all directions. After it

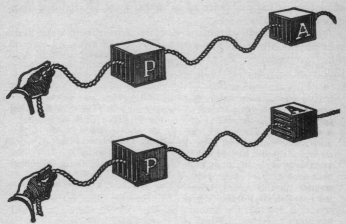

Fig. 36-3. Mechanical analogue of polarization experiment.

has passed through the crystal, it is vibrating in only one direction and thus is said to be **plane-polarized.**[7]

Now here is the same topic discussed in another textbook:

Polarization of Light—The wave character of light is demonstrated by the phenomena of interference and diffraction; the transverse wave nature of light is revealed by *polarization*. This phenomenon can be illustrated by a simple test using two thin plates of a mineral called *tourmaline*, the plates having been cut from the crystal in a particular manner. A beam of light is passed through one of the plates and, except for a slight tinting due to the color of the tourmaline, remains unchanged in appearance. It has, however, been profoundly altered, as a test with the second plate placed in the path will show. When the plates are parallel the light passes through both, but when one is turned the amount of light transmitted becomes less, and then they are at right angles the light is almost entirely quenched, and the overlapping region appears dark.

A somewhat similar effect can be pictured for a mechanical wave by supposing transverse vibrations in all directions to be set up in a rope stretched horizontally. When the rope is unobstructed the waves will travel freely along its entire length, but if the test is repeated with the rope passed through a vertical slit, the horizonal components of the vibrations will be prevented from traveling beyond the slit and only the vertical components will be transmitted. A second slit will produce no further change if it is

[7] Newton Henry Black, *An Introductory Course in College Physics*, The Macmillan Company, 1941.

vertical also, but if it is turned to the horizontal all vibrations beyond will be quenched.

The significance of the test with the tourmaline plates will be considered by the aid of Fig. 337. Light is regarded as a wave in which the vibrations are transverse; that is, in planes at right angles to the line of propagation. For natural light, it is supposed that in these planes, the vibrations occur in all directions, a few of which are represented by the radial lines on the incident ray in the figure. Tourmaline transmits only vibrations or their components which are parallel to the crystal axis. Thus, in the light transmitted by the first plate *P,* the vibrations are restricted to a single plane, as represented by the short dashes in the figure. This light is said to be plane polarized. The second plate, *A,* when crossed with the first as shown, extinguishes the light because the vibrations incident upon it have no components along the direction in which it is capable of transmitting. Plate *P* is used to polarize the light and is called the *polarizer,* and the plate *A* is used to analyze the polarization and is called the *analyzer.*

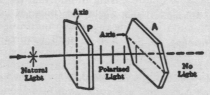

FIG. 337. Polarizing action of tourmaline.

It is believed that light waves, like radio waves, are due to magnetic and electric fields which continually build up and collapse, and which are right angles to each other. In specifying the plane of vibration of a light wave, the plane of the electric field is meant.

The term polarization implies a lack of symmetry around the axis of propagation. The fact that a light wave can be polarized is taken as evidence that the wave is transverse, as a longitudinal wave appears to be inherently symmetrical with respect to its direction of travel.[8]

As you can see, both of these authors try to describe polarization by means of a comparison. One student may find the analogy of a rubber tube more vivid, while another student may understand polarization through the rope analogy. If you find that you cannot come to grips with the presentation of an idea in one science textbook, try going to another. It may be that you will want regularly to consult two versions of every topic you study. In the interests of saving time, you probably will prefer to use the second text as your ace in the hole.

Sometimes, students will use the same technique in another way. If they find that they are having undue difficulty in grasping the science lectures they attend, they will try to sit in on other lectures on the same topcs given by a different teacher. This can often be arranged on a large campus.

How to adapt your studying to special situations

In some science courses, you will find that the textbook seems to be the core of the work. Everything you need to know is in it, and the lectures apparently serve the purpose only of making clear what you have already covered in the text. To many students, it is disappointing to find that the lecturer follows the text so closely that while the course is exceptionally easy, lectures are so unexciting that they would just as soon stay away from them. Your first task in such lectures is to listen carefully as the lecturer reviews the content of the course. Hold your note-taking to a minimum by reading carefully in your textbook before attending lectures. If you take your reading notes along with you to the lectures, you can spend your time reviewing them with the lecturer and thus save yourself a good deal of review time.

On the other hand, you will often find yourself in a course in which the lecturer seems to be teaching a course entirely different from the one the textbook had in mind. This kind of course is much harder for the student who is interested only in making high grades. For the student who is eager to understand various points of view, who wants to go as deeply as possible into a subject, who wants to broaden his outlook, the organization of this course is tailor-made. He has the opportunity to roam far beyond the limits set by a single textbook.

In such a course, you must concentrate your primary learning effort on the lecture itself. The notes you take must be far closer to complete than in the other type of course. Your study time must favor your lecture notes.

At the same time, do not neglect the problems assigned in your textbook. They are still rehearsals for the problems you will have to solve one day on an examination.

When a course concentrates upon lectures in the manner described, it is often useful to discuss with a friend a lecture you have just heard. The purpose of such a brief review is to make sure you have understood exactly what was going on and also to give yourself an opportunity to recite the material just covered.

In many courses, your instructor will issue a course syllabus, which can be helpful in many ways. First of all, the syllabus will usually contain all the reading assignments and all the test and report dates for the semester so that class time will not have to be spent on such announcements. In addition, you will find a list of lecture topics and often a brief outline of the lectures themselves.

You can expect to find no more than a list of the subtopics of each lecture. Yet they are useful in that they direct your attention toward what is to be covered in each hour. You can write the headings supplied by these notes into your notebook in preparation for the lecture. With the format of the lecture before you, your job is to listen and comprehend what is said under each of the headings. The syllabus topics also become review material for you, since you have a list of all the topics that have been covered in the semester. What you must know about these topics is, of course, the substance of the lectures themselves.

How to identify and remove stumbling blocks

A deficient background in mathematics may cause difficulty in chemistry or physics—particularly physics. Unless you can handle algebra fairly well, you will be poor at manipulating the equations you encounter in the sciences. Students who cannot understand calculus will find physical concepts tough to manage. So college advisors often will steer students away from physics if they are poor in math.

Should you plan to take college physics, review your mathematics. One way to do it is to get a tutor in the special areas of difficulty. A book especially designed to prepare students for the first-year physics course is *Review of Pre-College Mathematics,* by Claude J. Lapp and others (Scott, Foresman and Company, 1934).

There is another possible source of trouble that may hold you back in science. A special requisite of chemistry and physics is that you understand principles in the order in which they are taught. If you miss one link in the chain, you may not be able to understand fully what follows. Thus if you suddenly find that a formerly easy science has become impossibly tough, make certain that you have not misunderstood material that went before. Check through all the chapter titles in your textbook to see whether you can find any gaps in your knowledge.

It is because of this "building" nature of the sciences—each principle resting on one before—that we have stressed careful preparation of every assignment in a course.

How to profit from a science demonstration

One feature of the typical science lecture that often proves a pitfall for the student is the *demonstration*. Because of the elaborate preparations that are made for the demonstrations, because of the essentially theatrical nature of the presentation, some students seem to feel that their role at the demonstration is to sit back and enjoy it. Yet you must get more from the demonstration than the spectacle alone.

By definition, a demonstration is intended to make clear for you a principle or theory that your lecturer wants to drive home. No matter how complete your notes on a demonstration may be, they will be useless to you if you have failed to understand the theory being illustrated.

What kind of notes should be taken of a demonstration? Your primary job of note-taking is to make a clear diagram of the experimental set-up, labeling every item correctly. You will probably find that you can use symbols to represent the various kinds of apparatus. If you want to do this, try to copy the standard symbols used in the diagrams in your textbooks.

As you watch, make the mental connections between the events you are watching and the theory they are illustrating. Every step in the demonstration is understood to be "in relation to" the principle. As you study your lecture notes, each time you come to that diagram, think of how you would explain what you saw.

How to apportion time strategically before an examination

When you are ready to review for an important test in science—mid-term or final—don't forget to go over the material of the entire period covered by the examination. Inspect your quiz grades and quiz papers to see where your strengths and weaknesses lie. For example, if you are preparing for a final examination on a physics course in which your mid-term examination grade was a *C*, you probably ought to divide your study time to give the first half of the term's work two-thirds of your effort, the final half only one-third.

The reason for this is that review of the half will improve your understanding of the second half. Putting greater emphasis on the second half will mean that you are wasting time. Your mastery of the later work is only as good as your understanding of what went before. If your work during the first half of a term has been satisfactory, change the ratio back to two-thirds on the second half, one-third on the first.

You will find that although science courses are generally very difficult, you will have less trouble with them if you systematize your work as has been suggested in this chapter.

CHAPTER 8

HOW TO STUDY THE SOCIAL SCIENCES

PERHAPS the biggest surprise for the college freshman is his discovery of the social sicences. Before coming to college, he took courses in *social studies,* or something similar under a different name. He studied *geography,* but that was years before. Surely he had some *history.* He has heard of *psychology*—who has not? But when he gets to college, lo and behold! there are courses called *anthropology, government, economics, political science,* and *sociology.* And strangely, on the typical campus, more students major in the social sciences than in biology, chemistry, and physics combined, even though before leaving high school, most of them would not have been able to name, much less define, more than a few of the subjects in this category. As a bare minimum, most colleges require two years' work in the social sciences.

You surely understand the scope of *history* and *geography,* but do you understand what is involved in the other social sciences?

Anthropology studies man's physical characteristics, where he is found, his races, his adaptation to his environment, his primitive culture.

Economics studies production, distribution, and consumption of goods and services. It is concerned with the organization of management and labor, and how they are interrelated.

Government, sometimes called political science, studies forms of political administration, political theory, and political institutions.

Psychology studies the mind in all its operations.

Sociology studies the institutions and functions of human groups.

The social sciences are founded upon principles and theories just as the sciences are. They pursue fact wherever possible in support of these principles and theories. They investigate and predict. A great deal of your study time will be spent learning evidence for what has been established. This is the easiest part of your job, for it resembles most closely the kind of study you are used to from high school days. College study of the social sciences, however, goes beyond memorizing facts. The theories are far more important. In fact, you may often have more difficulty in understanding the principles of social sciences than in remembering the material.

Special problems

First, you will have the same problem you have whenever you enter a new area of study: the vocabulary will be strange for you. To make your life just a little bit tougher, the vocabulary or social science has a difficulty all its own—you will find that some new words you meet are used only by a single author in a field. Or a single word may be used to mean different things to different authors. And so you will have to learn words and definitions that you will find only in the writings of a single author!

Secondly, you may find that reading the social science classics presents certain special difficulties besides vocabulary. In science readings in most colleges, the student does not go to the original articles and notebooks of the scientists responsible for a particular observation or theory. Rather, he reads text-books written by men who are primarily teachers as well as scientists. They interpret and clarify for the student. In the social sciences, this is often not the case.

The student may have a textbook that he can use as a guide to material he is studying, but he also has original sources to read. And these are almost more difficult than the textbooks themselves. This problem is so important that it is given a great deal of attention later on in this chapter, where you are shown how to deal with social science readings in sources other than textbooks.

One point must be made now about how to cope with the presentation of social theory in original sources. If you find yourself experiencing heavy weather in trying to get through a particular author, turn to an interpretive article or book on that author. Once you have seen what others have to say about a particular theory, you will find that you can profit more from the original source itself. Finding a book or article on any of the great social scientists presents no problems. Your first stop would be a suitable encyclopedia, such as the *Encyclopedia of Social Sciences* or the *Encyclopedia Britannica*. The *Reader's Guide to Periodical Literature* will help you find current sources, and the card catalogue in your college library will also be valuable. Two hours of reading about a particular theory will often save you far more than that amount of time when you return to the original works.

As you read social science theory, you should learn to associate the theory with the scholar who originated it. This association will help you understand references made by your teachers and by authors whose works you will read. It is a good idea, however, to go one step beyond this. Repeat the process you used for learning rules of grammar; restate every theory you must learn in your own words. The best way to do this is to invent an example with which you can always associate the theory.

Reading a social science textbook

When you read a social science text you will, of course, bear in mind the principles of good reading discussed in Chapter 2. You will look at the beginning and the end of the chapter for an outline of the material that the author intends to cover. In addition to this, you will often find questions at the ends of chapters.

Here, for example, are the questions that appear at the end of Chapter 12, "Determinants of Length of Life," in *Population Problems* by Paul H. Landis (American Book Company, 1943).

- 1. What is meant by the "life span"? What possible factors have a bearing on its length?
- 2. Why is the length of life a suitable subject for the sociologist as well as for the biologist?
- 3. What factor is primarily responsible for greater length of life?
- 4. Compare the average length of life of peoples of selected nations. Do you attribute the differences primarily to differences in biological characteristics of peoples or to differences in culture?
- 5. On what basis do insurance companies predict the length of life of a population or of a particular group or individual?

- 6. What are the principal factors of environment that tend to terminate the potential life span prematurely? Discuss them briefly.
- 7. How might a better system of medical organization increase the average length of life?
- 8. Can the average length of life be raised in the future to the extent that it was during recent decades? Defend your answer.
- 9. Comment on the social importance of increased longevity. If you inspect these questions before reading the chapter on which they are based, you will know just what to look for.

Let us examine a typical chapter from a social science textbook to see how you will work through it in your studying. Do you recall the three steps in effective reading?

1. DETERMINE WHAT IS TO BE LEARNED.
   a. opening section clues
   b. sub-headings and illustrations
   c. closing section clues
2. READ FOR UNDERSTANDING.
   a. topic-by-topic reading
   b. writing notes from memory of what you find
   c. checking to fill in additional detail
3. MASTER IT SO THAT IT BECOMES PART OF YOU.
   a. first review at close of reading
   b. first recitation
   c. periodic recitation

Use these techniques now to work through an assignment in a representative freshman textbook in psychology.[1]

Your first objective is to determine what is to be learned from the chapter assigned. Keep that in mind as you read the *opening section.*

[1] John Frederick Dashiell, *Fundamentals of General Psychology*, Houghton Mifflin Company, 1937. Psychology was selected for this discussion because of the widespread student interest in this subject. Any of the other social sciences could have been used just as easily.

Chapter IX:

SENSORY FUNCTIONS

Sensitivity in General

The Importance of Studying Sensory Phenomena.
There can be no expression without impression, no response without stimulation. A man does nothing, is not active, in any manner involving the effectors studied in the last chapter, unless in some way he is being influenced by energy changes occurring inside or outside of him which play upon his receptors—provided we except a few cases of smooth muscle and gland excitation by hormones. The student interested in the phenomena of human nature and in their prediction and control must have some definite knowledge as to how men are sensitive to influences; to what kind of forces or influences they are sensitive; at what degree of intensity; and at what places on or in the body the influences must be applied. Many are the practical questions that turn upon such facts. What are the most effective colors for switch lights and street-crossing signals? Can all men see them equally well? What is the best form of illumination for a factory? How fine a difference can the average pilot detect in the directions of the motions of his airplane when it is enveloped in clouds? Do different pilots vary much in this regard, and can such variations be measured and tested? How good an "ear" and what kind of "ear" must one have to become a successful violinist? What are the essentials of a good musical tone? Just what is the nature of the differences of tones which proceed from various string, wood-wind, and brass instruments? In what way does the rolling of a ship excite nausea? When one is learning to operate a typewriter, what controls the speed and accuracy of the strokes? Why is the touch method of typing recommended? In learning to hold a billiard cue of a fencing foil precisely right, what receptors are involved? To put all this in a nutshell: no attempt systematically to understand the hows and whys of human behavior can be successful unless consideration be given to the *paramount rôle of stimulation in the initiating and in the controlling of behavior.*

A second reason for the study of human sensitivity presents itself as soon as we recognize the other centuries-old motive for psychological study—the analysis of one's own personal and private conscious experience. It is a fact that the great majority of thoroughgoing inquiries into the nature of consciousness have been highly analytical in character, and have discovered as the basis of consciousness sensations of one sort or another. One's awareness of an object perceived or of an event imagined or dreamed, the feelings of his emotional responses, and even the processes of thinking as he is conscious of them—all are held to be reducible to the primordial sensory experiences of particular colors, tastes, sounds, pressures, strains, and the like. This analysis of one's consciousness, while for the most part exceedingly difficult for the untrained, is well typified by some fairly easy and common analyses attempted by the average man. He may, for example, examine the experience he calls the taste produced by his lemonade to determine whether it has sour-ness enough or sweet-ness enough, or he may examine the taste of his breakfast cereal to see whether the sweet-ness and the salt-ness of the taste are properly balanced. To summarize: any systematic study of psychology from the introspective point of approach must recognize *the central importance of sensations* (that is, the individual's awareness occasioned by stimulations) *in the analysis of consciousness.*

In keeping with the aims of this book as announced in the first chapter, we shall, for the most part, approach the sensory processes in the objective rather than the subjective manner, though supplementing the former with the latter at a few points. Putting it more simply: our primary inquiry will be to see how our hypothetical subject reacts to the various forms of stimulation which we bring to bear upon him and what difference in his actions are explainable by the changes of stimulation; but we shall now and then amplify this account by asking him, "How does it 'feel' or appear?"

A more general reason for including sensitivity in our survey of psychology lies in the fact that this division of psychology has probably been more thoroughly worked out in its details than any other; and it would be an unfair introduction to the field if we did not give the reader some acquaintance with some of these details.[2]

From a quick reading of this opening section, you can see the *general plan* of the entire assignment. In a few moments, you will examine the *section headings* and *illustrations* of the chapter, and then read the *last section* of the chapter to see whether there is further help available in identifying what is to be learned. The brief section you have just read gives you insight into the importance of the chapter. Because not more than a minute or two will be needed to make a few notes on this topic, make them now.

Now you have read and understood this introductory section and can see the general scheme and importance of this chapter.

[2] Some of the vocabulary here is difficult. In these four paragraphs, you encountered sensory, phenomena, effectors, receptors, hormones, paramount, analytical, primordial, introspective, objective, subjective, hypothetical, and amplify. Learn the words you do not know, if you want to read this psychology textbook effectively. Use the card technique described in Chapter 5.

Quick inspection shows that the author gives you two kinds of headings within the chapter, one more general than the other.

1. in understanding behavior of others

   a. what are men sensitive to?
   b. how sensitive are they?
   c. where in the body are they
      sensitive?

2. in understanding our behavior

   a. perceiving objects
   b. imagining and dreaming.
   c. thinking

The main headings in the chapter:
    Cutaneous Sensitivity
    Gustatory Sensitivity
    Olfactoy Sensitivity
    Kinesthetic Sensitivity
    Static Sensitivity
    Organic Sensitivity
    Auditory Sensitivity
    Visual Sensitivity
    Some Quantitative Problems
    A Concluding View of Receptive Processes

These ten topics are the structure of the remainder of the chapter. As a result of a few minutes' effort, you understand that the chapter will study one by one the various senses and types of sensitivity of man. You will keep in mind as you read these sections that *the study of sensory phenomena helps us understand the behavior of man.*

As you get into each of these discussions, you will find it subdivided further. *Cutaneous Sensitivity,* for example, is broken down into *Stimuli and Receptors,* and *Some Special Phenomena.* It will probably be best for you to plan on taking notes under all the subheadings, but how much you will write will depend on the importance of each individual section.

Knowing the purpose and the general structure of the reading assignment, go on now to the last section to see what it can tell you about the body of the chapter. The title, *A Concluding View of Receptive Processes,* seems to promise general insights that can be valuable for understanding the rest of the chapter. (If you are alert, the four opening words of this section should be a signal to you in your reading.)

Let us now summarize the roles played by the different classes of receptors in the life economy in the light of the preliminary descriptions and analyses of human and animal behavior we have set forth in earlier chapters. The primary sources of human and of subhuman behavior are to be found in the metabolic processes occurring within the body and especially in the inadequate relations of external conditions to the processes. The *interoceptors* are the sensitive organs most directly implicated here. Next, the organism when it gets into action proceeds to make some changes in its environment. In this the *exteroceptors* act the part of advance guards through which the specific characters of the surroundings play upon the body and modify the directions of movements. Further refinement of the movements is secured through the co-ordinations made possible by the *proprioceptors.*

A simple illustration lies at hand in the behavior of a hungry child. The empty stomach sets up interoceptive impulses which initiate motion and locomotion: the child goes after food. The direction in which he goes is determined by the smell or by the sight of cookies or apples, the sight of doorways, and by other exteroceptive stimulations. The maintaining of his general bodily positions, and the effective reaching for and taking hold of and eating of a cooky or an apple, depend upon his proprioceptive organizations.

Coupled with a dictionary definition of the three key terms (interoceptors, exteroceptors, proprioceptors), the illustration of the child gives good insight into the concepts discussed. When you go on to read the body of the chapter, you will see how important these three terms are.

Now let us go on to study the effective use of other kinds of social science readings.

Reading other materials in social science

You will often have to read materials other than textbooks. This is because textbooks in many courses have so grand a scope that they cannot go deeply enough into all aspects of the subject they are covering. Another reason for assigning readings in sources other than textbooks is to teach you how to "look for yourself." By going to original documents, treatises by experts, and other specialized sources, you learn the tools of scholarship. Being able to locate and evaluate information is essential in your advanced college courses, and valuable all through life.

Reading in such sources sometimes causes great difficulty for the student who is accustomed to the style and format of textbooks. Besides being tailored to meet the time requirements of a college semester, the typical college textbook is written to accommodate the level of knowledge and ability of students in most colleges. The additional readings you will have to master in the social sciences are not subject to the same restrictions.

Let us examine two works, one a *history textbook* and the other a *history,* to find out how they compare in depth and difficulty. The topic is the emergence of the C.I.O. (Congress of Industrial Organizations) as a factor in the American labor movement. See first how a textbook, *The American Nation,* by John D. Hicks (Houghton Mifflin Company, 1955, 3rd ed.), covers this event.

One result of the labor turmoil that characterized these years of change and experiment was the division of organized labor itself into two competing camps. The American Federation of Labor, led since 1924 by William Green, adhered consistently to the Gompers policy of cooperating with capital as long as wages and working conditions remained satisfactory. With the capitalistic system as such it refused to quarrel, provided only that labor obtained a reasonable reward for the work it was called upon to do. Furthermore, the A.F. of L. still set much store by the crafts union type of organization, and opposed with vigor all attempts to organize all the workers in a given industry, regardless of their skill or lack of skills. The Federation, so its critics complained, had lost touch with the problems of the ordinary worker. After the destruction of the NRA in 1935, John L. Lewis, militant head of the United Mine workers, took the lead in the formation of a Committee for Industrial Organizations, the purpose of which was to promote the unionization of industries as units, and not in accordance with specified trades or skills. In this endeavor he was officially opposed by the A.F. of L., but, with the support of his own and several other powerful unions, he sent organizers into many of the great mass-production industries, such as automobiles, steel, textiles, rubber, aluminum, plate-glass, and furniture. Unmindful of LaFollette's warning as to the hazards of Communist infiltration, Lewis, to make haste, accepted the assistance of numerous Communist sympathizers. The effectiveness of their work was immediately apparent, but the presence of Communists and "fellow-travelers" in high places was to plague the

C.I.O. for many years to come. In most instances the C.I.O. plan of organization seemed to meet a long-felt need; old unions took on new life, and new unions were founded as needed. For co-operating with Lewis in this work ten unions were suspended in 1936 by the A.F. of L., and as a result, the C.I.O. assumed a permanent character that its prime movers had not first intended. Claiming to represent a membership of nearly four million workers as against the five million of the A.F. of L., the C.I.O. changed its name in November, 1938, to the Congress of Industrial Organizations, adopted a constitution after the A.F. of L. model, and elected Lewis as its first president.

What have you learned from this short piece, all there is in Hicks on this split of the two unions? Contrast it, for example, with the treatment in *The Coming of the New Deal* by Arthur M. Schlesinger, Jr. (Houghton Mifflin Company, 1958). Schlesinger devotes an entire chapter to what he calls "Emergence of the CIO." The total number of words in that chapter is approximately 4,500. By comparison, the Hicks treatment looks skimpy.

Schlesinger's book is more than 600 pages long, devoted to the events of but two years in American history. The Hicks work, on the other hand, recounts the "History of the United States from 1865 to the Present," and it runs only one hundred pages longer. How many pages would there be in Schlesinger's book if it covered all the material covered by Hicks with the amount of detail exemplified by the chapter on the CIO?

It is possible to make the contrast between a *history textbook* and *a history* even more dramatic by comparing a few sentences in Hicks' volume with the treatment by Schlesinger of the same matters. On the presence of Communists in the C.I.O., Hicks wrote:

> . . . Unmindful of LaFollette's warning as to the hazards of Communist infiltration, Lewis, to make haste, accepted the assistance of numerous Communist sympathizers. The effectiveness of their work was immediately apparent, but the presence of Communists and "fellow-travelers" in high places was to plague the C.I.O. for many years to come.

This is what Schlesinger had to say on the same topic. Remember that your purpose in reading this is to see the rich possibilities of history beyond the brief sketch that a textbook can give.

> If he [Lewis] had few ideas, he had a burning vision—the vision of a mass workers' movement, bringing "industrial democracy" to the nation by giving labor its deserved stature in American society.

And the very intensity of this vision introduced a new militancy into the life of labor. "The time has passed in America," said Lewis, "when the workers can be either clubbed, gassed, or shot down with impunity. I solemnly warn the leaders of industry that labor will not tolerate such policies or tactics." His old-fashioned militancy opened the way for new ideas and ideologies—Socialists or ex-Socialists like Hillman and Dubinsky, or like the young Reuther brothers, struggling to build a union in Detroit; Trotskyites, Lovestoneites, Stalinists. With the tolerance of a man indifferent to ideas, Lewis welcomed them all, confident that he could turn the zeal of each to his own purposes. Needing manpower for the battles of steel and rubber, he even suspended his old hatred of Communism. "Industry should not complain if we allow Communism in our organization," he observed. "Industry employs them." "Never refuse to work with anybody," he told the Newspaper Guild, "who's willing to work with you." He went so far as to declare an agnosticism about the Soviet Union. "To determine what is actually taking place in Russia is quite impossible—at least for me," he told Selden Rodman with unwonted modesty, adding, "I think we will solve our own difficulties in our own way." Lee Pressman left his government job and became Lewis's counsel in the CIO. Communists went into the field as CIO organizers. When someone expostulated to Lewis about the Communist influx, he is said to have replied, "Who gets the bird, the dog or the hunter?"

The CIO had a spirit of its own, however, diverging both from the Communists and from Lewis. Unlike the Communists, the CIO militants wanted a free and democratic America; unlike Lewis, they wanted a new America. But for the moment all united in their adherence to the Lewis gospel: "Let the workers organize. Let the toiler assemble. Let their crystallized voice proclaim their injustices and demand their privileges. Let all thoughtful citizens sustain them, for the future of labor is the future of America."

So we see how two sentences in a *history textbook* become two paragraphs in a *history*. While both serve their purpose, you can see that the textbook view of things is not enough for the proper study of history.

Did you notice that the authors of the two books in question had different attitudes toward what they were observing? Which was the more sympathetic toward Lewis? You will find such disagreement many times in your reading. One of the things you will learn from consulting a variety of sources in your social science studies is how to detect an author's point of view.

Whether you have an easy or hard time in reading will depend upon how you go about it.

The techniques for reading source material were discussed

in Chapter 2. Let us review them, and then go on to see how they are applied to social science readings.

STEP 1   Inspect preface, foreword, table of contents, index, and whatever other keys are provided in the plan of the book.

STEP 2   Read first chapter carefully to find the scope, importance of book, relationship of work to other works, and to become familiar with style of writing.

STEP 3   Read chapter by chapter:
inspect chapter to determine goals for reading,
read to find out just what is said,
write notes from memory to show that you have really understood and are ready to learn, going back only to check your accuracy in remembering or to pick up additional detail.

These techniques apply to the reading of an entire book, but often, in your courses, you will want only to read a single chapter of a given book. Even if this is the case, it is a good idea to look at the preface of the book so that you will be able to associate the name of the author with the ideas he represents. Then turn to the chapter that concerns you at the moment. Inspect it in detail for its plan.

To show how much information is available to you in a quick inspection, let us discuss two books that are often read in social science courses today. See what help their authors give the reader. The first is Volume 1 of *Democracy In America* by Alexis de Tocqueville, translated by Phillips Bradley (Alfred A. Knopf, Inc., 1946). This was originally published in 1835.

There is a one hundred page *introduction* by the translator that would not be helpful for you if you merely planned to read one chapter. But if you were going to read the entire book, you would find the introduction well worth your time. The author has written a brief *preface* that you will find helpful, because it spells out quickly the foundations of the country and system of government he is going to describe. There are a brief *synoptic table of contents* and a detailed *table of contents* showing the plan of the book, which proceeds from an inspection of the *Exterior Form of North America* in Chapter 1 through a discussion of all the aspects of freedom and government in the United States, ending finally with Chapter 18, *The Present and Probable Future Condition of the Three Races That Inhabit the Territory of the United States.* There is a five-page *conclusion* that takes a quick, sweeping look at the new world as it appears in the fourth decade of the nineteenth century. The *index* is ample, giving you a quick passport to whatever particular topics may interest you.

Now see how one chapter—the eighteenth, dealing with the present and future condition of the three races—reveals further helps for the reader. First of all, there is an untitled *introductory section.* Its first three paragraphs call attention to the fact that while de Tocqueville has often mentioned the Indians and the Negroes in America, he has not dealt with them systematically. He now proposes to discuss their role and that of the Anglo-Americans in the new world.

Further inspection of the chapter reveals that there are five more *subdivisions* within it, each titled. The first is called *The present and probable future condition of the Indian tribes that inhabit the territory possessed by the Union.* The other subdivisions are devoted to the relations between the whites and the Negro and non-white elements; the chance of duration of the Union; the republican institutions and their chances of duration; and finally the causes of prosperity in the United States.

Examining the first subdivision in detail, we find it *further* subdivided into nine topics. And this form of outlining is present throughout the volume. Surely the reader receives a good deal of help—if he is willing to take it.

As you read *Democracy in America,* then, there are many signposts along the way to guide your reading, and this arrangement is not a rare one. Let us go on to inspect another book that is widely read today: *Constraint and Variety in American Education,* by David Riesman (Doubleday Anchor Books, 1958).

To set the tone of the book, there are a *preface, prologue,* and *epilogue.* Less than twenty-five pages long in all, they help you develop a picture of the author, and his goals, methods, and philosophy.

The *table of contents* tells many things: the chapter names themselves could be three general topics entitled "The Academic Procession," "The Intellectual Veto Groups," and "Secondary Education and 'Counter-Cyclical' Policy." While these titles are not especially revealing, each is further subdivided. Examine the *subtitles* of the third: *The Secondary*

*School's Vulnerability in the Community, The Social Studies as
a Case in Point, The Twilight Case of the Junior College,* and
nine more as well. Surely the structure of this general topic
begins to emerge clearly. Each subtitle has its own detailed
*subheadings. The Secondary School's Vulnerability in the Com-
munity* is organized under the following topics:

> Some public schools are freer than many colleges, but in general
> the high schools today are in the position of the colleges a century
> ago, monitoring indifferent students and being monitored by the
> community.

> The enormous variety of pressures on the schools—from their
> domination by the upper social strata to their partial control by
> the previously underprivileged—and their relative freedom amid
> the interstices of competing pressures.

> New pressures on the teacher's personality as well as her politics.

Do you see how helpful this is? With even a cursory examination, you know the form of the book and the main point to be
made in each individual section. Your attention is directed
toward what it is you must extract from the work, and now you
can study it quite effectively with the methods you use in
studying textbooks. Now let us take one of these individual
sections from *Constraint and Variety in American Education.*

First, what questions does the section's title—"Altered Patterns of Pressure on the Teacher"—suggest? Remember that
when you see any title or subtitle you must ask yourself at once
the questions that this section must answer. Questions here
would be: "What were the previous pressures on the teacher?"
"What are the new pressures?" "What change has taken place?"

> The harassment of the public school teacher has been traditional
> in the smaller American communities, but this used to take the
> form (particularly if the teacher was a woman) of policing her
> private life, her smoking and gallivanting and church-going, with-
> out much direct interference in her conduct of the classroom.
> Today, especially in the larger places, the teacher is much freer
> to lead her own private life, but what we might term her academic
> freedom is under a great deal of pressure. Lack of concern over the
> teacher's private life reflects the general urbanization of America
> and the decline of puritanical vigilance over teachers, ministers,
> and other exemplars; meanwhile, however, concern over the
> teacher as a person has taken on a new aspect; the teacher is re-
> quired today to be a "good guy," warm and friendly, not too
> eccentrically dedicated to interests in which the community can-
> not share. Moreover, the personality of the teacher has become

more closely intertwined with the subjects taught: the high schools, which could remain fairly remote from immediate community preoccupations when attended only by a few, are now under a service-minded pressure to teach the social studies, and in many places they are also under pressure to teach a kind of syncretistic and neutral religion, as well as to teach tolerance, democracy and citizenship, and all other good things.

Teaching these topics, which contain more obvious dynamite than the limited traditional curriculum did, however, both draws on what is in the papers and risks getting into them. High school teachers can become labeled by their students as "controversial" as soon as any discussion in the social area gets at all heated or comes close to home. While a college student usually has to take the trouble to write home before he can get a parent steamed up about what a teacher has said in class, and in fact is quite likely to protect his teacher against his less enlightened parents, the secondary school student is still living at home with parents whose jealousy of the teacher is not mediated by distance either of space or status. The high school teacher has in fact lost relative status in recent years as more and more parents are themselves high school graduates. And while the kindergarten teacher gains admiration because she can control several dozen preliterates whose mothers cannot always manage even one, the high school social studies

Altered Patterns of Pressure on Teachers.

1 Regulation of private life (smoking etc.) once big thing; now teacher must be a "good guy," not an eccentric interested in scholarly things.

2. Today less interference with private life, but people look more closely at what goes on inside classroom — especially in social studies: teachers deal with ticklish stuff today, parents know a lot about school subjects.

teacher has a harder time being one-up on American-born parents who can claim to know as much as she about civics or UNESCO.

If you were to take notes on what you have just read, you would ask yourself the question: How are the patterns of pressure upon the primary and secondary school teachers of today different from those of previous generations?

If you have been able to do this well from memory, you are ready to go on in the chapter.[8]

Some of the vocabulary in the selection may have given you trouble: *harassment, urbanization, puritanical, exemplars, intertwined, preoccupations, syncretistic, preliterates.* Do you know them all? If you do not, get out the index cards and your dictionary.

Even when books are not arranged in as helpful a manner as you would like, there still are ways in which you can get to the heart of an assignment before you actually begin to read. Let's have a look at a book with fewer obvious helps than the books just discussed: Harrison Brown, *The Challenge of Man's Future* (The Viking Press, 1954).

Subtitled *An Inquiry Concerning the Condition of Man During the Years That Lie Ahead,* this book deals one by one with the factors necessary for man's survival on earth in the years to come. Against the population growth pattern, Brown plots our needs for food and energy, and our chances for satisfying these needs. This is a provocative book that calls for thought and action by each of us to promote the necessary concern of government to meet "the challenge of man's future." Let us assume that in one of your social science courses you have been assigned the reading of the chapter entitled "Food."

First you would examine the entire book briefly. There is a *preface* of but a few pages that can be read quite easily. Beginning in the third page, which is the next to last, you read:

> . . . the present position of machine civilization is a very precarious position. . . . Whether or not it survives depends upon whether or not man is able to recognize the problems that have been created, anticipate the problems that will confront him in the future, and devise solutions that can be embraced by society as

[8] Notice that such material as this has no specific details and figures that you must find and remember in reading. In general, this absence of specific detail is an aid in studying: your attention is focused on ideas rather than on detail. Yet, many students, accustomed to high school homework, would rather memorize facts and figures than master ideas. These students find this kind of reading quite difficult. Their problem is that they find it hard to pinpoint what it is they are supposed to learn. Chapter 2 showed how to find the main ideas in a book, and the remainder of the present chapter gives further information on techniques for doing this in social science readings.

a whole. . . . In the light of what we know of the nature of man, it would appear that the possibilities of solution are remote. . . .

I believe man has the power, the intelligence, and the imagination to extricate himself from the serious predicament that now confront him. The necessary first step toward wise action in the future is to obtain an understanding of the problems that exist. This in turn necessitates an understanding of the relationships between man, his natural environment, and his technology. I hope that this study will in some measure contribute to that understanding.

The preface has given you an understanding of the scope of the book and the author's thesis that the world is in trouble but can get out of it if we try hard. There are *an index, a list of suggested readings, chapter titles,* and *numbered sections within the chapters,* but that is the limit of the help the reader receives in peering into the heart of the work before actually beginning to read. There are no handy section headings that we have come to depend on in our reading for study purposes. This book is typical of many in its arrangement, and you will have to learn to study such a book if you want to get on in the social sciences.

Don't think that you must begin with the first word in the chapter and plow on through to the end. A quick check of the chapter organization will do much for you. Let us turn now to the chapter "Food" to see how this works. It begins:

All living things require energy if they are to survive. Most animals, including man, obtain their energy by ingesting other living things and burning their organic matter with oxygen:

Organic matter + oxygen ———→ carbon dioxide + energy

In the case of higher animals, such as man, organic matter is eaten, oxygen is taken in through the lungs, the oxygen reacts with organic matter in the body, carbon dioxide is expelled, and the energy is used by the body for various activities. . . .

Since the opening paragraph moves so deliberately to make a point, it would appear that our chapter summary must lie elsewhere—if one exists at all. After all, what you have read thus far is certainly not an original thought. Now turn to the *first sentences of the first few paragraphs* to see what you can learn in this way:

- 1. All living things require energy if they are to survive.
- 2. A man lying in bed and performing no external work requires a certain minimum energy intake.

- 3. A man who weighs 125 pounds and who is engaged in moderate activity requires about 2,600 calories per day, while a man weighing 200 pounds requires 3,700 calories per day.
- 4. The main sources of food energy are carbohydrates, the most important of which are starches, (the main constitutents of potatoes and cereals) and sugar.
- 5. A second important source of energy is fat, which provides about twice as much energy per pound as do carbohydrates.
- 6. We know from experience, however, that a person who consumes a diet consisting only of carbohydrates or fats will soon perish.
- 7. Protein is the principal constituent of the cells which make up the human body, and a liberal supply is needed in food throughout life for growth and repair.[4]

It is evident by now that the first section of the chapter is designed to give you a picture of the life-sustaining requirements of man. It would be easy to sketch in a heading for the first section of your notes: *Man's Food Requirements*.

Let us go on to the end of the chapter to see what we can find there in a few moments. We will read only the opening sentence of each of the last eight paragraphs:

1. In the one-half of the world which is badly undernourished, an increase in food production of approximately 50 per cent is necessary if people are to have adequate nutrition.
2. Such increases are clearly possible in principle.
3. Thus we see that when we consider population limitation solely on the basis of potential food supply, enormous increases of numbers of human beings are possible in principle.
4. However, it must be emphasized that an enormous food-production potential is no guarantee against starvation.
5. In the undernourished half of the world, most people are farmers barely able to produce sufficient food for their own needs.
6. At the present time there is insufficient food production to provide adequate nourishment for the people of the world, and the population is rising quite rapidly.
7. The underdeveloped areas are in the position, however, of being unable to provide new capital at the necessary rate.
8. Thus far we have seen that increased food production in the world requires increased industrialization.

This brief look at the end of the chapter has disclosed a clear outline of the food production problem. Increased food production is necessary and possible; the potential to provide it is not the whole story; parts of the world are already suffering

---

[4] The author apparently uses the first sentence of a paragraph as a topic sentence. By reading the seven sentences just quoted, you have a recognizable and unified development, do you not? This knowledge will help you a great deal as you read through the entire book.

badly; the world's population is exploding; areas that must develop food resources don't have the financial capacity to do so; increased food production demands industrialization, which in turn will require greater development of natural resources (the apparent subject of the next chapter, entitled "Energy").

So the heart of the chapter is summarized in the last eight paragraphs. Do you see that you have the entire chapter at your fingertips? Your task now is to fill in the details of the argument.

Take one further look at the chapter just to convince yourself of the tremendous possibilities inherent in inspecting a chapter before plunging into it. The chapter has nine numbered sections, and we know that Brown makes the first sentences of his paragraphs count for a great deal. The opening sentences of his sections should be particularly revealing for you as reader:

- 1. All living things require energy if they are to survive.
- 2. Since World War II the average American has consumed annually about 250 quarts of milk, 360 eggs, 170 pounds of meat, poultry, and fish, 190 pounds of grain, 130 pounds of potatoes, 65 pounds of fats and oils (including butter), 120 pounds of citrus fruits and tomatoes, 360 pounds of other vegetables and fruits, 110 pounds of sugar, 20 pounds of beans, peas, and nuts, and 20 pounds of chocolate, coffee, and tea.
- 3. The total land area of the world amounts to about 36 billion acres.
- 4. For the entire time during which man has existed on the earth he has competed with other animals for food.
- 5. The land areas of the world provide man with his food, but they provide him, in addition, with a multiplicity of products which enable him to clothe and shelter himself and to produce a variety of goods which increase the comfort of his daily life.
- 6. The food production of the world can be increased in a variety of ways.
- 7. Low crop yields can result from any one of a number of causes.
- 8. Plants can be limited in their growth rates by a variety of factors.
- 9. In the one-half of the world which is badly undernourished, an increase in food production of approximately 50 percent is necessary if the people are to have adequate nutrition.

So you see that the opening sentence of each of the sections of the chapter tells you a good deal of what the section contains. Knowing the point of each topic as you come to it makes the reading of each section meaningful. Surely the few minutes spent in getting the feel of a chapter will help you study.

This method of taking your bearings before actually reading applies as well to magazine or journal articles. Once you have sifted them to identify what you want to know, apply the study techniques you have already learned.

HOW TO MAKE THE BEST USE
OF A SCIENCE LABORATORY

      A science major must work at acquiring a body of information to use and build upon during the rest of his life. And not only in his specialty. He needs to learn all he can of every science course he will ever take. Specialization, to be sure, is important—without it one cannot become expert in anything. But the exact point at which one branch of science begins and another ends is not as clear today as it was a generation ago, and the scientist finds it imperative to go back and forth across scientific boundary lines in order to pursue his work. Physical chemistry is a union of physics and chemistry; biologists and chemists have a new partner, the biochemist. Such blends as these are becoming common throughout science, which means that if you are going to major in one branch of science, you cannot ignore the others. Mathematics too must be emphasized in your training—modern scientific investigation depends on it.

Even if you are not planning to major in science, a selection of science courses is sure to be valuable to you. The fact is that we are living in the Age of Science, and to be in touch with our times we must have at least some understanding of scientific thought and development. Mastering the material to be found in just one year of elementary science at college is a sound basis for that understanding, but the chances are that you will want to build upon it, going beyond the bare science requirement demanded by your college.

We may differentiate two classes of science—*descriptive* and *investigative*. Descriptive science depends largely upon the observation of the physical world. It is concerned with classifying and identifying the substances around us. Obviously, biology—botany and zoology—falls primarily into this category. Think of the botanist identifying collected plant specimens.

On the other hand, we have the investigative scientist, who

studies the nature and meaning of phenomena in a theoretical manner. The physicist intent upon exploring the nature of the atom is a good example. Yet, when he has progressed to a certain point, his work becomes descriptive in that he must develop broad classifications and laws of behavior for the phenomena he has investigated. Thus, while both extremes are far apart, they invariably meet again.

Whatever type of science interests you, a considerable portion of your hours in science courses will be spent in laboratory work. You can expect anywhere from one to four hours of laboratory work per week in a science course. Your laboratory hours help you master the principles and facts you find in readings and lectures by affording you the chance to actually see for yourself. But the laboratory does more than merely reinforce your learning.

Most important, the laboratory gives you experience in the *scientific method*. All science is based upon the scientific method. Seven hundred years ago Roger Bacon stated that the true nature of the physical world can be adduced from observation and experience. Thus it is not enough to be told that fire consumes matter and produces carbon dioxide. This theory does not possess scientific validity until it has been demonstrated and observed in an experiment.

In your laboratory work you will be verifying what your textbooks and lectures tell you, while sharpening your ability to observe and establish truths. The laboratory can be the most exciting place in the world for you, and this depends largely on *your own methods of work*. Do you understand the use and care of your laboratory equipment? Are you well prepared each time you enter the laboratory? Can you work effectively right through the session? These are the questions on which your satisfaction in laboratory work depends. They are discussed fully below.

Know your tools and how to use them

Before a session begins, your teacher usually will make some remarks concerning the particular project ahead. Pay close attention so that you can avoid the destructive slips that result from insufficient care or knowledge. Good laboratory work is by nature deliberate. You have a good deal to accomplish, but there is time to do it cautiously and completely, paying attention to every detail of procedure.

In physics and chemistry laboratories, the procedure is somewhat different from that of the biology laboratory even though the over-all goals are the same. Instead of dissecting and examining specimens closely, you spend most of your time experimenting with substances under varying conditions of temperature, pressure, etc. The tools of these laboratories are generally intricate. With the exception of the microscope used in biology, there is nothing to compare with the elaborate hardware of physics experiments and the glassware of chemistry. Proper care of equipment means keeping it clean and ready for use, making certain that measuring equipment is as accurate as needed.

Proper use of equipment is so important in the chemical laboratory, for instance, that the first laboratory sessions are usually devoted to acquainting you with instruments and procedures you will use throughout the year. Such a session is well illustrated in this experiment adapted from a freshman chemistry laboratory manual.[1] See how a variety of instruments and procedures used in simple problems can give you the working knowledge you need.

THE USE OF THE BALANCE

Discussion: Objects and materials to be weighed fall into two general classes, those of which only an approximate weight (to the nearest gram) is required and those of which an accurate weight (to the nearest centigram) is demanded. Approximate weighings are made on platform scales, which are kept in the laboratory. Such scales must always be tested because they are exposed to the fumes of the laboratory, and become rusted. If the scales are found to be out of order, do not adjust them yourself, but report to the instructor. Substances should not be placed directly on the platform, except pieces of certain metals as zinc and aluminum, or porcelain and glass objects. In weighing on the scales, put a piece of paper of about equal size (a weighing paper or filter paper) on each platform. The object to be weighed is put on the left platform. When the weight is less than 10 grams, the rider on the graduated beam on the front of the scales is used. If the object weighs more than 10 grams, weights are added to the right platform until the pointer swings the same number of spaces each side of the middle division.

Accurate weighings are made on beam balances, which are very sensitive and must be protected from the fumes of the laboratory. Such balances are kept in special balance rooms. They are inclosed by a glass case to avoid air currents during the weighing. *Never attempt to weigh a warm object on a chemical balance.* The up-

[1] Joseph A. Babor, W. L. Estabrooke, and Alexander Lehrman, *Laboratory Manual in Elements of General Chemistry*, Thomas Y. Crowell Company, 1931, pp. 11–13.

ward current of warm air rising from it will make it appear lighter than it really is. Never place anything directly on the pans of the balance, all materials to be weighed must be in a container, such as a watch glass, crucible, weighing tube, etc.

Materials: A platform scale, beam balance, crucible and cover, small evaporating dish, set of weights, crucible tongs.

Directions: The instructor will explain the use of the scales and the analytical balance.

(a) Heat a clean porcelain evaporating dish in the flame for about 5 minutes. Set it aside to cool. Then heat a crucible and cover in the flame until red hot. Remove the flame and allow crucible to cool. When cooled to room temperature, weigh the evaporating dish and the crucible and cover on the platform scales.

	Scale	Balance
Weight of evaporating dish	....	....
Weight of crucible	....	....
Weight of crucible cover	....	....

(b) Weigh the same objects on the analytical balance. Weigh the crucible and cover together to check your results. Account for the differences in weights on the two weighing instruments.

Of course, this work occupies just one part of a laboratory session. In the same session, you can expect to carry out many other procedures. If you do the work described just as carefully as you can and think about what you are doing, your subsequent work in the laboratory will go smoothly. If you do not, you may find yourself having to learn procedures over and over again each time you go to the laboratory. Needless to say, you will waste a good deal of time.

Did you notice that you ask to check the weight you establish for the crucible and cover by first weighing them separately and then together? This kind of safeguard against human error should become a regular part of your work in the laboratory.

How to use a laboratory manual

Your laboratory manual is of greatest importance. It was devised to act as your personal guide through laboratory projects. You can and must consult it before, during, and after a laboratory session. It is a tutor sitting at your elbow, saying:

- This is the *point* of what you are doing today.
- These are the *materials* you will use.
- This is the *equipment* you will need.

- This is the *procedure* you will follow.
- These are the *observations* you should make.
- What are the *conclusion* you will draw?
- What is the *general inference* you can make?

If you make use of your laboratory manual *before* each session in the laboratory, then your laboratory experience will be interesting and profitable. Later you will be shown how to use the manual during the laboratory procedure and afterward in review. Now let us see how you should prepare for the laboratory. Three steps are involved.

STEP 1—READ YOUR TEXTBOOK FIRST

The laboratory manual does *not* completely explain the reasoning behind what you will do in the laboratory. It only supplements the textbook, just as your experiment supplements your lectures and demonstrations.

You miss out on valuable instruction if you do not take advantage of the textbook explanation behind the phenomena you will observe in the laboratory. And you miss out on it just when you need it most, because the weekly laboratory sessions come and go quickly, bringing new material that piles up rapidly in a mass of facts, ideas, and theories to understand and absorb. There is no way to repeat laboratory work, any more than you can listen again to a lecture that has gone by. Unless you have prepared for each step in a laboratory session, you miss its point. Reading your textbook is the first step toward understanding what the manual will tell you to do and why.

Your textbook

- (1) Has the space in which to describe and explain principles more fully than a manual can;
- (2) Brings to your attention pertinent experiments other than the ones you will perform in the laboratory;
- (3) Supplies reference material not found in a manual—charts, tables, glossaries, and great amounts of background information;
- (4) Shows you pictures of organisms and substances that cannot be supplied in the ordinary laboratory because of the expensive and intricate equipment they entail;
- (5) Compares organisms and substances you will see with others not available to you.

Step 2—Read Your Manual for Main Ideas

Unless you have read your manual before coming to the laboratory, the first part of your time there must be spent catching up on this reading. The laboratory manual is a road guide for each session in the laboratory. Read it before starting, to find out where you are going and how to get there. Read it through quickly immediately after you have read the assigned pages of your text. Look for two things as you read:

- (1) What is the theory or principle of the work you are going to do? Your reading in the textbook should have taught it to you. Have you already learned it well enough, or must you go back to the text again?
- (2) Are any of the terms new to you? If so, look them up so that you do not waste valuable time trying to interpret what you are supposed to do.

Step 3—Read Your Manual Again to Visualize the Experiment

If you have been able to discover the main ideas of the experiment you will perform, you are now ready for the final reading of the manual before the laboratory session. This time, keep a picture of the experiments in mind as you read. This is a slow, careful reading in which you see each piece of apparatus as it is mentioned, each material, each procedure.

Read the questions the manual asks. Some of them can be answered before you get to the laboratory, because they depend on knowledge you already have. Answer them. You will free yourself for answering questions that can only be answered in the laboratory. These questions are your cues to the importance of the work you will be doing.

As you read each step, ask yourself why it is included in the procedure. You may want the help of your textbook again for this. If you cannot grasp most of the reasons without help, you may have to spend more time reading your textbook next time you go at an assignment.

Now let us apply the procedures just discussed. As our examples, we will use the laboratory manual quoted earlier in this chapter: *Laboratory Manual in Elements of General Chem-*

istry. The textbook we will use is *Principles of Chemistry,* by Joel H. Hildebrand (The Macmillan Company, 1940).

You have gone about one-third of the way through your chemistry course. The present experiment is on *weak electrolytes, ionic equilibrium,* and *indicators.* Chapter 8 of your chemistry textbook, *Electrolytic Dissociation,* is assigned for study. It is eighteen pages long and covers more ground than the one experiment we will deal with.

In accordance with the procedure you will use for all science readings, you read the opening page or two of the chapter to determine the scope of the chapter. You find that the process of *solution* is described, and the term *ion* introduced and defined. Of course you will spend some time later on to make sure you understand both and can remember them adequately. You next check the section headings to see the specific topics that are treated in the chapter:

Abnormally Great Lowering of the Freezing Point
Independent Migration of Ions in Electrolysis
Discharge of the Ions at the Electrodes
Formulas of Ions
The Properties of Dilute Aqueous Solutions of Strong Electrolytes Are the Sum of Independent Sets of Properties, Hence Independent Substances Are Present
Heats of Reaction in Dilute Solutions of Strong Electrolytes Depend on the Reacting Ions Only
Weak Acids and Bases Are Less Ionized Than Strong Acids and Bases in Solutions of the Same Concentration
Weak Salts
Ionization of Weak Polybasic Acids in Steps
Ionization in Other Solvents Than Water
Ionization of Water

In addition to these section headings, you find other study guides in several tables of information, one diagram, and twenty-one separate problems to help you test your understanding of the chapter. All of these will help you get to the heart of the chapter.

As you do your reading, you note words that are new for you. On the first page of the chapter, for example, you encounter aqueous, solvent, dipole, and electrostatic. Do you know them all? Notice, too, that one of the chapter subheadings, *The Properties of Aqueous Solutions of Strong Electrolytes Are the Sum of Independent Sets of Properties, Hence Independent Substances Are Present,* mentions the mathematical concept of independent sets. Do you understand what it means? If you do not, you must find out. You can see that coming to science courses with a good background in mathematics can save you study time.

Now that you have the framework of the chapter established and have set your sights on what it is you are suppose to learn, you are ready to read through the chapter. As you come to the end of each section, you stop to recite the gist of what you have learned, writing it in your notebook. You then work the exercises at the end to the chapter to make certain you have comprehended clearly and can put the information to work. Finally, you review your notes to see that they are in good form.

We will not reprint here the entire chapter of the chemistry textbook dealing with the experiment and its related topics. A short excerpt will show you how a textbook supplies background material and explanation necessary for complete understanding of the experiment you will perform.

Weak Acids and Bases Are Less Ionized Than Strong Acids and Bases in Solutions of the Same Concentration.

There are some acids and bases which show the properties of hydrogen and hydroxide ions, respectively, to a much less extent than do strong acids and bases in solutions of the same concentration. Solutions of HC_1, HNO_3 and H_2SO_4, at the same concentration, say 0.01 normal, would have about the same sour taste, but 0.01 normal acetic acid, $HC_2H_3O_2$, would not taste nearly so sour. The first three acids would show almost identical colors with an indicator like methyl violet, sensitive to that degree of acidity, but it would require approximately normal acetic acid to show the same color. The same weakness on the part of acetic acid is shown in power to conduct current. While, therefore, the properties of acetic acid indicate that it yields hydrogen ion in water, they also indicate that only a little of the hydrogen of the acid is ionized. Again, while the effect of the acetic acid on the freezing point of water is greater than that of an un-ionized substance like sugar, it is not double the latter, as is approximately the case with an acid like hydrochloric acid. Its heat of neutralization is no longer 13,700 cal., as with a strong acid, but has a different value, and includes the heat of dissociation of the acid during its neutralization.

There are a number of such weak acids, including carbonic acid, H_2CO_3, hydrogen sulfide (hydrosulfuric acid), H_2S, silicic acid, H_2SiO_3, (also many poly-silicic acids), nitrous acid HNO_2, arsenous acid, H_3AsO_4, sulfurous acid, H_2SO_3, and hydrocyanic acid, HCN, hypochlorous acid, HC_{1O}, etc. The **degree of ionization** is the fraction or percent of the total electrolyte present, which has been broken down into ions. For example, if 0.1 mole of acetic acid is dissolved in 1 liter, 0.0013 mole of H+ is liberated; since every H+ produced requires one molecule of $HC_2H_3O_2$ to split up,

0.0013 moles of the acid have dissociated, which is 0.0013 ÷ 0.1 or 1.3 percent of the acid taken. It is to be noted that as a weak acid is diluted the degree of ionization increases although the concentration of H+ diminishes.

The most important weak base ordinarily encountered is ammonium hydroxide, NH_4OH. It is this weakness which makes it useful in cleansing, for although it does not yield enough free hydroxide ion to be injurious in washing, yet, if the little it does yield is used up, more can dissociate, the undissociated portion acting as a sort of reserve for hydroxide ion.

Weak Salts. Most salts are highly ionized when in solution, even though they be salts of weak acids or bases, like sodium acetate or ammonium chloride. There are, however, a few exceptions, including lead acetate, $PB(C_2H_3O_2)_2$, the iodide of cadmium, $Hg(CN)_2$, and ferric sulfocyanate, $Fe(CNS)_3$. These salts are poor electrolytes, and their reactions in solution show the presence of relatively few ions. For example, all ordinary soluble chlorides give a precipitate of lead chloride, $PbCl_2$, on the addition of lead ion to their solutions. With mercuric chloride, however, no precipitate is obtained, indicating that there is less chloride ion in a concentrated solution of mercuric chloride than in a saturated solution of the rather insoluble lead chloride. If, however, silver ion is taken, a precipitate is formed, for silver chloride, $AgCl$, is much less soluble than lead chloride, and $HgCl_2$ yields enough chloride ion to precipitate it.

Now that you have read a short section of the textbook to get the flavor of the kind of material you will encounter in your textbook, let us go on to read the manual to see how we can apply the techniques developed above.

Remember, you are to read your manual twice. The first time is to pinpoint the theory or principles underlying the work you are going to do, and to check yourself on all the vocabulary used in the description of the experiment. As you read, you find that the quality of your textbook determines whether you find the manual tough or easy.

Your second reading of the manual will be a careful thinking through of the problem you are going to undertake in the laboratory. How many of the questions can you answer on the basis of what you have read? Do you understand the development of the experiment step by step? Go back to your textbook if you do not. Above all, make certain that you know what to do throughout the experiment. Visualize each step in the procedure.

Weak Electrolytes, Ionic Equilibrium, Indicators

Discussion: Electrolytes which are only slightly ionized are called *weak electrolytes*. Since the concentrations of the ions in equilibrium with the molecules in a solution of a weak electrolyte are very small, the values for the ionization constants are small. If the concentration of one of the ions in the solution is materially increased, in order that the value for the constant remain the same, the concentration of the other ion must decrease. The change in the concentration of the hydrogen ion may be determined by using a suitable indicator. Thus a solution of acetic acid has a pH less than 5, i.e. the molar concentration of H+ is greater than 1×10^{-5}. By adding solid sodium acetate to dilute acetic acid, the concentration of the acetate ion is increased, and this molecular acetic acid allowed to form, and as a result, the concentration of the hydrogen ion is decreased below 1×10^{-5}, but still above 1×10^{-7} mols per liter. Methyl orange is an indicator which changes from pink to yellow when the molar concentration of a hydrogen ion is reduced below 1×10^{-5}. By using methyl orange as an indicator, we can "observe" the change in pH of acetic acid when sodium acetate is added. Phenolphthalein changes from colorless to pink when the pH becomes greater than 9, i.e. when the molar concentration of the hydrogen ion decreases below 1×10^{-9}. A solution which is alkaline to methyl orange is, therefore, acid to phenolphthalein.

When ferric chloride reacts with ammonium thiocyanate in solution, ferric thiocyanate molecules impart a red color to the solution. One of the equilibria in the solution is

$$Fe(CNS)_3 \rightleftarrows Fe^{+++} + 3\ CNS-.$$

What are the other equilibria? ....
.... Mercuric thiocyanate is very slightly ionized, hence when mercuric chloride solution is added to the solution containing the ferric thiocyanate, the concentration of the thiocyanate ion is decreased due to the formation of molecular mercuric thiocyanate, more ferric thiocyanate ionizes to maintain equilibrium, and as a result there is a decrease in the intensity of the red color.

Materials: Acetic acid, hydrochloric acid, sodium acetate, sodium chloride, ferric chloride, ammonium thiocyanate, mercuric chloride, methyl orange, phenolphthalein, test tubes.

Directions: (a) Take 10 c.c. of distilled water in each of two clean test tubes. What is the pH of distilled water? ....
.... To one tube add 2 drops of methyl orange. What is the color? .... Is the solution neutral, acid, or alkaline? .... Account for the color of the indicator. .... To the other tube add 2 drops, not more (if more is added a precipitate of the indicator will form), of phenolphthalein solution. How does distilled water react towards phenolphthalein? ....
.... Explain ....
....

(b) To 20 c.c. of water add drops of acetic acid. Divide the liquid into two parts and add 2 drops of methyl orange to each. What inference do you draw from the color of the indicator? ....
.... To the first add some solid sodium chloride, and shake. Is there any change? ....

.... To the second add some solid sodium acetate, and shake. Explain the difference in behavior .... Repeat the experiments, using hydrochloric acid instead of acetic acid. Does the addition of sodium chloride decrease the concentration of the hydrogen ion? .... Why? .... Why does the addition of the sodium acetate, which does not furnish an ion in compound with HCl, reduce the H+ concentration? .... Formulate the equilibria in the four cases ....

(c) To 10 c.c. of water add 1 drop of ferric chloride solution and 3 drops of ammonium thiocyanate solution. Formulate the reaction .... Then add 1 c.c. of mercuric chloride solution. Explain the result .... Formulate the change ....

You see that there is a great deal of detail in a typical experiment, and if you are to work well in the laboratory, you must familiarize yourself with what you are going to do before you get there. Did you notice that some of the information asked for can be supplied before performing the experiment while other information must wait for actual observation? If you prepare carefully, the work you will do in the laboratory will carry out plans you have laid before beginning. With this advantage, you can devote yourself to *thinking* about what you are doing in the laboratory while you are doing it. The resulting improvement in learning will be worthwhile.

How to use your laboratory time

There is a special feature of laboratory work that differentiates it from your other college work. In listening to a lecture or in takng part in class discussions, you may think actively and participate to a certain extent, you may take good notes—but you still tend to think of yourself as part of an audience. In the laboratory, by contrast, the accent is upon independence and individual work.

Bearing this in mind, here are five points that can contribute greatly to your success in laboratory work.

1. BE READY TO WORK WHEN YOU ARRIVE

While your instructor usually will start a laboratory session with some discussion of the work that is going to be undertaken, be ready to start out on your own once he has finished. This means that you must have studied your textbook and manual.

Above all, you must have the desire to work when you arrive at the laboratory. Laboratories are less formal than other college classes and, because the sessions are usually longer, they tend to be more leisurely. The atmsophere is relaxed, there is no strict rule against conversation, and there is little central direction. Unless you are on guard, these conditions can distract you from making the most effective use of your time. If you are to accomplish the work scheduled for the period, you need to keep constantly focused upon it and to respect the need of others to do the same.

When you arrive at your laboratory table, lay out the tools you will need for your work and keep unnecessary paraphernalia out of sight. After your instructor has completed the preliminaries, open your manual and get to work.

2. Use Your Laboratory Manual Properly

If you have familiarized yourself with your textbook and manual before you arrive at the laboratory, you will have a good grasp of what you are to do and why. Now you must make every *observation* and answer every *question* that the manual requires. Perhaps you will be tempted to cut corners, for you will know some of the answers before you are halfway through a procedure if you have done your reading well. But far more important than speed in laboratory procedure are understanding and thoroughness. Each step of the work that you complete satisfactorily will help drive home to you the points being made. It is important in the long run not to skip over them, but to perform every step called for without omitting a single detail.

3. Do Your Own Work

The unwary can fall into the trap of collaborating with others, when the best way to learn is by doing your own work. College science laboratories have seen some of the cleverest joint enterprises ever organized. The ingenuity that students can show in working together on a project in order to reduce the amount of work done by any one student is something to marvel at. Unfortunately, most of the members of such combinations suffer for their parts in the scheme. The typical plot is organized in this way: several students with little interest or ability divide the work facing them into tiny, easily performed parts. Readings and observations made by each student are shared with the group. While the students find that they do not have to work very hard under this plan, they will also find that they do not learn very much either. Secondhand information is not as meaningful as firsthand experience, and the resulting losses are bound to show up when examination day arrives.

4. DON'T WASTE TIME

The drawings you make in the laboratory are not intended to hang in the Louvre. The object of sketching an equipment layout is to help you recall just how you conducted certain experiments. This is extremely important if others are to understand just how you arrived at the conclusions you report. The object of drawing a specimen you observe under the microscope or on your dissecting table is to help you remember what you have seen and make it easy to identify individual parts of a whole. It is not to make a pretty picture, elaborately colored and lettered.

But if your drawings are to serve their purpose, they must be completely accurate. When you come to use a drawing during your review sessions, you should be able to recognize easily everything you have put down. This includes the labeling of parts of drawings as well as the drawings themselves. It includes the items you put down in your laboratory manual in response to the questions you are asked in the manual.

With whatever free time you have—and on some days it can be a considerable amount if you have prepared well and work efficiently—you can get a good deal of studying under your belt. For example, while you are waiting for a specimen to finish baking, or just after you finish your work, use your time for thinking about what you have been doing, so that the point of the experiment will be clear in your mind. You can use spare time to memorize, and to organize materials for your laboratory report. You can go back to your textbook to review its presentation in light of what you are observing in the laboratory. You can work ahead in your textbook, looking toward your next laboratory session or an examination. Indeed, you may find that you are capable of doing a great deal of your studying and review right in the laboratory.

Even if you do not find yourself with much free time on your hands, stop working periodically to stand back and look at what you are doing. It is so easy to get lost in a profusion of detailed procedures you are carrying out and completely miss their significance. It is easy to go through all the steps in an experiment without knowing why.

5. Ask Questions When You Must

Consult your teacher and laboratory assistants whenever you need help. These men do not like to spend time going over material that is clearly explained in your textbook, but they do stand ready to help you at all times.

One kind of difficulty you may have is awkwardness in handling laboratory equipment. Rather than use it badly, ask for help. Forcing a tool can damage it. Using it inexpertly can hurt a specimen being observed. Carelessness can cause injury to you and others. Your textbook can set you straight, and it is likely that if you have trouble understanding your textbook, then so will other students. By asking questions, you help yourself and other students as well.

A final word

Don't forget that your laboratory manual is as much a study material as your textbook and your lecture and class notes. Use the procedure described in pages 57–60 for careful review arranged at regular intervals over the period of the entire semester or year. With this review and the procedure that has been described for carrying out your laboratory work, you will learn effectively and do your best work on examinations.

CHAPTER 10

GETTING ALL YOU CAN FROM YOUR COLLEGE LIBRARY

THIS chapter is dedicated to helping you find and use the wealth of materials provided by your college library. The establishment and maintenance of a library represent a staggering effort by thousands of people—authors, editors, printers, librarians, and many others—and it is significant that universities and colleges are evaluated to a large extent on the number of books in their libraries. Harvard has more than five million; Yale more than three; Illinois, California, Columbia, and Chicago more than two. A first-class library is a prime factor in attracting scholars to a campus.

More than any other unit of the college, the library is the focus of studying. You can learn more by working in the library than you can by any other single activity. You can work at a more rapid pace than you can in the classroom or the laboratory. You can find all points of view on any topic. You can choose your own hours for working.

Of course, the library is essential to making the highest grades you are capable of. It is the place where you will develop the ability to find and evaluate information. It is the place where you will find the books you are assigned to read. It is also the place where you will work independently without a specific assignment, and one of the marks of the good student is his knowledge of sources and information he has not been asked to find. It brings joy to the heart of the teacher to read evidence in an examination paper that a student has taken the trouble to go off on his own to find out more about a subject than a textbook and other assigned readings could give.

Acquaint yourself with your college library

A college library meets two needs. First, it is a study hall equipped with books and other reading matter you need for your course work. Secondly, it is the laboratory in which you will carry on much of the research you will do in college.

As a study hall, it is unexcelled. Ample table and chair space is provided, as well as good lighting. The books. encyclopedias, and periodicals you need are close at hand. In contrast, a dormitory room can be the center of a conspiracy of distraction and interruption. When this is so, the individual student cannot do more than hope for peace and quiet. An additional drawback is that no one student can hope to own all the reference materials he will need for his work. The only reference book every student should have with him when he arrives at college is a good desk dictionary.

As a research laboratory, it provides the opportunities you need to become skilled in library research techniques. Your knowledge of how to use a library will be of great use to you throughout your entire adult life.

But while all the materials may be there, your individual skill in using library facilities will determine whether or not you are effective in carrying on your work. The same research task can require two hours of one student while another student will need one hundred. One student can find all he needs within the library; another will never find what he is looking for.

Your tools in finding the reading matter you want are the *card catalogue,* the *reference room,* special and general *bibliographies,* special *reading rooms,* and the aid of *librarians.*

In the first weeks of your freshman year, take an unhurried sightseeing tour of your library. Most colleges will arrange such tours for groups of students in freshman English classes or for students taking part in freshman orientation programs. You will be shown all parts of the library, and you probably will be taught how to use the card catalogue in finding books. You may be shown how to complete a call slip to order a book from the "stacks," [1] how to locate individual issues of periodicals that are kept in bound volumes, and how to locate encyclopedias and other reference tools. If such a tour is not available at your library, you certainly should go on a tour of your own.

When you go about on your own, note the special rooms in which you will be spending a good deal of time during your four years of college. No matter what your major, if your library has a special room containing books in your field, it will also have a card catalogue in that room that will save you a great deal of time in the future. Instead of having to cope with the general catalogue, which may have millions of entries,

---

[1] In most libraries, the stacks are the area where the bulk of the book collection is kept. Ordinarily you do not have direct access to the stacks, but must submit a call slip to the librarian, who will see that you obtain the book you want.

you will do well to use the more limited catalogue in your special library room.

To learn as much as you can about the card catalogue, spend a few minutes looking up some books you are familiar with. First find the books under title, then under author. Try chasing down some of the other subjects under which the books you are looking for may be found. You will see later in this chapter (page 190) just which part of a card shows the other subjects under which the books are listed. If you want to borrow a book, obtain a call slip and order it. The practice gained will make you more familiar with library procedure.

If you wait until you have a research assignment to go to the library, you may find that the lost time spent in aimless hunting about will actually be greater than the time you will spend in a trip arranged early in your first semester at your own convenience.

Library work habits

Three kinds of note paper are suggested for library use. While you may develop a better arrangement than the one proposed here, if you are doing your first work in a college library, adopt the system suggested here. It is standard practice for many researchers. First there is the 3-by-5 card that you will fill out each time you come across a lead in your search for sources of information. For example, you are doing a paper on *semantics* and find a reference to a book by Irving J. Lee, with specific emphasis on one chapter in particular. You would immediately write a card like the one on the following page.

Notice that your card includes these items, which are common to every bibliographic entry: author, title, place of publication, publisher, date of publication. If there is more than one edition of a book, then your card would include the number of the edition of the book.

One card for each reference! Having a separate card for each book or article you use will make it easy to keep track of your work in progress. In addition, you will want to arrange a bibliography for any paper you write, and having a separate card for each source will make it easy to arrange your bibliography in the form desired. While you are using your cards to track down books and articles in the library, you would do well to keep your cards separated according to type (book or journal article) and alphabetized within each group. This practice will make it easy to chase down items in a card catalogue. When you find a catalogue card for a book you are looking for, write its call number down on your card so that you will be able to locate it each time you come to the library for it without having to look it up again in the catalogue. When you have located all

Lee, Irving J., *Language Habits in Human Affairs*, New York: Harper, 1941 (see Chap. V.)

the cards you are looking for in a particular session with the card catalogue, you can work on writing call slips for each book or article.

The second kind of note paper you will use is the call slip itself. This slip is needed for ordering books from the stacks. While they are always available in the library, many students keep a small supply clipped to their 3-by-5 cards and fill them out as completely as they can when they first find a reference they want to inspect.

Half-sheets of notebook paper are useful for the notes you will take on your readings. They provide a great deal of room, are easy to store, and not as bulky as 5-by-8 cards, which some students use. Several half-sheets may be pinned or clipped together without difficulty. One sheet or more for each entry is advised—never more than one source on a sheet, because you must keep your notes on sources separate from one another for use during writing. Keep a good supply of sheets on hand and cultivate the habit of getting all you want to extract from your source so that you do not have to go back to it too often. If you find an apt quotation for an argument you will present in a paper, get it down correctly at once. Correctly means correct to the last comma. If you extract from a paragraph, omitting certain portions, indicate the omission by points of ellipsis (. . .) . When you find a good presentation of a point of view you will want to explore in a paper, write a paraphrase. There is room on a half-sheet.

If you do not have a deliberate plan of attack when you go to the library, you will find that it is very easy to waste more time than you spend in study. I am reminded of a former student of mine who was unable to benefit from the library. This student complained that going to the college library was a waste of time for him because it took him so long to get down to work. He explained that by the time he had collected all the things he needed, made his way to the library, found a place to work, found the books he was after, and got down to work in them—there was no time left to do his reading.

One of his mistakes was that he simply did not leave sufficient time in which to work. There are details of procedure that are time-consuming. Yet, if you organize your briefcase properly early in a semester, you will need little preparation each time you go to the library. Establish a supply of essential things and check that supply from time to time.

His more serious error was that a trip to the library very often turned out to be a social event at which he would cultivate his many friends on the campus. Before he left his dormitory, he would manage to meet and chat with at least one or two of his friends. More often than not, this would lead to a coffee break. Because there was no bell ringing at a specific time to tell him that he had to go to the library, he managed to dawdle until there was little time left in which to work.

Getting to the library and then beginning to work at once requires self-discipline that this student did not have. Of course, you must consider library time as much a part of your work schedule as any of your classes, lectures, or laboratory periods.

Library guides to information

It is essential to know where to find materials you will need in any research you undertake. There are four outstanding sources for the names of books and articles you will need:

- 1. Bibliographies that are given in books you already know.
- 2. Bibliographies given in encyclopedias.

- 3. General and special bibliographies.
- 4. Card catalogues and periodical indexes.

Note that the order given is not necessarily the order in which these sources are used by researchers.

GUIDE 1—YOUR TEXTBOOKS

Your textbook in a course is probably your best first guide to the information you will need for any research you do in that course. Take the names of books and articles given in footnotes and at the ends of chapters dealing with the specific topic that interests you. The books listed in chapter bibliographies are general references that will broadly treat the subject you are after. Books and articles listed in footnotes may be special references that might fortunately take you to the heart of your research problem. At the very least, they will take you into the general "neighborhood" you are looking for. When your author is kind enough to give critical notes with his bibliography (known as "annotating" a bibliography), he saves you the trouble of examining all the sources cited to find out whether they will be useful.

When you have listed all the titles you have been given, go to the library for copies of the books and articles you want to examine. Read chapter titles and indexes in these references to test their helpfulness in meeting your needs. For example, if you were reading a chapter called "Probability and Likelihood" in the book *Statistical Methods in Research* by Palmer O. Johnson,[2] you would find this bibliography at the end of the chapter:

1. Kendall, Maurice G., *The Advanced Theory of Statistics*, Vol. I. London: Charles Griffin & Company, Ltd., 1945, pp. 164–185.
2. Kolmogoroff, A., "Grundbegriffe der Wahrscheinlichkeitsrechnung," *Ergebnisse der Mathematik und ihrer Grenzgebiete*, Vol. 2 (1933), No. 3.
3. Mises, Richard von, *Probability, Statistics and Truth*. New York: The Macmillan Company, 1939.
4. Nagel, Ernest, "Principles of the Theory of Probability," *International Encyclopedia of Unified Science*, Vol. 1, No. 6. Chicago: The University of Chicago Press, 1939.
5. Pearson, Karl (ed.), *Tables for Statisticians and Biometricians*. London: Biometrika, University College.

If you were pursuing some part of this subject further for a research problem you were doing, you would secure a copy of these works from your library to see whether they contain information that would help you. You would surely find that each useful reference would serve a second purpose—it would lead to still more sources of information. As you work, you find that some books and articles are mentioned again and again, a measure of their importance. It is essential that you consult them. Remember, as you study a new source, to use the table of contents and index in the manner described in Chapter 2.

GUIDE 2—ENCYCLOPEDIAS

You have probably had some experience with encyclopedias, beginning long ago with the simplified volumes designed for children, where you looked up facts in much the same way as you would consult *The World Almanac*. As need arose, you may have used the encyclopedia as an expansion of the dictionary. For example, *Webster's Collegiate Dictionary* defines chemistry as "the science that treats of the composition of substances, and of the transformations which they undergo," and the *Encyclopedia Americana* expands this into more than thirteen pages on chemistry. A further extension of encyclopedia use—particularly pertinent to your needs in college—involves broad surveys of fields that interest you, plus reference to the bibliographic leads which the articles provide. Often your textbooks will provide neither text nor bibliography on a subject you want to investigate—but in any case you will want always to include encyclopedia reference in connection with any research.

To determine how up to date an encyclopedia is, look at the last date on the copyright page—the page on the back of the title page. Here are three encyclopedias which almost every library contains:

1. *Encyclopaedia Britannica* (24 volumes). If you had no other general encyclopedia available to you, this one would probably meet all your needs in college. The *Britannica* is a model of scholarship. Revisions are constantly made, and yearbooks bring new information to the reader. The most important new information is in science and technology, of course. The articles on the arts have not required much change. In fact, for cultural subjects, the eleventh edition of the *Britannica* is unsurpassed. If the humanities are your primary interest, you might consider buying a used copy of the 11th for your personal library.

2 Prentice-Hall, Inc., 1949.

2. *Encyclopedia Americana* (30 volumes). The articles in the *Americana* are generally shorter than those in the *Britannica* and so might be more useful under certain circumstances. It is considered stronger in technical subjects than the *Britannica*.

3. *New International Encyclopedia* (25 volumes). Several supplementary volumes have appeared since the latest revision of the *International* in 1922. Its shorter and more numerous articles, compared with the other two encyclopedias mentioned, make this the handiest reference of the big three. It is well regarded in biography and history.

These three outstanding encyclopedias all provide bibliographies as well as information useful for you in doing the research you will have to do in college. There are other important encyclopedias, of course. Two more that you may use at one time or another are the *Encyclopedia of the Social Sciences* and *The Catholic Encyclopedia*. If you care to read a comprehensive treatment of the encyclopedias available, go to *A Research Manual* by Cecil B. Williams and Allan H. Stevenson (Harper & Brothers, 1951).[8]

But some skill is needed in using these great collections of knowledge. For example, every term that ever interests you may not be found easily in the way it will be found in a good dictionary. In general, you will have to look up details of a specialized subject under some broad category. Information concerning *hydrometallurgy* will not be found as an entry in the *Britannica*, but it is discussed in an article entitled *Copper*. You will find that often your first step is to seek out the proper articles for explanation of a particular term. The dictionary will be useful in giving you leads. Moreover, the *Britannica* and *Americana* both have excellent indexes.

A point to consider when you consult an encyclopedia is that much of what you seek may be dispersed in separate articles. Thus, your research papers may require information that cuts across several areas of knowledge. (It goes without saying that they will also send you far beyond encyclopedias for all the information required. In one sense, high school research papers mislead students, making them think that all a research paper is for is to find the correct article in an encyclopedia and then write an abstract of it.) When you are doing a paper, list all of the topics that might contribute to your research before going into the encyclopedia. Then search out all the pertinent entries.

[8] This valuable publication offers much more than discussion of encyclopedias. It goes into every phase of library research and then into the preparation of a research paper from beginning to end. It is a volume you should consider buying as a valuable addition to your personal library.

Even when you have exhausted all your original leads, you must not stop prematurely in your search. The *cross references* that articles supply should be searched through to see whether additional useful information is waiting.

A paper on the Brook Farm experiment of nineteenth-century America might call for searching an encyclopedia under these headings: Brook Farm, transcendentalism, Nathaniel Hawthorne, Margaret Fuller, and Theodore Parker. In the eleventh edition of the *Britannica,* you would soon find other names mentioned in the Brook Farm article, and you can add them to the list you were going to use. The information found in the *Britannica,* plus the leads to other sources, make a good start toward a well-documented paper on your subject.

GUIDE 3—BIBLIOGRAPHIES

Bibliographies are listings of publications relating to a common subject or author. Consult the bibliographies that exist in the areas you are studying. Thus, you will find the public speeches and other writings of many of the great figures in history listed in articles or books that are available in your library. You will find important events catalogued in the same way. These bibliographies are arranged in much the same way as the bibliographies at the end of a chapter in one of your textbooks. Sometimes the compiler of the bibliography will do more than merely collect the standard facts of author, title, place of publication, etc. When he supplies some commentary on the items in the bibliography, we call his effort an annotated bibliography.

Publications that have made their appearances through the years are listed in *standard* bibliographies, while more recent publications are listed in *current* bibliographies. Before undertaking a term paper or any other research paper, familiarize yourself with existing writing by consulting appropriate bibliographies. Your instructors and librarians can supply you with names of appropriate bibliographies.

Examine these three standard bibliographies to see how they are arranged.

- 1. *Cumulative Book Index.* The H. W. Wilson Company. New editions are published regularly.
- 2. Graham, Bessie. *The Bookman's Manual.* R. R. Bowker. 1948.
- 3. Winchell, Constance M. *Guide to Reference Books.* American Library Association, 1951.

Current bibliographies appear in practically every area of learning—science, literature, technology, religion, etc.

GUIDE 4—CARD CATALOGUES AND PERIODICAL INDEXES

Card catalogues and indexes to periodical literature are the last sources of information leading to your goal in research. Here is the procedure to follow in using them. List the general subjects under which your topic might be classified in these sources. List all the authors whose work you have encountered in your previous searches. Then pursue them all one by one through the indexes and catalogues until you have exhausted your list. It may be, while you are working in this manner, that you will encounter some additional categories under which to continue your work. Write these new leads down at the end of your list and work through them when you have searched the other categories.

Before you begin your research, write a complete bibliographic note on each entry you may want to examine so that you will have the information you need when you are ready to begin. The best place for writing the information is, of course, the call slip, but remember that you will also need many of the bibliographic entries for the paper you will one day write. Therefore, you must keep a permanent record of each item on a 3-by-5 card.

In using card catalogues and periodical indexes, be certain that you exhaust all the leads they contain. Every book or pamphlet a library possesses is represented by at least three cards; all give the same kind of information concerning the item, but each is found in a different place in the catalogue. They are grouped by author, by title, and by subject. The cards giving an author's entries are usually placed in the following order: (1) complete collections arranged in chronological order, (2) selections from complete collections, (3) single works given alphabetically by titles, (4) single works in collaboration with others, and (5) edited works or translations. There is frequently one more section: (6) works of biography and criticism in reference to the author, alphabetically listed by secondary author. It is wise to examine a few cards that precede and a few that follow a series of entries that interest you, just to make certain that you have not missed a trick.

As you work in card catalogues, you will become familiar with the various types of notations used on the cards. Unless you are interested in library work as a profession, chances are you will not use most of them. Just to show you what these items mean, you will find on page 228 a typical card with its entries explained.

Libraries differ in the amount of information they ask for on a call slip, but the minimum would be author's name, book title, call number, and volume number when a work runs to more than one volume. In the case of *The Travels of Marco Polo,* the example used, you would write "Polo, Marco," "The Travels of Marco Polo," and either "915" or "G370.P72," depending upon whether your library uses the Dewey decimal or the Library of Congress catalogue system. Of course, your call slip will also show your name and whatever other identifying information the library desires.

It is not necessary to memorize the cataloguing system your library employs, but it is useful to have a general understanding of it. You probably know, from your high school days, that the Dewey decimal system employs numbers to designate subject areas. Most colleges use the Library of Congress system, which employs letters of the alphabet to show subject areas. Thus, the 900 series in the Dewey decimal includes all works of history, while the letter G designates geography and anthropology in the Library of Congress system. The number G370.P72 used for Marco Polo's book indicates that it is in the G series and has as its author a person whose last name begins with the letter P.

A periodical index—and there are many—is your guide to articles published in magazines and scholarly journals. It is indispensable in library research, because it helps you find the most recent developments in your field of interest. Unlike the card catalogue, it appears in pamphlet and book form. Some indexes are published monthly and some less often, but all supply the information you need to locate articles: name of publication, volume number, date, author, article title, and page numbers.

No single index attempts to keep track of all the scholarly journals that are published throughout the world. *General* indexes, of which there are several, catalogue many publications in a wide range of subjects, and many *special* indexes concentrate on restricted areas of learning. Even so, some of the special indexes are voluminous publications because of the amount of activity in their subjects. You should familiarize yourself with at least two general indexes and be able to use their resources easily and effectively. If you follow the same procedures with the periodical index in regard to searching procedures and note-taking from the index, you will find it a great help in using a library expertly.

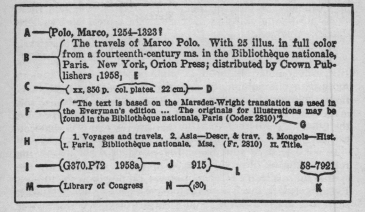

KEY:

A. Author's name and dates
B. Title and description
C. Page count: front matter and text
D. Volume size (height)
E. Kind of illustrations
F. Additional information quoted from book
G. National Library, Paris—number
H. Cross references
I. Library of Congress system catalogue number
J. Year of publication and position of edition in that year
K. Key number for librarian's order of card replacements from Library of Congress
L. Dewey decimal system catalogue number
M. Card publisher
N. End of printed matter on card

Familiarize yourself with these general indexes:

1. *Reader's Guide to Periodical Literature.* This is the guide you will probably use most often as you begin to do research. The magazines indexed by the *Reader's Guide* are those of general circulation. Entries are arranged alphabetically by author, subject, and title. When you go to the index, be prepared with a list of entries that interest you.

2. *International Index to Periodicals.* This is a companion index for the *Reader's Guide.* It is arranged in the same way, but indexes a great number of scholarly journals not included in the *Reader's Guide.*

On page 194 you will find part of a page from *Reader's Guide,* to show you what information is included in typical entries and how the information is arranged.

To help you understand the cryptic style of the *Reader's*

Guide, here is a "translation" of the first item given under "IMMIGRANTS in the United States":

> "Man Who Found His Country" by B. Smith, Jr., illustrated, *The Saturday Evening Post*, volume 231, pages 22-23 plus carryover, issue of October 4, 1958.

As you use indexes, you will find that the symbols and abbreviations employed will become second nature to you. When you make notes on an entry in one of the indexes, be sure to record the page numbers of the article that interests you, so that you can go right to the article you want to read.

In exploring your college library, you should inspect the reference room to see the range of subjects covered by the special indexes and where the indexes are found in the library. Examine two or three indexes to see the list of periodicals each surveys. You will generally find such lists inside the front cover of any issue of an index. A few titles will suffice to show the variety of indexes that exists for the convenience of the researcher: *Art Index, Chemical Abstracts, Education Index, Psychological Abstracts.*

Special indexes are valuable beyond the requirements of the student actively engaged in research. By consulting the appropriate indexes regularly, you can keep up with articles appearing in your field of interest. When you meet a title that interests you, just read the article. This is far better than subscribing to all the journals you might want to consult from time to time.

One point must be reiterated now. Many beginning researchers overlook the help that librarians can give. Besides knowing the location of books and other library resources, librarians are expert in suggesting research leads. Consult them freely until you can get around in the library unaided. One warning: don't approach a librarian asking for "the book that tells everything about. . . ." Rather, ask for a bibliography in the general field that includes the subject you are researching.

In the college library, you have a unique opportunity for enjoyment. There is time in college for wandering about through certain collections accessible to the student. Books you might otherwise miss are met in this way, and entirely new areas of learning discovered . . . a beautiful volume of poetry, a novel by an author you had never heard of, a collection of color plates by a naturalist, the work of an oriental philosopher. A chance meeting in a library can sometimes mean more than years of formal study.

IMMIGRANTS in the United States
Man who found his country. B. Smith, jr.
il Sat Eve Post 231:22-3+ O 4 '58
Mike Smelas of America. R. A. Graham.
America 98:101 O 26 '57
Salute to a lady. E. Corsi. il Read Digest
70:57-9 Mr '57
We will bear true faith. H. R. Kuehn.
America 97:613-15 S 14 '57
See also
Naturalization
Refugees
also Hungarians in the United States;
Irish in the United States; and similar
headings
IMMIGRATION and emigration
See also
Quarantine

Australia

Rotary brings out a Briton. il Rotarian 92:
4-5 Je '58
Welcome, neighbors! il Rotarian 93:26 S '58
See also
Immigrants in Australia

Brazil

Stars and bars along the Amazon. M. D. Ross
and F. Kerner. Reporter 19:34-6 S 18 '58

Canada

Canada: bonanza-land for Americans. L.
Gross. Coronet 42:108-12 Ag '57
Haven for immigrants. Time 71:31 Mr 3 '58
Refugee school finds a home; Sopron univer-
sity. il Bsns W p 197-9 Ap 6 '57
Suez starts a rush of migrants. il Bsns W
p 185+ F 23 '57
United States and Canada magnets for im-
migration. H. F. Eckerson. bibliog f Ann
Am Acad 316:34-42 Mr '58
See also

Europe

Intergovernmental committee for European
migration

France

Lift for France. il U S News 43:94-5 Ag 23
'57

Ghana

Immigration quota for Ghana. D. D. Eisen-
hower. U S Dept State Bul 37:111-12 Jl
15 '57

Great Britain

Body blow from Punch. America 96:690 Mr
23 '57
Exodus from Britain; cartoons. N Y Times
Mag p56 Mr 3 '57
Long, long queue to leave Britain. L. Birch.
Reporter 16:20-2 Mr 7 '57
Psychological emigrant. Time 69:25 F 18 '57
Suez starts a rush of migrants. il Bsns W
p 185+ F 23 '57
Two out of five. il Newsweek 49:42+ F 18
'57
Wanted: skilled help. map Newsweek 51:39
Ja 13 '58
Youths leave Britain. il U S News 42:100+
Mr 8 '57

HOW TO WRITE A TERM PAPER

MANY occupations and professions demand regular report writing. In fact, the difference between moderate and outstanding success in your career may depend upon your ability to research and report. Moreover, if you go to graduate work, you will find that a common requirement for a degree is a large and complex thesis. Behind that report will stand many hours of library or laboratory work. But even if your interests do not go beyond getting good marks while in college, you will find that the term paper is often weighed as heavily as the final exam in determining your final grade.

In this chapter, you will find answers to questions that trouble the student who has never done a term paper as well as he should: how to set up a work schedule, how to find the general area you want to work in, how to prepare your preliminary bibliography, how to prepare your working bibliography, how to outline your paper, and how to prepare your final bibliography. The final topic in this chapter is a discussion of how to write one special kind of report—the book review.

The *purpose of writing a term paper* is to demonstrate that you can use the tools of scholarship and, at the same time, work toward becoming expert in a subject.

There are many good ways to go about doing a term paper. Ask several scholars how they work, and you will find a variety of patterns; ask successful college students, and you will find others. This is because writing a paper is an art. As you gain experience in writing, you will develop your own individual techniques.

But if you have not yet written a paper of college quality, follow step by step the plan that is discussed in this chapter. If you know of any techniques that work better than some of those suggested, by all means incorporate them in the general method shown here.[1]

Set up a work schedule

You have read in this book that a work schedule is important for *effective study,* for *writing a theme,* for *final review before examinations.* Term papers must also be scheduled carefully if you are going to be able to complete each part of the preparation in time to get on with the next part. Of course, it is essential that you do not fall behind in your work or hand your paper in late. In some cases, teachers will deduct credit if you do not meet deadlines.

You may have no idea of the amount of time you will need for carrying a term paper through from assignment to completion if you have never written one before. Take your lead from the *date* on which the paper is *assigned* and the date on which it is *due.* If your teacher thinks it advisable to make an assignment two months or more before the date on which a paper is due, he must think that you will need that much time to do a good job.

There is no yardstick for determining precisely how long you will take on any one of the steps that go into the preparation of the completed paper. But you should set up a schedule for yourself, something like this:

GOAL 1—topic approval   due on . . .
GOAL 2—bibliography   due on . . .
GOAL 3—complete outline   due on . . .
GOAL 4—final draft   due on . . .

Beginning students often miss deadlines because they underestimate the amount of time they will need to complete the job. When you have scheduled your goals, attach the schedule to the wall in front of your desk. Remember that you will have to make plans for getting the work done *while keeping up with your daily course work.* The first time you do a paper, be especially generous in allotting time to each part of the work.

Choose a topic

You will find within the limits of a single college course a tremendous number of broad and interesting subjects. It is

[1] Undoubtedly, you will have instruction in one of your English courses in how to write a term paper, but it may not come until after you have written a few papers in other courses. For that reason, it is well to give some attention to the matter now.

ridiculous to hear students complain that "there is nothing to write about." Whether this attitude comes from the mistaken notion that an undergraduate's paper must be entirely new and fresh, or whether it comes from a lack of interest on the part of students, nothing can be further from the truth. Topics are available in abundance!

Each student brings to his topic his own background, his own ability to reason, and his own ingenuity in finding and using available information. This is his contribution. You are not expected to blaze new trails in a term paper.

Lack of interest may cause certain students to have difficulty in finding a topic. Unfortunately, you will not be equally stimulated by every course for which you have to write a paper. If you are called upon to write a term paper, your best method of choosing a topic may be to *relate your course to your major interests*. It is entirely possible to blend an interest in medicine, for example, with work in literature or economics. A study of the portrayals of physicians in the work of a particular playwright or author may fill the bill in the first case; practices of establishing medical fees, or the growth of health insurance, may be what you want in the other.

There are other ways to find topics, of course. Look over the *chapter headings* in the textbook you are using in any course. Each of them represents an opportunity for further study. A *question* asked by a teacher during class discussion, a *reference* at the close of a chapter you are reading, a *footnote* comment—any of these may suggest a topic to you.

Don't expect the *title* of a first-rate paper to jump out at you. What is more likely is that you will be attracted by an isolated statement you encounter. It may be that you do not agree with it, or that you find it striking enough and convincing enough to upset an opinion you have held. As you think about it, you may realize that it merits further investigation.

An excellent source of topics is the *list of suggested topics* which your teacher may furnish. Your teacher will not suggest an area for study unless he knows that material is available in your library to implement your study. He also knows most of the areas that are within the grasp of his students. Before you look elsewhere, study his suggestions.

The best reason for rejecting suggested topics is that they do not interest you. The factor of interest in writing a paper is so important that it makes other factors minor. But before you can be certain that you have found a topic, there are three other considerations that must be recognized:

- Check your library resources to see whether they are adequate to support your paper.[2]
- Sample the sources you will use to see whether you are biting off more than you can chew.
- Check with your teacher to see whether he will give preliminary approval for your selection.

Writing a paper involves some reading of a specialized nature, which will be described shortly. This reading is extremely important, for there is nothing more dismal than the sight of a student who has spent a month or more in reading for a paper only to find out that he cannot manage the topic he has chosen.

A quick check of your library resources will reveal whether you have too narrow or too broad a topic. If you have selected too broad a topic, you can easily cut it down to size in most cases. But attempting to expand narrow topics may take you into fields you do not care to study.

In checking to see what your library contains and whether you are skillful enough to use the materials, there is a definite procedure to follow. First of all, you must use your familiarity with the organization of books. What information can you gather from a *table of contents,* from a *preface* or *foreword,* from an *index?* When you have located the parts of your references that can do you the most good, you are ready to show how well you can skim a book. Go quickly from *subheading* to *subheading* within a *chapter* to see what you can find. When you have found the parts of a chapter that concern you, read quickly through them to see what kind of information they give, how readily they can yield what you need, how deeply they go into the subject you are studying. When you feel that you have met this requirement, you can go to your teacher to present the topic for approval—Goal 1.

Prepare your bibliography

Knowing how to develop a bibliography is important. By the time you have finished your bibliography, you will be well into the final work involved in a term paper. The bibliography is the center of your entire project. It is your test of whether you can do the paper, your guide to the paper in progress, and an important part of the paper itself. Thus, the bibliog-

---

[2] It is sometimes possible to arrange for interlibrary loans if books you need are not found in your library but are available elsewhere. When you are confronted by a problem of this kind, consult your librarian to see what help he can give you.

raphy you will need for a term paper will actually consist of three bibliographies:

- (1) The *preliminary* bibliography, consisting of early leads to the information you will need. While you will eventually use most of the sources you encounter, some of the sources will not be useful for your purposes. Note that this bibliography is far from thorough; it contains enough sources to verify that you have a topic which can be developed.

- 2. The *working* bibliography, consisting of all the sources you work through during research, whether they find a place in your paper or not. Many of the books and articles you include in this list will turn out to be unproductive. Others will help you think about your topic, but will have no direct bearing on your paper. Still others will serve only as leads to additional sources. The working bibliography, then, is an inventory of resources, some of which turn out to be more useful than others.

- (3) The *final* bibliography, consisting of all the sources you cite in the paper and all other sources you believe can help a reader who wants to read along lines you have not fully developed in your paper. This is the bibliography that your reader will see. Its form is particularly important, because your reader's ability to find the references depends on the accuracy and completeness of your bibliographic style.

Let us study each of the bibliographies in turn.

PRELIMINARY BIBLIOGRAPHY

When you have decided that a topic is interesting and shows promise as a term paper, begin recording the sources you will use in doing your preliminary research. Your first few leads will generally come from the source that suggested the topic to you—a footnote reference, a list of books and other sources at the end of a chapter, an encyclopedia article, a lecture, discussion with one of your classmates. Whatever their origins, be sure to note these references properly. The best way to do this is to start a file of index cards. Each lead you collect will have its own card, containing all the information you need for locating the source.

Some bibliographic references made in books are incomplete. Yet their value justifies the work required to track them down. In a course in English history, for example, you may have been reading S. T. Bindoff's *Tudor England* (Penguin Books, 1950).

A term paper is assigned in the course, and you hope to choose a topic that will reflect your interest in art and architecture and yet meet the requirements of a history course. In the appendix entitled "A Note on Further Reading," you find several references to works on "the history of ideas, scholarship, literature and art." Two books on architecture are included. Out come your index cards. A new file is set up for architecture, and each card is marked *arch.* plus a serial number. The references are not complete, but they may suffice. Below are two leads to possible papers on the architecture of Tudor England. You are still far from choosing the final topic, but these leads may be helpful in guiding you. You might have found

---

Arch. 1

Gotch, J. A.
Early Renaissance
Architecture in England,
1901.

Arch. 2.

Garner, T. and A. Stratton,
The Domestic Architecture
of England during the
Tudor Period,
1911, 2 vols.

these same leads in many other ways. For example, knowing you had a term paper to do on the Tudor period, you might have searched your library card catalogue for books under the entry *Tudor England* or under *Architecture,* and come upon the same items.

However you come across your first references, consult them as soon as possible to see whether the general subject is *appealing* and *suitable* for your course.

To avoid too broad a topic, you might focus upon the building of that period as a *reflection of the political and social spirit that existed.* In short, how did the events of the period shape its architecture? This suggestion is intended only as a guide to get you started thinking about what a good term paper subject might be. After you have secured the two books mentioned and examined them carefully, you might find dozens of topics that would be more suitable.

Let us take another example: In a class in sociology or in American civilization, you may have read a book by Max Lerner, *America as a Civilization* (Simon and Schuster, 1957). His section on the press interests you. The bibliography supplies approximately two dozen titles on the press. What can you find in these references that may lead you to a term paper topic? Here is the first paragraph of Lerner's extensive bibliography:

> On the press, see Morris L. Ernst, *The First Freedom* (New York, 1946) for an affirmation of the principle of a free press and an attack on recent trends toward monopoly, and E. B. White, "The Vanishing Marketplace of Ideas," *The New Yorker* (March 16, 1946). The most significant discussion on press liberties and responsibility is *The Report of the Commission on a Free Press* (Chicago, 1947). I have dealt with this topic in "Freedom in the Opinion Industries," *Ideas Are Weapons,* and "Seven Deadly Press Sins," *Actions and Passions* (New York, 1949). For an excellent study of the daily press, see Alfred McClung Lee, *The Daily Newspaper in America* (New York, 1937), and Gordon W. Allport and J. Faden, "The Psychology of Newspapers," *Public Opinion Quarterly* (Dec. 1940). The role of the newspaper in American daily life is considered in Bernard Berelson, "What Missing the Newspaper Means," in Paul Lazarsfeld *et al.,* eds., *Communications Research: 1948–49* (New York, 1949), pp. 11–29.

Each of these articles and books can become an excellent guide to the research materials you would want to use in doing a paper.

As you narrow a large field down to a subject you can handle, you will be dipping further and further into the sources that are available to you, because one book leads to many. *Each item you find must be recorded on an index card.* Even if a source will ultimately yield only a small amount of information, make a card for it so that you can locate it easily whenever you want it. The process of preparing a preliminary bibliography is one of alternately *finding sources* and *skimming them quickly* to determine their usefulness for your paper.

In looking through a source, you may find particular sections of it that show great promise. When you do, make a record of the pages or chapters that you will want to see again when you begin the systematic and thorough reading of sources. After you have skimmed a source, its card may contain additional information:

(call #) Landis, Paul H., Population
          Problems. American Book
          Company, New York, 1943.
Chap. 3. quick survey outstanding
population growth theories,
comments on each, leans toward
sociocultural approach.

Good source for population statistics.

It will only take a few hours of library work, then, to tell you:

- Whether or not you have a subject worthy of a term paper.
- Whether your library contains the books and other source materials you will need for your topic, and whether you can obtain the additional sources you may need through an inter-library loan.
- Whether you can read the authors you will need with the necessary degree of understanding.

And you already have the beginnings of your working bibliography. Your preliminary bibliography is ready to be copied from your cards and presented to your teacher. Until he gives you the required approval of your topic, there is nothing further to be done.

WORKING BIBLIOGRAPHY

Upon receiving approval for your topic, you are ready to go on to a careful, systematic search for sources of information on your topic. The main guides to this information were described in Chapter 10 of this book.

Still using your index cards to record the leads you find, go through the *special bibliographies* that may exist in your field of interest, *encyclopedia articles* if you have not already covered them, *card catalogues,* and *indexes to periodical literature.* If your topic is of current or recent interest, *The New York Times Index* will help you find your way.

Above all, don't make the common mistake of using only an encyclopedia article or two. As you will see when you first work seriously in encyclopedias, they are not exhaustive in their treatments; they are only surveys for ready reference.

Use special bibliographies with care, wasting no time on entries that are obviously going to be fruitless for you. For example, if you are doing a paper on the youth of Mark Twain, most of the entries in a Twain bibliography will not help your research. You will be less prone to search out fruitless leads as you acquire experience in research.

Check every cross reference in the card catalogue of your college library for additional leads. Do not be content with one periodical index alone when there are others available that appear attractive.

As you go into your reading, remember that Goal 3 is in sight—your *outline.* The outlines that will help you most in your writing will be flexible. While they will contain practically every item you will cover in your writing, they will not be in final form until just before you are ready to type your paper. Let us see how this works out.

Outlining and writing the paper

1. Construct your first rough outline of the paper. Don't strive now for good outline form. It is enough merely to *list the subjects* you will cover and try to *set up limits for each topic* you will discuss so that you know where each one begins

and ends. The purpose of listing subjects is to facilitate filing your reading notes.

2. When you have listed all the individual topics that will go into your paper, *assign a Roman numeral to each of them*. Then go through your cards and number them according to the appropriate outline topic. Group your cards according to the numbered sections of your outline. In cases where one source yields information bearing upon more than one section of your outline, make duplicate cards for each section of the outline.

3. Take notes as you go, grouping your notes under their assigned Roman numerals. The notes are sometimes the product of *paraphrasing* and *summarizing,* sometimes *direct quotation*. You may also want to outline *brief comments* upon what you are reading.

Your index cards will not be adequate for the lengthy notes you make on many sources. Use half-sheets of paper. Copy *exactly* that material you will want to use *verbatim*. Note the exact location of any *reference* you will use in your paper. Take pains to interpret accurately material you paraphrase or summarize. Make certain that your half-sheets are marked with the proper Roman numerals indicating portions of your outlines.

The kind of note you will take on a given source will depend on what you want to accomplish.

For example, if you were writing on some aspect of the life of Benjamin Franklin, you would surely use his autobiography as a primary source. Read this paragraph from that entertaining document:

> I had hitherto continu'd to board with Godfrey, who lived in part of my house with his wife and children, and had one side of the shop for his glazier's business, tho' he worked little, being always absorbed in his mathematics. Mrs. Godfrey projected a match for me with a relation's daughter, took opportunities of bringing us often together, till a serious courtship on my part ensu'd, the girl being in herself very deserving. The old folks encourag'd me by continual invitations to supper, and by leaving us together, till at length it was time to explain. Mrs. Godfrey manag'd our little treaty. I let her know that I expected as much money with their daughter as would pay off my remaining debt for the printing-house, which I believe was not then above a hundred pounds. She brought me word they had no such sum to spare; I said they might mortgage their house in the loan-office. The answer to this, after some days, was, that they did not approve the match; that, on inquiry of Bradford, they had been informed the printing business was not a profitable one; the types would soon be worn out, and more wanted; that S. Keimer and D. Henry

had failed one after the other, and I should probably soon follow them; and, therefore, I was forbidden the house, and the daughter shut up.[8]

This brief glimpse of one aspect of the character of Franklin and of the manners of his time can be used by the student in a variety of ways, depending upon the kind of paper being written. For example, if your emphasis were on his personality, you might quote in full this picture of practical Ben. Or to save space, you might use a brief synopsis of the pertinent material, as shown below. (The Roman numeral in the upper right-hand corner refers to the section of the paper in which you deal with this topic.)

If you were developing an account of Franklin's years of struggle to become established in Philadelphia, you might use a brief synopsis with your attention on his efforts to pay off the outstanding debt in his printing business, as on page 205.

4. As you collect notes, read them through from time to time

> Franklin Autobiography   V
> pp. 76-77
>
> During this period, Ben courted a young woman and wanted to marry her. He demanded a dowry of 100 pounds "to pay off my remaining debt for the printing house." Her parents decided against this because the recent failures of two fellow printers made Ben and the printing business appear bad risks.

---

[8] *The Autobiography of Benjamin Franklin and Selections from His Writings*, A. S. Barnes & Company, 1944.

to be sure that you understand them, to discover duplications or disagreement among your sources, and to find out where your sources are not providing the solid body of information you need. You may have to search further to fill gaps in your notes, or it may be that the information you are seeking cannot be found. At any rate, reading yor notes as you proceed in your research will make you aware of your needs. Most important of all, it will help you think about your paper as you progress, it will cause you to make still further modifications in your outline, and it will suggest language that may be used in the final paper.

5. When you have covered all your material for a section of your outline, then begin writing that part of your paper. At the same time, continue the research that remains to be done. While some of your teachers may not agree with this advice, it is a fact that many experienced writers use this technique

> *Franklin Autobiography   VII*
> *pp. 76-77*
>
> *At one point, Ben considered marrying a "very deserving" young woman if she were brought a dowry large enough to pay his debts — 100 pounds. He suggested that her parents mortgage their home if they did not have ready cash.*

of writing while they are still reading. There are several advantages to doing so:

• You will find out whether you really have all the information you need for each part of your paper. If your sources for one section of a paper are insufficient, it is probable that your reading for other sections is not all it should be. Finding this out early gives you plenty of warning to change your research practices while you still have time.

- You will be able to estimate the length of the entire report by determining the length of a single section.
- You gain time for editing and rewriting long before the due date of the report.
- Once again you are forced to think through your paper so that you can be sure your conception of the material is correct. Restructuring an entire outline at this point, if necessary, is easier than having to junk an entire first draft of a paper a few days before it is due.

Thus, you are doing all these things at the same time:

- 1. Completing coverage of your bibliography,
- 2. Perfecting your outline,
- 3. Writing parts of your first draft.

So by the time you have completed the research for a paper, you will find yourself well along with the first draft. At that point, stop to examine the project from the perspective you have gained through extensive reading, careful planning, and considerable writing. You are approaching Goal 4—the final draft. Go on to complete the first draft.

Let a few days elapse between completing the first draft and reading it through. Allow the material to get cold so that you can be as objective as your teacher will be when he reads it. If you recall, you were advised to complete even ordinary freshman themes early in order to do a good job as reader and editor of your own work.

Chapter 4 contains a fuller discussion of how to edit your work, but a few suggestions are in order now:

- (1) When you pick up a paper you have written, read it through from beginning to end without making any changes in it. What over-all impression does it give? Does the paper accomplish what it set out to accomplish?
- (2) Is the arrangement of elements as effective as it can be? Do you, as reader, learn what you want from the paper easily, or do you find yourself wandering between ideas without understanding their connection?
- (3) If the general form of the paper pleases you, read it once more. In this reading, focus on one section at a time.

Are the paragraphs arranged in the best possible order? Are the individual sentences placed correctly? And are the elements within sentences as effective as possible?

Do not begin to rewrite as soon as you find a section that needs help. Instead, make notes on what you find. A professional editor writes his comments in the margin of a paper he is working on, or he attaches notes to the pages suggesting changes. You can do the same. Be sure that you are not completely altering part of the paper so that it no longer suits adjacent sections. Remember that your paper is a single unit even though it has subdivisions created to help your reader. When you have finished examining your paper carefully and making notes for necessary changes, go through the notes once more to make certain you are improving the paper, not hurting it. Then begin to rewrite.

When the rewriting is done, you may prepare the final draft. It is not always possible for a student to use a typewriter in preparing a paper, but it is important to make the final draft as attractive as possible. If you must do your papers longhand, use ink, maintain wide margins, cover one side of a sheet only, and make your charts as clear as possible. Obey the special instructions your teacher gives. Some teachers insist on double-spacing even for handwritten reports. Others will require double-spacing only between paragraphs. Cover your report with a title page, and be sure to number each page accurately. Your last tasks before handing in a paper are to proofread it and check to be certain that you have arranged your pages in correct sequence.

Final bibliography

The concluding section of a term paper generally is the easiest of all your tasks. It is no more than a listing of all the sources you have used in writing your paper. There are many forms possible for setting up your bibliography, the main consideration being that you supply all the information a reader will need for finding each of your sources.

- Credit *every* source you have used, whether you have quoted directly or not.
- Be consistent in bibliographic form.

Crediting sources has already been discussed in this chapter. Some students are dismayed by the number of references they must include in a term paper; others are prone to think that the more references they use, the better their papers. Use as many references as are necessary to satisfy the requirement of honesty in giving credit where credit is due, but don't write footnotes without justification. Several quotations making the same point over and over again waste valuable space. They are not a mark of scholarship. This device will win you no friends among your readers, nor will it improve a poorly conceived and executed paper.

For a book, all the basic bibliographic information you must supply boils down to author, title, publisher, place of publication, and date of publication:

Trevelyan, G. M., *English Social History,* Longmans, Green and Co., New York, 1942.

When you cite this book in a footnote to your paper, you add the page or pages used: . . . 1942, pp. 6–8.

In citing an article printed in a journal, other information is needed. After supplying the author's name, give the article title, name of the publication, volume and issue number, date, and pages on which the article appears:

Blake, William E., "Education and the Anti-Philosophical Attitude," *American Association of University Professors Bulletin,* Vol. 42, No. 4 (Winter, 1956) , pp. 667–678.

The two sample forms supplied here are intended only as guides. Your teachers will probably supply their own *style sheets* at the time they assign your term papers. If they do not, you can use these entries as models for your bibliographies.

In your bibliography, it is customary to list first the book titles, arranged *alphabetically,* according to authors' last names. Articles are grouped together after books, and they too are arranged *alphabetically* according to authors' last names.

Here are a few of the abbreviations commonly found in footnotes in your college books, along with their full forms, and their meanings:

cf.	*confer,* compare
et. al.	*et. alii,* and others
f.	and the following page
ff.	and the following pages
ibid.	*ibidem,* in the same place
op. cit.	*opere citato,* in the work cited
p.	page
pp.	pages

Cf. is used by an author to suggest that the reader compare a statement made by the author, or someone he is quoting, with another statement made elsewhere. Thus, we see ". . . Cf. Jones,

The Struggle, p. 23." In referring to a book that has more than two authors, a writer may name the first author and then add *et al*. Thus, "Jones, F. W. *et al*." In referring to a topic that is discussed on more than one page in a book, an author may write "p. 434f." or "p. 434ff." The abbreviation *ibid*. is used to avoid repeating a complete footnote. Thus when a writer makes reference to the same source more than once he uses *ibid*. for each *successive* reference to the work. If the page number is different in the second reference, the author writes *ibid*., p. 63. If a footnote refers to a book already cited in an earlier, but not immediately preceding, footnote, the author may write, "Jones, *op. cit*." This reference may also be used with the page number following the abbreviation. The abbreviations for page and pages are well known by now.

As you find your way in scholarly techniques, these forms will become second nature.

Writing a book review

The task of a book reviewer is to judge how well a book has achieved what it set out to do. This is much different from the job you had in high school when you wrote book reports. Most high school students feel that book reports are designed only to tell their teachers whether or not they have read the books assigned. In discussing a novel, therefore, full recounting of the plot was important. The events of a history or biography had to be told in detail.

Judging how well a book accomplishes its purpose is quite another matter. You would do well to acquaint yourself with the art of book reviewing as it is practiced in dozens of fine magazines, such as *The New Yorker, Harper's Magazine,* and *Saturday Review*.

Keeping in mind that a review is an appraisal rather than a summary, read the opening section of this review from *Saturday Review*, September 17, 1960:

"GOOD-BYE DOLLY GRAY: THE STORY OF THE BOER WAR"
By Rayne Kruger (*Lippincott. 488 pp. $7.50*)

By Thomas R. Adam
This spirited account of the Boer War, its origins, conduct, and consequences should be assigned reading for the Pentagon and State Department. Furthermore, their putative masters—the informed public—would be well advised to dip into its lively pages for a glimpse of the cold fatality of wars by governments on gov-

ernments, with the peoples concerned little more than suffering
stooges. Modern Africa stems to an incalculable degree from this
sorry conflict. Tribal society, conquered in the name of "civilization," watched the higher culture of the machine gun devastate
land and people in a stark struggle to decide which white faction
should dominate the other and make off with the loot.

In less than 500 pages Mr. Kruger—a kinsman of Oom Paul,
himself, though one would never guess it from his impartiality—
attempts to delineate both the setting and course of the war. The
politics, personalities, and culture of Victoria's England, Cecil
Rhodes's South Africa, and Paul Kruger's Transvaal are given a
family-album treatment, which is enlivening though somewhat
intimate for the general reader. And while the military course of
the war is detailed with a sense of human drama, the author's skill
has embroiled him too deeply in the creation of characters for
complete reliance on all his judgments. Still, this is history in the
tradition of Thucydides.

Does the reviewer like the book? Has the book accomplished
its purpose—implicit in its title? The first sentence of the review characterized the book as *spirited* and recommended the
book as required reading for responsible American officials.
The second sentence said that a well-informed public should
read it as well. Sentences three and four make clear why the
book is important today. Clearly, the reviewer thinks the book
commendable and important.

In the second paragraph of the review, we see the scope of
the book clearly defined and some of the content criticized as
to appropriateness for the general reader. Finally, the reviewer
expresses some reservations concerning how well the writer
succeeded in his task.

Do you see how the reviewer comes to grips with his task?
While he inevitably must discuss the content of the book, he
prevents his review from becoming a mere résumé of what the
author said. Everything about the book is discussed critically.
And that is what you must attempt to do when you review.

In the remainder of the review—and only about one-third
has been reprinted here—the reviewer deals with the subject of
the book. He relates it to the world situation confronting us
today, and concludes with this brief paragraph:

This work is too serious, timely, and honestly researched to be
titled with a snatch of marching song, denigrating it to a Noël
Coward nostalgia for British imperialism.

Thus, the review keeps to the theme of judging the book, not
telling its story. While the reviewer's background enables him

to do a closer job of criticism than most freshman students could, you can see here what is expected of a reviewer.

Here is an example of an extremely brief review of another work of history, taken from *The New Yorker,* February 1, 1958. Although your reviews generally will run to at least three times as long, you will benefit from seeing how so short a review accomplishes its purpose. It demonstrates in a nutshell *how you should write about a book:*

> FIRST BLOOD: THE STORY OF FORT SUMTER, By W. A. Swanberg (*Scribner*).
> A fine account of the seven months of compromise, stupor, and corruption in Washington, and of swashbuckling idiocy in Charleston, that culminated at dawn on April 12, 1861, in the opening engagement of the Civil War. It is usual, and perhaps correct, to suppose that by then disaster was inevitable. Nevertheless, as we read this scrupulously objective record, it is difficult not to believe that it could have been prevented—by an energetic Buchanan, by an honest Floyd, by a less senile General Scott, by a maturer Governor Pickens, by a sane Seward, by a resolute Lincoln, or even, quite possibly, by a self-confident Major Anderson, the Hamlet to whom fate gave the command of Fort Sumter. Mr. Swanberg, of course, makes no such explicit statement, but it is an earnest token of his achievement here that he has illuminated for us not only a moment in history but the nature of the men whose characters did much to create it. Maps and photographs. A Book-of-the-Month Club selection.

Without retelling the events described in the book, the reviewer quickly gives us his judgment. Words such as *fine, scrupulously objective, achievement, illuminated,* represent the reviewer's appraisal of how well the author achieved what he set out to do.

Incidentally, you almost always will find in the *preface* a statement of the author's purpose. Understand this purpose before writing your review. Nothing is more unfair than negative criticism of a book on the ground that it failed to do more than the author intended to have it accomplish.

CHAPTER 12

HOW TO WRITE A TOP-NOTCH EXAMINATION PAPER

EXAMINATIONS are the pay-off! Every college student must take them—usually several sets of them each year. No matter how good your recitations, reports, and term papers are, your college record will be unsatisfactory if you do not do well on tests.

Some students always do *better* on tests than the rest of their work would seem to promise. They go through a semester in lackluster fashion, perhaps doing work that is only barely passing, and then they come up with an outstanding final-examination paper. Because college grades are based heavily on test scores, these students make final grades far above the merit of their work. On the other hand, certain students do excellent work during a semester and then fall short of expectations on their examinations. Their final grades drop markedly.

There is no doubt that some students have the knack of writing good examination papers, while others do not. This chapter shows you how to acquire the knack, so that you can make better grades than ever before.

Main types of examinations

There are four main types of examinations: essay, brief essay, quick-scoring, and oral. Let's take a quick look at each:

● 1. An *essay* test is a test in depth, demanding thorough exploration of a limited number of broad topics. You are asked to recall information, differentiate between what is important and what is not, perceive relationships between ideas, and then write a well-organized, clearly expressed paper that shows the results of your thought. Your ability as a writer is almost as important as your knowledge of subject matter. The essay test is used most often in courses that demand a great deal of reading —the social sciences and the humanities.

● 2. The *brief-essay* test is designed to cover a greater number of topics than can be included on an essay test. Your answers in the brief-essay test are a paragraph or two in length, discussing specific topics without relating them to one another, in contrast to the essay test, in which each answer is many paragraphs long and thoroughly integrated. Your ability to write a good paragraph is on display in the brief-essay test, but you do not have the responsibility of developing a complete theme. In this sense, the brief-essay test is easier than the essay test. The social sciences and the humanities lend themselves to this kind of test, but some science courses also use it.

● 3. The *quick-scoring* test is composed of the familiar true-false, multiple choice, matching, and identification types of questions. The widest range of subject matter can be covered in a quick-scoring test, and no demands are made on your ability as a writer. By contrast, your reading ability is of great importance in taking such a test. The quick-scoring test can be given in almost any course.

● 4. The *oral* test can be of several types. It can last anywhere up to several hours. The setting can range from an informal conversation with one teacher while both of you are seated in easy chairs to the ordeal of standing before a panel of teachers. You can be subjected to a series of brief questions on a wide selection of topics. You can be given a few broad questions that you are expected to explore fully. The oral test is found commonly in four situations: (1) as part of an honors course, (2) as a senior examination covering all the work done in your major courses, (3) as a comprehensive examination before receiving your degree, and (4) as part of a foreign-language final examination. In the last case, the test is designed to test your speaking knowledge of the language.

Many final examinations combine two or more types of tests, to balance out the special abilities demanded by the various tests. College final examinations are not restricted to one hour in length. They can run to three or four hours at a sitting, and in some cases can be spread out over several sessions.

Later in this chapter, you will find out just how to take each kind of test so that you can do your best work. But there is special study you must do in preparation for every test, so let's take a look at that most important of all college work: *review*.

Final review strategy

If you have *worked at* this book thus far, you have already made substantial progress toward doing your best in the tests you will have to take all the way through college. Good habits of study, good reading and writing, careful lecture and laboratory work—all these qualities result in good test performance. You have formed, or are on your way to forming, the habit of regular and purposeful study. You read and look and listen carefully for the main ideas your teachers will ask for on tests. Above all, you periodically review all the material of each course you are taking. The week does not pass without your going back over notes to recite the heart of what you have been studying. *Each session of this kind is a miniature review for examinations.*

There remains only the need to work out effective procedures for getting all you can from your study and review *during the final weeks of a semester*. Don't forget that in those weeks you will have to do more than just review for your tests! You will still be attending classes and meeting new material to learn. But your final review must commence during this period, so dovetail it to your other work.

The way to begin is to *survey your final review requirements in every course you are taking*. One month before final examinations, set time aside for taking stock in each course of

- (1) What you know well,
- (2) What you should know better,
- (3) What you do not know at all.

	Mon.	Tues.	Wed.	Thurs.	Fri.	Sat.
9	English	Geology	English	Geology	English	Geology
10	Spanish	Economics	Spanish	Economics	Spanish	Geology
11		Economics				Geology
12						
1	Math.	Math.	Math.	Math.	Phys. Ed	
2					Phys. Ed	
3						

This means going through your notes, your laboratory manuals, and your textbooks that you have not outlined in yor notes.

To show how this is done, let us use the sample program discussed on pages 6–7 in Chapter 1.

In your *freshman composition*, you have been writing themes all semester long, and the chances are that you will have a final impromptu theme instead of a test, so you will not have to study for it. If an *English usage* test is scheduled, you may have some reviewing to do. The bulk of your reviewing will be done for your courses in *economics, geology, mathematics,* and *Spanish.*

Take stock of every topic covered in each of these courses. As you discover a topic you do not feel strong in, make an entry in your notebook for that topic, including where you will find the material to be studied, and how long a period you will need for studying it.

In *economics,* for example, you may have:

Economics		
topic	source	time
Federal Reserve System	Textbook pp. 81-96 Lecture notes pp. 28-32	3 hours
operation of commodity markets	Textbook pp. 103-121 Lecture notes pp. 41-45	3 hours
...	...	...
	Total Time Needed	... hours

Do this for each of your courses. When you have, you are ready for the next step in the process.

Create a new study schedule for the final weeks of the semester. Adapt the work schedule you have been using during the semester to fit in additional hours where they will do the most good. (See Chapter 1, page 12.) Some of the additional time you will need is found by adding hours to your work schedule and by foregoing some of your social life for the weeks remaining in the semester. If you have been working well all through the semester, you probably have found yourself using fewer study hours than you had originally scheduled.

If you start your final review early enough, you will find that there is time enough to do right by all the topics you know need attention. *One month before the end of a semester is the best time.* If you wait until time gets short, your review schedule will be dangerously crowded. The groundwork is laid in your day-to-day homework and reading assignments. You cannot prepare adequately for a test in a few days if you have neglected to study all semester long. This cannot be overemphasized. The final review is just the last in your program of periodic reviews and recitations for each course.

Do you recall the steps in effective studying that were given earlier in this book?

- Identify what is to be learned,
- Learn it,
- Master it.

The final step results from the review and recitation you conducted all by yourself with your notebook. By the end of a semester, you have recited these notes many times. You probably have understood and committed to memory all but the most recent material. A glance at a section heading in your notebook is enough to recall what you have written. This is real mastery of material. When you have arrived at this stage, the final review is almost routine.

Final review procedure

If you have followed the procedures discussed in Chapters 2 and 3, by the end of a semester you have refined the organization of your notebook so that:

- (1) All related information on a given topic that you have gathered from various sources—lectures, reading, discussions—now appears in the same section of your notebook.
- (2) A good deal of material has been taken out of your notes. Now you have progressed sufficiently so that elementary information and skills are second nature to you.
- (3) Misconceptions, ambiguity, and redundancy have been

edited during your day-to-day review. What is left is the hard core that you need for your tests.

● (4) The sectioning of your notes—the arrangement of topics under appropriate titles—now reflects the larger topics that have emerged as the semester went on.

Thus, the bulk of your notes has been reduced, and your study materials are in proper focus. You can now put the finishing touches on your understanding of the material.

● If you are preparing for an *essay test*, spend your time outlining essays that you must be prepared to write.

● If you are preparing for a *brief-essay test,* spend you time identifying all possible subjects for such essays and preparing brief notes for the paragraphs you will write in answering the questions.

● If you are preparing for a *quick-scoring test,* you will spend your time reading all the material you can be quizzed on, identifying the questions that can be asked.

● If you are preparing for an *oral test,* you will spend your time thinking through all your topics and what you might want to say about them.

Preparing for an essay test

If your notes have been well taken and carefully studied, than any essay test you face can demand nothing more from you than you should demand from yourself as you study. That is why you have been told to go through the exercise of periodic review and recitation so often during a semester. Each session of study is your rehearsal for the real thing.

When a teacher prepares an essay test, do you think he looks with a fine-tooth comb for the least important, the most minute jots of information with which to plague you? Certainly not. *The material that receives greatest emphasis during a semester is the subject matter of an essay test*. In preparing for an essay test, then, your first important job is to *select the major themes* that will be the most logical candidates for questioning. In an essay test, you will have to answer three or four major questions during a two- to three-hour period. Your teacher may give you a choice among five or more questions from which you will select the ones you can answer best. The most sensible review procedure for you to follow is to *make up questions based on the outstanding areas of the course and then outline your answers.*

You know what is most important in each course you take, so this procedure is not difficult.

For example, if you are taking a course on the history of the American labor movement, you might expect a question such as:

Compare and contrast the practices and philosophies of the A.F. of L. and C.I.O. in the period immediately following the creation of the C.I.O.

Do you recall the discussion of the philosophy of John L. Lewis quoted in Chapter 8 of this book?

In any of several social science courses, you might read Harrison Brown's book cited in Chapter 8. A reasonable question based on this reading might be:

Discuss the problem of food production and the world population explosion.

Of course, these are not the only questions that can be developed on the topics mentioned. Scholars in these areas would be able to do far better than the above sample questions. They would ask that the information be related to other sources that had been assigned during the semester. They would always go beyond asking you merely to report on what you have read; they would ask you to think deeply. As you go over the major topics in a course, you must bear in mind that comparisons and contrasts must be drawn, conclusions attempted, hypotheses devised. As you come to the end of a course, the major topics of the course should be fairly obvious to you. In preparing for tests, put yourself in the place of the teacher and ask what questions *you* would write if you were conducting an examination.

This point must be re-emphasized: it is not enough merely to identify the topics you will be tested on. You must go on to *actually writing possible examination questions,* for this process will lead you to the next step—*thinking through and outlining possible answers.*

As you do this, you are not merely working toward top test grades. You are also working in the most direct way possible toward *effective use of knowledge.* And your ability to *use* knowledge is just as important as the knowledge itself. If you can list the ten most important areas of a term's work (and ten is an arbitrary number—there may be more, there may be fewer), you are reviewing and perfecting your grasp of the entire subject. By going on to the next step—writing questions and outlining suitable answers—you are demonstrating and perfecting your ability to handle the material. Proper preparation for an essay test may teach you more than all the lectures you have attended in a course. Outlining answers to all conceivable important questions for an examination is also an excellent aid in learning how to organize your thoughts and express them well.

Here are two guides to use in outlining during review:

- 1. For every essay question, adopt a position and stick to it. "Man's survival on this planet is possible only if. . . ." "The fundamental difference between the philosophies and practices of the A.F. of L. and the C.I.O. was. . . ."

Either of these sentences, if completed, takes a position that must be maintained throughout your essay if you are to end up with a unified, effective discussion.

- 2. Gather supporting evidence and memorize key facts. THIS IS ESSENTIAL. One claim or generalization piled upon another proves nothing. Facts, facts, facts. Be as specific as you can.

Read these two sentences in response to the first question:

- "Man needs a certain minimum daily food intake."
- "A man weighing 165 pounds requires as many as 4,500 calories a day if he is engaged in heavy physical labor."

Which sentence has the greater impact?

Keep these guides in mind as you prepare your outlines before a test. For a sample outline, go back to Chapter 4, pages 66–67, where the question of comic books was discussed in several ways, each approach suggesting a different outline. As you go over the broad organization of your notes in a course, you should be developing and strengthening your point of view concerning the major problems of the course. Having a point of view and being able to express it clearly and succinctly will help you in every question of a test.

Preparing for a brief-essay test

Teachers are leaning more and more toward tests that demand answers in the form of brief essays, usually no more than a paragraph or two in length. These paragraphs leave no room for evasion and padding. You must come right to the point, answer the question with the material it asks for, and then stop writing at once so that you have time for the rest of the test. Because you must express yourself crisply and pointedly in the brief essay, this type of test is quite difficult for many students.

Review for the brief-essay test is just as extensive as for the essay test. You must survey all you have studied, to find areas of weakness needing special attention. Your review is divided into two phases: (1) you must "spot" typical subjects for brief essay questions, and (2) you must think through good answers to each question you find and decide on a topic sentence that will set the tone of your response.

As you become accustomed to taking brief-essay tests, you will find yourself continually looking for questions while you study during a semester. You may spot some during lectures. Do you recall how in Chapter 3 you were told that it is good practice to use the left-hand pages in your lecture notes for special items that require attention? As a lecture proceeds, you may feel that something the lecturer has just said could easily become a brief essay topic. Make an appropriate entry on that left-hand page. When you are doing your reading for your courses, you will come across material in the same way. Again, an entry in your notebook will help you when the time comes for final examination review. In class discussion, the same technique will come in handy. Your skill at recognizing possible questions and automatically recording your impressions will help you greatly.

If you follow this practice steadily throughout a semester, you will find yourself with a first-class collection of brief essay subjects that you can review just before examinations. Whatever subjects you miss during the semester will be found in your final review.

What constitutes suitable material for a brief essay? If you think of the space limitations of the brief essay, then you will be guided in selecting topics properly. In *history*, for example, identifying some historical figure or event lends itself to the brief essay. In *sociology*, *anthropology*, and *psychology*, there are terms and ideas to be defined and illustrated. In *literature*, a question on the meaning and importance of a school of writers could be treated in brief essay form. In a science such as *biology*, a description of a process or anatomical feature could be answered in a brief essay.

In Chapter 2 of this book, pages 21 to 24, you read a selection on *photographic memory*. Look back at it again now if you have forgotten its substance. The treatment of the topic might well form the basis for several brief-essay questions. For example:

a. "Discuss the validity of the term *photographic memory.*"
b. "Describe the characteristics of *eidetic imagery.*"
c. "Give the gist of Allport's findings in his experiments on *eidetic imagery.*"

The key to your answer is the topic sentence. All that is needed after the topic sentence is the evidence to substantiate your statement.

In answering the three questions based upon *photographic memory,* you might begin in this way:

a. "Discuss the validity of the term *photographic memory.*"
Answer: What is commonly referred to as photographic memory is a form of eidetic imaging that is far from photographic. . . .
b. "Describe the characteristics of *eidetic imagery.*"
Answer: Eidetic imagery is neither truly reproductive or static, and the longer the time between exposure to a scene and imaging, the greater the chance for distortion. . . .
c. Give the gist of Allport's findings in his experiments on *eidetic imagery.*"
Answer: Allport, experimenting with a group of sixty 11-year-olds, found that the children were able to image later with unusual vividness and detail complex scenes that they had observed for thirty-five seconds. . . .

A student who is not sure of himself or has little information to supply in a brief essay betrays himself quite readily by the way in which he opens his answer. In question C, for example, he might begin in this way: "Professor Allport was extremely interested in the subject of eidetic imagery." This tells the reader nothing.

The brief essay must convey information if it is to be a good one. The opening sentence must be particularly telling. If you take the trouble to write out or even just think through the opening sentence of the answers for possible brief-essay questions, your answers will command respect.

Preparing for a quick-scoring test

The quick-scoring test will ask you only to read carefully and completely, and then write your answers in the form of words, numbers, letters, or marks on an electric scoring sheet.

Many students feel that quick-scoring tests are easier to take than any other. For one thing, they dislike writing. For another, they know that they will have the opportunity to guess answers. They feel that they can tell from the wording of a question just how to answer it, even when they are uncertain of the material.

On true-false questions, they have an even chance of guessing correctly.

However, most quick-scoring tests penalize guessing by deducting twice as much credit for an incorrect answer as they give for a correct answer. Under this system, the student who relies heavily on guessing cannot make a respectable grade.

Quick-scoring tests are not the soft touch they are sometimes thought to be. Questions of a thoughtful and searching nature can be expressed in quick-scoring form. In addition, you will find that some questions depend upon other questions in a test, so that your entire understanding of a complex problem can be discovered through a series of quick-scoring questions.

Without a doubt, you must be thorough in your preparation, not relying on intuition or test-wiseness to carry you through. Only when you are completely at sea on a given question can you even consider testing your luck. But make sure of the scoring of a test before you do.[1]

There is no sure-fire way to study for the spot questions you will meet on some examinations. You will find, however, as you become accustomed to spot questions that certain kinds of material lend themselves to spot testing: factual information with which an author illustrates his material, true or false interpretation of theoretical material, dates, definitions—in short, everything that you should learn if you do your work with a critical and questioning mind.

You will be preparing for spot questions if you ask yourself, "Does the author have any facts to back up his statements? What are these facts?" "What exactly do the terms mean which I have learned for this course?" "What are the important theories, dates, definitions, historical incidents, thinkers, and formulas upon which this field of study is based?" This is what you will find on spot tests and there is no trick which will help you prepare for examinations. If you are *thinking* while you study, these facts will stick in your mind automatically. Star such items in your notebook, lecture notes, lab manuals, and outside reading notes. This will not only help you build a firm foundation in your courses, but will also outline information that you may expect to find on spot tests.

As illustrations of true-false questions that can be written for material in a course, let us go back to the selection on *photographic memory* once more. Here are five questions which might be asked on that material.

[1] Before a test begins, the examiner will usually inform you of how the test is to be scored. If he does not, you have the privilege of asking about it. Under almost any system of scoring used nowadays, out-and-out guesswork is a bad risk.

TRUE	FALSE	Eidetic imagining is more common among children than among adults.
TRUE	FALSE	To merit the name "photographic," memory must be complete in every detail.
TRUE	FALSE	Specific eidetic images soon fade from the memory of the subject.
TRUE	FALSE	Allport found evidence of imaging of almost photographic fidelity among his sixty child subjects.
TRUE	FALSE	Interest in the picture shown will influence the amount of detail the eidetic imagist can repeat.

As the end of the semester approaches you will find it helpful to review for the spot question by merely going over your materials and looking for all starred items. This kind of study will give you information you will need for documenting essay questions and will also strengthen your grasp of the factual material you have learned.

Preparing for an oral examination

Since, in practice, the oral examination is used to test your over-all grasp of large bodies of information, there is no effective short-term preparation for it. The best review for oral examinations is carried out for months before the test.

What you must do is to systematically go through all the notes you have accumulated from readings, lectures, and class discussions. Test papers saved from individual courses are also helpful. When you have finished one reading, go back to the beginning and read again. Concentrate on the areas that you know least well. As you read, think of how you might express yourself orally if you were questioned about what you are reading. If ever there were a place for reading aloud, this is it.

Think of the course material you are covering in terms of its broad areas—literature by centuries and movements, history by eras, psychology by schools of thought, etc.

If you are told who will examine you, can you guess from their areas of specialization what they are most likely to ask you? Are you aware of the attitudes these men hold on the subject? Are there students who can tip you off to the idiosyncracies of certain examiners? There are many tricks of the trade that more experienced students can give you.

How about reviewing with others?

Many students like to study with their friends before a big test. If a study group is organized successfully and managed intelligently, it can serve a worthwhile purpose. But no student should think that group study is designed to replace individual work. Rather it should serve only as a check on the subject matter to show whether an important section of a course has been overlooked for one reason or another. In addition, it should be a means of learning how much the student really does understand of every topic in a course.

The general rules for organizing a study group are these:

• (1) The group should be composed of no more than five students who work well together.

• (2) There should be a brief planning session to agree on the purposes of the group and a plan of procedure. This meeting should be no later than three weeks before a final examination, and everyone should leave the planning meeting with a definite assignment to review intensively that segment of the course in which he will later lead discussion.

• (3) At the next meeting, a few days later, each member should appear with an outline of the material for which he is responsbile. He will distribute copies of these notes and go over them with the others.

• (4) There should be two or three more meetings devoted to quizzing one another on the various topics of the course. Each student should prepare questions he thinks may appear on the test, and the entire group should work together discussing reasonable answers.

Under these conditions, such group effort can be worthwhile. Experience will tell you whether you can benefit from working in this way and will influence your decision about whether or not to participate in further ventures of this kind.

An experiment in group preparation for a test

A number of years ago, the author spent one hour with a group of worried freshmen who were preparing for their first college final examination. Each of the thirty students in the group was asked to prepare five quick-scoring questions based on the course in question. Quick-scoring questions were chosen because the final examination was to be of that type. In a few minutes, 150 questions were ready.

Each student read his questions aloud in turn. When a question was read that more than one student had prepared, the entire group wrote the question into their notebooks. In this way, students ended up with almost fifty questions for later study.

When the students came to the test, they found that almost all the fifty questions appeared on it. In addition, it was found that of the 150 original questions, 63 were on the test. Needless to say, the class average on that test was very high.

The tactics of taking an examination

If you want to avoid trouble and get the best grades possible with your knowledge and skill, get right to work when you sit down. Have a definite routine to follow from the moment you take your seat in the examination room.

GET SET FOR THE TEST

Have nothing with you except the materials you will need for taking the test. To carry notes or a textbook into an examination, unless you are specifically authorized to do so, is a serious error. Not because they are temptations, but because you will feel impelled to study them until just before the test gets underway. Don't worry yourself by finding things you have not learned. Relax and follow directions. If you miss a single instruction your teacher gives because you are boning up in a last-ditch effort, you will lose much more than you gain.

Examine your test papers. Do you have all the question-and-answer sheets you will need? Write your name and other identifying information wherever needed. There is no point in wasting the time allotted to the test itself on these housekeeping tasks.

GET RIGHT DOWN TO WORK

ON AN ESSAY TEST

1. *Read* all the questions through quickly to select those you will answer—if you have a choice. If you find ambiguity in the language of the questions, ask your teacher for help at once.

2. *Underscore* the key words in each question you are

going to answer: *describe, compare, identify the main elements,* etc. Your essays will be organized in accordance with these words.

3. *Set up* a time budget. In the case of a test in which there are four questions of equal weight (this information will be supplied on the question sheet) and you have two hours in all, take about twenty-five minutes for outlining and writing each essay. Reserve the final twenty minutes for all-important editing. Guard against getting all wound up in one question you particularly like and forgetting about the others until there is insufficient time left for answering them. If the test questions are of unequal weight, budget your time appropriately. It is common to hear students exclaim midway through a test that they had "just noticed that all the questions were weighted differently." The time to find this out and to plan your work is before the test begins.

4. *Think.* Here the distinction first arises between outstanding students and those who will merely get by. Can you now demonstrate to your teacher that you have thought carefully about the problems in front of you by writing maturely and persuasively? As ideas come to mind, you are working on the next step in the process.

5. *Outline* briefly the answers to all the questions you are going to work on. Don't bother with detail, but think of the broad ideas of the essay you will write. Check with your teacher as to what ways of outlining are permissible. You may be able to use the first pages of your examination booklet, the back of your examination booklet, or a separate sheet of paper.

Outline all the essays before you begin writing the first one. Students sometimes write themselves out on the first few questions of a test and then draw a blank on the last questions because they have become fatigued.

6. *Choose first the essay you feel you can do best,* and get to work—with one eye on your watch. It is far better to work ahead of the time schedule you set up than to immediately fall behind it by tackling the most difficult question on the test for you. Besides, you will not feel as good after working hard on a tough question as you will if you can get off to a flying start.

Remember the importance of setting the tone of your response by stating your attitude on each question at the start. Then hit hard with facts and more facts. Nothing can give greater strength to an answer.

One good essay on the first question you select will build your confidence for the entire test. After you have done this essay, choose the next one you feel most like doing, and so on until you have finished.

7. *Read* through your outline before you undertake an essay. Add to it any important ideas you will want to develop under the main headings you set up at the start. You may want to reorganize the outline. Do so with numbers and arrows. Don't waste time making your outline look beautiful.

8. *Remember* that you are being judged on how well you write as well as on how much you know. The student who wanders along in an essay, citing a fact here and a fact there in unconvincing manner, cannot hope to do well on a test. The most important idea to keep in mind as you outline an essay and as you actually write it is that *you are answering a specific question*. If your essay fails in this—no matter how brilliant the information and style—it is not satisfactory. A good way to work is to imagine that you are being asked a question in class, that your teacher and classmates are listening to your words and criticizing your effort. Write for them.

9. *Edit* your work for clarity, completeness, accuracy, mechanics of style, and appearance. You may find that you can increase the effectiveness of your writing by underscoring important ideas, by using Roman numerals to make divisions clear. Don't undertake any substantial rewriting unless you are blessed with a good deal of extra time—an unlikely occurrence. Your answers should represent your best writing. Whatever corrections you add should not make your work difficult to read.

On a Brief-Essay Test

1. *Budget your time.* This means, first of all, finding out how many questions you must answer. Then, on the basis of how the test questions are scored, set up goals for your work during the test. A question that is worth ten points should be given twice the time and twice the amount of writing you allot to a question worth five points. You will find that it is not easy to estimate the time you need for writing when you are new at the game of taking college tests. Going beyond the kind of answer expected cannot give you more points than are allotted to the question. But it will rob you of time needed to complete the test.

Don't forget that you must leave time for editing your answers. Your time budget must take this into account. While you work at your answers, check the time frequently in order to keep to your schedule.

2. *Underscore* the key words in each question in your first reading of all the test questions before undertaking to answer any of them. As in the essay test, the key word or words of a question will help you organize your answer.

3. *Read again* the questions you cannot answer readily. A second reading may be enough to trigger the recollection you need. As you read, think of the meaning of the question, taking special note of the important words in the question. Even if you cannot recall at once what you need to know, this second reading will help plant the question in your mind. Later in the test, while you are working on some other question, the answer to the troublesome question may come to mind. When this happens, stop your work to make a quick note of the thought that has come to you.

4. *Read* once more the first question you are going to answer, and get to work. Answer each question as directly as you can. A good aid in writing an effective brief essay is to say to yourself, "If I were premitted only a one-sentence answer to this question, what would that sentence be?" You must hit the nail on the head in every answer if you want to make a top grade. From the first sentence on, you must give your teacher the feeling that he is reading the work of someone who really knows what he is talking about. Above all, do not deliberately answer wide of the mark. You will get no credit for answering a question that has not been asked. And you waste time needed for the remainder of the test.

5. *Review* all your answers for clarity and accuracy. If you write poorly, your grades will suffer no matter how good the content of your answers.

(Read again the discussion on pages 226–28 of how to write an essay test answer—particularly in regard to writing and editing. What is said there applies here as well.)

On a Quick-Scoring Test

1. *Estimate* how far along in the test you should be after half an hour, one hour, etc. Write that estimate in the margin of your answer sheet, where you can see it during the test. Don't forget to include time for checking your paper.

2. *Make certain* that you know the symbols that are to be used in writing your answers before you begin to work. Why get halfway through a test before you discover that you are not following directions in regard to the form of your answers?

3. *Answer* at once every question you can answer easily, after reading carefully for comprehension. Where in the course

did the material come up? What are the implications of the question? Knowing the background of the question will help you decide the best answer to it.

4. *Skip* any question you are not sure of after one careful reading, but *star that question* so that when you come back to the question sheet for the second go-around you will be certain not to miss it.

5. When you have gone through the entire test once, *check back* to see whether you have overlooked any pages of the test. Because they are concentrating so hard on their work, students frequently overlook an entire page of questions.

6. *See* how much time you have left and then go through the test questions once more at a pace that will give you at least one more chance to each unanswered question. By now, some of them can be answered easily, but others will demand a great amount of time. Obey the instructions of your teacher in regard to guessing. It is foolhardy to guess wildly if you are subject to heavy penalties.

7. *Read quickly* the entire test in the remaining time to make sure you have not mismarked questions whose answers you know. This is particularly important in machine-marked tests. It is quite common for students to mismark an entire column by failing to align question and answer sheets properly.

If you come across any questions whose answers you want to change, make certain that your reasons for doing so are overwhelmingly correct. Don't begin guessing wildly because of panic late in a test. You take a real risk of ruining correct answers.

ON AN ORAL TEST

Be yourself. Your examiners realize that the situation puts you under a strain, and will make allowances for that.

You may be asked for definitions that can be given in one sentence.

More likely, your questions will demand answers that resemble brief or even full-length essays. Thus, before attempting an answer, try to establish in your mind the exact direction you want your response to take. Be guided by the key words in the questions, and then come quickly to the point in the first sentence of your answer. If you find that you have gone part of the way through a discussion and realize that you are on the wrong track, do not hesitate to ask for permission to start again. If your second answer is correct, you will not lose credit for the false start.

Observe the standards of good speech. The language of your spoken answers will count as heavily as that of your written answers on an essay test.

The emphasis in most oral examinations is on finding out how clearly you think. Try to reason carefully. A foolish stab at an answer is not what the examiners are after.

The jitters and what to do about them

There is all too much talk about the fear students have of impending examinations. The best attitude toward tests is one of *healthy respect*. To be sure, no student can be entirely happy about an oncoming test.

• If you are superbly prepared for a test, you may wonder whether you will do as well as you expect.

• If you are half-prepared, you wonder whether your instructor will be so uncooperative as to ask only about that half of the course you have not studied thoroughly.

• If you are not prepared at all, you wonder whether there is any chance whatsoever of passing.

When you come right down to it, there are probably two causes for the pre-examination jitters. One of them is lack of proper preparation and the other is psychological inability to perform on examinations. It is beyond the scope of this book to deal with the latter cause, but the first is by far the most frequent. If you follow the study procedures described here, you will enter your examinations with confidence and with the assurance that you know all the material about which you will be tested. There are very few cases of pre-examination jitters among students who do have this confidence which comes from being properly prepared.

The Dear Prof letter

A test is a contract between your teacher and you. He offers you a group of questions which he believes you should be able to answer. Make certain that you remember this while you are working on a test and when you get your grade.

To make excuses for yourself or to ask for special consideration is not living up to your end of the contract. Many students feel impelled at the conclusion of an examination to write a note to the teacher offering him unsolicited advice on the fairness or unfairness of the test, explaining that he has done well because the teacher is such a great guy or that he has done badly because his great aunt is ill, that he would like to take other courses with the teacher or that he never did have an aptitude for French literature and was never going to take another course in it. There are many variations on those themes. Alas, they are unappreciated. You have questions to answer. Do so. Write nothing else.

Every campus has its legend concerning the student who managed to pass a course without being able to answer a single question on the final examination. Don't try to become a legend.

Years ago, a student wrote his American literature teacher the following letter in lieu of an examination paper:

> DEAR PROF:
> I can't answer any of the wonderful questions you have devised, and it pains me because I know how hard you must have worked putting them together. Now I know that I cannot pass your course without passing the final examination, but Ruthie doesn't know that. And Ruthie means a lot to me. Let me tell you about Ruthie.

The letter continued in a glowing mood about the glories of this paragon of young womanhood, about how she expected so much of the poor student, about how he did not want to fail her. The legend has it that the student received an A for Ruthie's sake, but there is some doubt as to whether the story has any basis in fact.

One final word on tests

In many courses you will take in college, you will have more than one major examination during a semester. You may have a second test at mid-semester or perhaps even more. These tests will usually run for only one hour, the duration of regular class meetings.

What has been said about preparing for final examinations applies here, too. But there is one feature of these tests that is different from most final examinations. You have the opportunity to see your paper after the teacher has read and evaluated it. You may even be able to review it in class with your teacher.

A returned test paper can provide valuable help in preparing you for the other tests you will take during that semester and throughout the rest of your college career. If you examine the paper carefully to see the kind of errors you have made, you may be able to avoid similar errors in the future.

For example, you may find that you have misunderstood some of the semester's work, or you have understood the work but failed to convey your thinking properly. Perhaps you have overemphasized details and given scant attention to important ideas. You may have organized your answers badly. You may have read the test questions badly. You may have prepared on the wrong topics. Whatever the mistakes you have made, take proper steps to avoid the same errors in the future.

By the same token, you must look carefully at those parts of the test you did best. What were the characteristics of certain answers you gave that made them outstanding? If you can discover the pattern of those answers, you may learn something significant about your grasp of the subject and about how to write a top-notch examination paper.

INDEX